Computer Mediated Communication and the Online Classroom

Volume One: Overview and Perspectives

Edited by

Zane L. Berge
Georgetown University
Mauri P. Collins
Pennsylvania State University

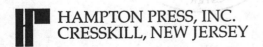

HAMPTON PRESS, INC.
CRESSKILL, NEW JERSEY

Printed in the United States of America

Library of Congress Cataloging-in-Publication Data

Computer mediated communication and the online classroom / edited by
   Zane L. Berge and Mauri P. Collins.
       p.   cm.
    Includes bibliographical references (p.) and index.
    Contents: v. 1. An overview and prerspectives -- v. 2. Higher
education -- v. 3. Distance learning.
     ISBN 1-881303-08-X (v. 1). -- ISBN 1-881303-09-8 (pbk. : v. 1)
     1. Educational technology. 2. Computer-assisted instruction.
3. Distance education. 4. Interactive media. I. Berge, Zane L.
II. Collins, Mauri P.
  LB1028.3.C6396   1995 v. l
  371.3'078--dc20
                                    94-23868
                                        CIP

Hampton Press, Inc.
23 Broadway
Cresskill, NJ 07626

CONTENTS

Preface

Editing the books in this series has been a new experience for us. We "met" online via the Internet while Mauri Collins was living in Las Vegas, NV, and Zane Berge in Springfield, VA. Collins was among the first 100 subscribers to IPCT-L (for which we thank Patty Crossett for her inspiration). Berge set up the LISTSERV discussion group, "Interpersonal Computing and Technology" (IPCT-L@GUVM), at Georgetown University in February 1992. We did not meet face-to-face until shortly before the first editorial board meeting in Pennsylvania, where the final selections from among the proposals were made. Since then we have spent countless hours together online, reading, editing, discussing, revising, and writing.

In Spring 1992 a debate was raging on IPCT-L, sparked by one contributor who asked how access to and use of computer-mediated communication in and out of the classroom could be justified to administration. As the contributor pointed out, CMC consumes computing time and resources, the connection to regional and national networks is expensive, and in these days of budget constraints and restraints, it is becoming increasingly necessary to justify such expenses to administrators.

Our discussion centered on the value to students, staff, and faculty of open access to the Internet from educational institutions. The Internet is an open communication channel that allows for free and open expressions in ways that are sometimes vulgar and profane and, at first glance, may not appear to contribute anything to the academic process. The contributor pointed out that this kind of discourse was not something that could be pointed to during the budgetary process as adequate reason to continue to pay the connection and usage charges that allow faculty and students free access to both internal and external resources.

Many members of the list responded to this challenge and pointed to benefits they had realized, both in terms of classroom accomplishment and personal and scholarly growth—their free access to many and diverse resources including local, national and international libraries and databases; and the colleagues they had "met" via CMC and with whom they subsequently collaborated—all attributed to their access to networked computers.

Another contributor, Dr. Gerald Phillips, Emeritus Professor of Speech Communication at the Pennsylvania State University, suggested that, although administrators might be unable or reluctant to follow our networked discussion, they do understand documentation and that list members should get together and write a grant to research the scholarly uses of electronic mail with Berge and Collins (the IPCT-L moderators) as leaders in this effort. He also mentioned in the same message that a book might even emerge from this effort.

After some extended discussion, we (Berge, Collins, and Phillips) decided that, although a research project might be beyond our scope, a book on computer-mediated communication would be feasible. Very early on, we settled on *Computer-Mediated Communication and the Online Classroom* as the title and determined that the desired content was to be examples of the uses of CMC in teaching and learning, written in such a way as to provide exemplars for those who are searching for ways to integrate CMC into their own classrooms and to justify continued support of network access to administrators. We contacted Hampton Press with our idea, and they expressed sufficient interest to ask us to submit a book proposal.

A call for chapters, distributed only through IPCT-L and a number of other electronic discussion group lists, brought us 93 chapter proposals via electronic mail. These were forwarded, again via electronic mail, for blind review, and then reviewed once more by our editorial board at their first face-to-face meeting in June 1992. Thirty-five of these proposals were finally accepted (with three subsequently dropping out) and notices sent.

To ease the distribution of common materials (e.g., the table of contents, instructions to authors, etc.), the editors set up a private listserv discussion group and subscribed all the authors and co-authors, the editors, and the editorial board. This allowed rapid dissemination of information and gave the authors and the editors a forum for discussion, suggestions, and questions. However, chapters were not posted for general critique to the list, although some authors did share drafts with one another. Only the two chapters considered critical to the content of the other chapters were posted. These were Santoro's introductory chapter on computer-mediated communications, and Sudweeks, Collins, and December's chapter on internetworking resources. We posted these chapters so that the other authors could reference them, instead of re-explaining, for example, some of the basic file retrieval tools.

The initial "Instructions to Authors" detailed a time line for drafts and revisions, with all drafts being sent and returned via electronic mail. Through all subsequent revisions, the drafts were edited online using an evolving set of "copy-editing symbols" and returned to the authors. It was not until the final revisions had been accepted that the authors sent in hardcopy and disks.

It became evident that the book, as originally planned, would run in excess of 500 pages. After some discussions and a look at the "natural breaks" in the subject areas, we proposed to the publisher that there be three books, not one. After some deliberation, the one book did become three with the series title: *CMC and the Online Classroom*. The three volumes are "CMC and the Online Classroom: An Overview and Perspectives," "CMC and the Online Classroom: Higher Education," and "CMC and the Online Classroom: Distance Learning."

Toward the end of the process, we asked the authors if they had been involved in any similar publishing efforts, in which all text, up to the final hard copy, was handled via electronic mail, and what their reactions were to the process. Reactions were mixed. Some of those who replied were evidently pleased with the system we had developed, the access the listserv provided to the other authors, and the speed at which their queries were responded to. One chapter was written by authors residing in Australia, Singapore, and the United States, who collaborated using electronic mail, and the Sudweeks's chapter made the round trip from the eastern United States to Sydney, Australia no less than six times on one particular day. Several authors remarked on how different and harsh it felt to see the editor's comments, in capital letters, on the screen, even though they were used to editorial commentary on paper.

The most consistent request for a change in process was for a more comprehensive table of contents, and for chapters be made available online for general discussion. We decided not to do this because, with the number of authors involved, we felt it would be very time consuming for all concerned. Many of the authors commented that the amount and speed of information and feedback flow helped them significantly in drafting their chapters; they could ask questions and get help from the editors or other authors in a most timely manner.

Among the editors, publisher, authors, or potential authors, there were over 1,200 email messages, exchanges of drafts, or postings in relation to this set of books, in the first year or the project (with hundreds more since then). This figure excludes the information exchanged privately among authors and some "broadcast" announcements to the 50+ authors, editors, and publisher. Without question, that amount of information and feedback could not have been exchanged via traditional mail in that time frame. One author noted that our process allowed us to exchange a quantity of information that otherwise would have been too time consuming using other communication channels. He continued by saying that he did not take as much advantage of the potential as he might have and concluded that we have come a long way down the line in bringing the editing process online, "but it seems to me . . . that there's a long road out there yet." We agree.

This set of volumes is perhaps the first to be electronically coordinated and edited online from start to finish. The concept was suggested, conceptualized, announced, accepted, drafted, edited, redrafted several times, and made ready for delivery to the publisher online. Was all the work worth it? It certainly was from the perspective of the authors and editors. In the final analysis, however, how well we have travelled this road is to be answered by our readers.

Dr. Gerald Phillips, Emeritus Professor of Speech Communication, Penn State University and book editor for Hampton Press, deserves a great deal of the credit (and none of the blame) for this book. He instigated the initial discussions on IPCT-L, suggested the book, put the editor's names together in the same sentence for the first time, and provided us with invaluable encouragement, guidance, and advice. Gerry Santoro has been an inexhaustible source of technical information, and Brad Erlwein assisted in the original selection of the manuscripts. Mark Evangelistia has patiently helped us set up and keep the Listserv lists functioning. Both the Academic Computer Center at Georgetown University and the Center for Academic Computing at Penn State University have been generous with their computer resources. Our appreciation to Dr. Susan Stoler, Academic Computer Center, Georgetown University for giving Zane Berge the flexibility in his schedule and support to meet the demands of this major project. Michael Day served as our "editor's editor," and we thank him for his stylistic and substantive revisions to this Preface, the glossary and the introduction to each of the books.

Above and beyond all, we thank Nancy Biggs Berge for her patience, tolerance, and hospitality, and for living with the time demands involved in our editing three books in one year (to say nothing of three issues of the IPCT Journal, two conference presentations, two book chapters, and three articles). We dedicate this book, with love and gratitude, to all our children: Jenna and Mark Berge, Doug Collins, Kim and Mike Snyder, Sarah and Simon Waghorn, Krys and Hozz Hosmer, and Jay, Ben, Norah, and Joshua Strebel.

Z.L.B.
M.P.C.

September 1994

About the Contributors

George Baldwin is Professor and Chair of the Dept. of Sociology and Human Services at Henderson State University, Arkadelphia, Arkansas.
BALDWIN@HOLLY.HSU.EDU

Zane Berge is Director of the Center for Teaching and Technology and Assistant Director for Training Service, Academic Computer Center, Georgetown University, Washington, DC.
berge@guvax.georgetown.edu

Marie (Mauri) Collins is a doctoral student in Instructional Systems at the Pennsylvania State University, University Park, PA and is Instructional Television Program assistant at WPSX-TV.
mauri@cac.psu.edu

Norman Coombs teaches History and Black Studies at the Rochester Institute of Technology, Rochester, New York.
NRCGSH@ritvax.isc.rit.edu

John December is a doctoral student in Communication and Rhetoric at Rensselaer Polytechnic Institute, Troy, New York.
decemj@rpi.edu

Jill Ellsworth is a faculty member in the Technology Department at Southwest Texas State University in San Marcos Texas, teaching in an interdisciplinary program for non-traditional adults.
JE@WORLD. STD. COM

Linda S. Fowler is an instructor and developer of international technical courses for AT & T.
lfowler@attmail.com

Tom Gentry is a Professor of psychology and cognitive studies at California State University, Stanislaus.
Gentry@deneb.csustan.edu

Joseph Kinner is Associate Professor in the Department of History, Gallaudet University, Washington, DC, and currently involved in the development of Distance Learning and Interactive Multimedia.
JGKINNER@GALLUA or jgkinner@GALLUA.GALLAUDET.EDU

Raleigh C. Muns is a practicing reference librarian at the University of Missouri - St. Louis.
SRCMUNS@UMSLVMA.BITNET

Anne Pemberton teaches high school English to Special Education students at Nottoway High School, Nottoway, Virginia.
apembert@PEN.K12.VA.US

Gerry Santoro, is a Senior Consultant at Penn State's Center for Academic Computing and an Affiliate Assistant Professor in the Department of Speech Communication.
gms@psuvm.psu.edu

John Sarraille is a professor of computer science at California State University, Stanislaus.
john@ishi.csustan.edu

James N. Shimabukuro is an assistant professor at Kapiolani Community College, which is part of the University of Hawaii system, teaching freshman and advanced composition courses in a computer classroom.
jamess@uhunix.uhcc.hawaii.edu

Katy Silberger is a librarian at Marist College Poughkeepsie, New York
JWEZ@MARISTB.BITNET

Fay Sudweeks is a doctoral student in computer-mediated communications in design at the University of Sydney, Australia.
fays@ARCHSCI.ARCH.SU.OZ.AU

Michael Szabo is Professor of Adult, career and Technology Education at the University of Alberta where he directs a graduate program in Instructional Technology.
Mike_Szabo@act.educ.ualberta.ca

Daniel. D. Wheeler is an Associate Professor in the Department of Educational Foundations at the University of Cincinnati and is also Director of Educational Services for KIDLINK, an international telecommunications project.
Dan.Wheeler@UC.edu

Robert Zenhausern is a Professor of Neuropsychology at St. John's University.
drz@sjuvm.stjohns.edu

Introduction

Volume One: Computer-Mediated Communication and the Online Classroom: Overview and Perspectives

Zane L. Berge

Georgetown University

Mauri P. Collins

Pennsylvania State University

As used in this book, the term *computer-mediated communication* (CMC) signifies the ways in which telecommunication technologies have merged with computers and computer networks to give us new tools to support teaching and learning. CMC describes the ways we humans use computer systems and networks to transfer, store, and retrieve information, but our emphasis is always on communication. In our model, the computer network is primarily a mediator for communication rather than a processor of information. As it is currently used to support instructional purposes, CMC provides electronic mail and real-time chat

1

2 Berge & Collins

capabilities, delivers instruction, and facilitates student-to-student and student-to-teacher interactions across a desk or across the world. These uses are enabling and promoting several paradigmatic shifts in teaching and learning, including the shift from instructor-centered distance education to student-centered distance learning and the merging of informal dialogues, invisible colleges, oral presentations, and scholarly publications into a kind of dialogic virtual university.

Considered together, the chapters in this volume revolve around the questions: "What do we know about teaching and learning?" and "How can educators and learners use CMC productively as we move into the 21st century?" *Computer-Mediated Communication and the Online Classroom: Overview and Perspectives*, the first in a 3-volume set, provides an overview of several themes relating to the use of computer-mediated communication both in class and in distance learning. These themes include accommodation of different learning styles and the empowerment of learners, regardless of physical challenges or social/cultural differences. Further, learners may now use the same tools and methods that professionals use; at the same time, pioneer educators using CMC are taking an interdisciplinary, project-oriented approach to teaching and learning—all of which creates authentic practice.

We find that CMC is changing instructional methods in several ways, including: (a) generating improved technological tools that allow classes to use a fuller range of interactive methodologies, and (b) encouraging teachers and administrators to pay more attention to the instructional design of courses. Both of these factors can improve the quality, quantity, and patterns of communication in the skills students practice during learning—a change that requires, in many cases, both teachers and students to learn different roles.

Educators often categorize the use of instructional CMC in three ways: for conferencing, informatics, and computer-assisted instruction (CAI). Computer conferencing provides e-mail, interactive messaging, and small and large group discussion. Informatics (repositories or maintainers of organized information) include library online public access catalogs (OPACs), interactive access to remote databases, program/data archive sites (e.g., archives of files for pictures, sound, text, movies), campus-wide information systems (CWIS), wide-area information systems (WAIS), and information managers, such as Gopher and Veronica.

In CAI, the computer is used to structure and manage both the presentation of information and the possible responses available to the human user. Uses of computer conferencing, informatics, and CAI include:

- mentoring, such as advising and guiding students
- project-based instruction, either within the classroom or in projects involving community, national, or international problem solving
- guest lecturing, which promotes interaction between students and persons in the larger community
- didactic teaching, that is, supplying course content, posting assignments, or other information germane to course work
- retrieval of information from online information archives, such as OPACs, ERIC, and commercial databases
- course management, for example, advising, delivery of course content, evaluation, collecting and returning assignments
- public conferencing, such as discussion lists using mainframe Listserv software
- interactive chat, used to brainstorm with teachers or peers and to maintain social relationships
- personal networking and professional growth and such activities as finding persons with similar interests on scholarly discussion lists
- facilitating collaboration
- individual and group presentations
- peer review of writing, or projects involving peer learning, groups/peer tutorial sessions, and peer counseling
- practice and experience using emerging technologies that may be intrinsically useful in today's society
- computer-based instruction, such as tutorials, simulations, and drills.

As the authors in this volume discuss the various methods, it becomes clear that there are many benefits to using CMC, but there are also some limitations that must be recognized. As the reader moves through these chapters, it will become apparent that one of the greatest benefits of CMC is its ability to liberate instruction from the constraints of time and distance. The convenience of access from home, school, or office permits many students and instructors to better meet travel, job, and family responsibilities. Educators and trainers, especially those involved in distance learning, have been searching for the "Holy Grail" of instruction for a long time—to be able to teach and have students learn anything, anytime, anywhere. To a large degree, CMC now can fulfill two-thirds of this desire.

CMC promotes self-discipline and requires students to take more responsibility for their own learning. Using CMC, instructors can vary a course's instructional design to include everything from structured projects to open projects in which students are free to work on "messy"—but authentic—problem solving. On the other hand, because students must manage their own learning, this newfound independence may be a hindrance to those students who need more structure.

No one can deny that we have entered an information age in which power comes to those who have information and know how to access it. If we consider which factors of CMC will be most important to education in the information age, it seems that our goals should be to develop self-motivated learners and help people learn to find and share information. If designed well, CMC applications can be used effectively to facilitate collaboration among students as peers, teachers as learners and facilitators, and guests or experts from outside the classroom.

One of the more important aspects of CMC use in instruction is that it is text-based. Facility in writing is essential across the entire curriculum, and with the present technology one cannot communicate on a computer network without writing. Just as important, if used effectively, CMC encourages and motivates students to become involved in authentic projects and to write for a real audience of their peers or persons in the larger world community, instead of merely composing assignments for the teacher. At the same time, we must recognize that not all students can express themselves well in writing, and, even for those who can, the act of writing and using online text-based applications can be a time-consuming struggle.

In this regard, there is an emerging body of literature, added to by several authors in this volume, who speak from their own experiences concerning the empowerment of persons with disabilities, physical impairment, disfigurement, or speech impediments, which hinder their equal participation in face-to-face encounters. CMC promotes an equalization of users. Because CMC is, at present, primarily text-only, the consequent reduction in social cues leads to a protective ignorance surrounding a person's social roles, rank, and status. Further, it is impossible to know if another person took several hours to draft a one screen response, or several minutes. Responses are judged by the ideas and thoughts conveyed, more so than by who is doing the writing. As a result, the lack of social cues and the asynchronous nature of the medium affords those with physical limitations or personal reticence the possibility of participating fully and equally in communicative activities within a mainstream environment. However, researchers realize that when social context cues are minimized nonreticent personalities can be encouraged to become overly zealous in their responses, or to become publicly inflammatory and aggressive on a personal level in ways that generally do not occur in other media. Second, it has been noted that some students prefer the social aspects of the classroom and are unsettled by the lack of face-to-face interaction in CMC, or the lack of a (sometimes) charismatic lecturer during presentation.

Another potential benefit of CMC is in promoting multicultural awareness. With the demographic make-up of many countries changing so rapidly, it is becoming increasingly important to develop communication skills for a culturally diverse community and world. Still, although CMC enhances some of these valuable skills for the 21st century, we must remember that because the bulk of CMC is conducted in English and in the written rather than in the spoken word, it may perpetuate some cultural hegemonies.

Many authors recognize CMC's capability, under certain circumstances, to reduce the sense of isolation sometimes felt by students and teachers. However, still others believe that the lack of social cues and face-to-face interaction increases the sense of isolation for persons using this medium to teach and learn. They point out that CMC may interfere with face-to-face relationships or be addictive.

However, as the chapters in this volume make clear, we cannot deny its value as a teaching tool. We simply need to remember that responsible use of CMC means using it in addition to other media, not as a replacement. As educators, our job is to provide options to fit a variety of learning styles, and it is in this regard that CMC can help the most. There are technical benefits to using CMC, such as the ease of circulating and archiving files and documents (e.g., teacher messages, student work, assignments).

On the other hand, the learning curve, with regard to learning the system and the technical "how tos" of the computer and telecommunications, can be steep. The cost of buying and supporting systems or accessing other networks is a significant "overhead" item in schools and colleges today, as is the cost and inconvenience of upgrading, repairing, or replacing hardware. Further, computer systems are not 100% reliable, a fact that adds to inconvenience and wasted time. With so many systems to learn and sources to tap, information overload has become a problem as some users struggle with the lack of criteria to help them to decide what to keep and what to discard from the swiftly flowing stream of incoming information.

All these factors—the idea that teachers, information designers, and instructional developers can use CMC to promote collaboration, cooperation, the sharing of ideas, and as an equalizing medium—means that the roles of students and teachers will change. No longer perceived as the sole experts and information providers, teachers become facilitators and guides. Conversely, students are no longer passive learners, attempting to mimic what they see and hear from the expert teacher. They become participants, collaborators in the creation of knowledge and meaning. Yet we must attempt not to reproduce or augment the problems associated with the gap between technology "haves" and "have nots" when we design CMC and computer conferencing applications and curricula. Every software, networking, or curriculum innovation reflects, to some degree, the unarticulated assumptions about the world view of the culture that created it. We must be aware of this fact and strive to create and use CMC innovations that allow for multiplicity, for change, for difference.

In response to increased pressure on universities and instructors to provide instructional delivery systems that go beyond the traditional "chalk-and-talk" form of lecture, computer-mediated conferencing has emerged as a tool for instructional communication not bound by prescribed meeting times or by geographic proximity. Successful integration of CMC into the curriculum, however, depends on one's ability to design and use CMC applications that meet course goals, delivery goals, or both. As part of course planning, we must address issues such as course goals, hardware availability, and student readiness. Large expenditures on CMC for the classroom will not help unless teachers understand how the technology helps fulfill the goals of the course. To this end, the chapters in this volume provide examples and practical advice.

Chapter 1 provides a foundation for understanding the terminology and processes of computer-mediated communication. Gerald M. Santoro defines CMC and gives examples of the various ways in which computers are used to mediate human communication, especially in support of instruction. This chapter describes how typical members of the academic community use computers for direct, human-to-human communication, informatics, and computer-aided instruction. Santoro describes the basic functions of electronic mail, group conferencing, and interactive messaging systems before going on to discuss the purposes of online databases and campus-wide information systems. This chapter provides the basic concepts and context necessary for understanding the more specific and in-depth information provided in later chapters.

In Chapter 2, Jill H. Ellsworth addresses the second half of our title, "And the Online Classroom." In an effort to expand access, meet learner needs, and overcome problems encountered by nontraditional, commuter students, she instituted CMC in two courses requiring intensive interaction between student and faculty. For many students, CMC provided a new avenue for learning—one not reliant on time, location, or instructor—that allowed them to access information in an exploratory fashion. Further, CMC gave many students a chance to use electronic mail, computer conferencing, and synchronous communication with their peers to independently build their own useful knowledge structures.

CMC's flexibility and variety allows instructors to meet numerous learning and personal needs, especially when working with individuals with special needs and those who are less mobile or shy. However, many CMC applications require that students first take the time to learn considerable information and skills and be provided with access to computers and software that can be costly.

Ellsworth determined that CMC enhances both the teaching and the learning process. In considering the major benefits of CMC, her students said that they appreciated the timely feedback, the accessibility of faculty and resources outside of class hours, and their ability to get more out of the class.

James N. Shimabukuro, in Chapter 3, examines the potential impact of computer-mediated communication on writing instruction by developing a future scenario in a college setting. However, the scenario is equally relevant to other instructional levels. He next describes the growth of computer networks, using a generational model:

First: Local Area Network (LAN)
Second: Wide Area Network (WAN)
Third: Remote Access Network (RAN); and
Fourth: Global Access Network (GAN).

In the fourth generation model, the traditional college campus is no longer the focal point of instructional delivery; instructors and students are electronically linked around the world, and they seldom, if ever, meet face-to-face. Faculty offices do not have to be grouped at a single geographical location; instructors are able to work out of home offices, often far removed from a physical campus. A campus may house conferencing and administrative facilities, but traditional classrooms have all but disappeared—the future campus is primarily the geographical base for the mainframe or whatever system functions as the network server. Shimabukuro has based his future scenario on the ways the university community might use CMC in a fourth generation network, and he closes his chapter with a discussion of the consequences and implications of this model for classroom teachers today.

Joseph Kinner's and Norman Coombs's chapter (Chapter 4) outlines the problems and opportunities of adaptive computing and provides vignettes of persons who have made significant use of adaptive computing in school. The chapter gives an in-depth report on a pilot project that enabled two courses using the Internet to unite classes of hearing and deaf students from Gallaudet University and the Rochester Institute of Technology into a single, virtual classroom. Two-thirds of the participants were hearing impaired, and one was blind. The success of this project demonstrates ways in which CMC can mainstream disabled learners into the educational system.

Kinner and Coombs take the position that the personal computer equipped with adaptive technology is one of the most empowering and liberating tools in the lives of persons with physical disabilities. The computer, along with the CMC it enables, opens education and the entire information world to a new population. Further, it has been demonstrated that CMC can enable this population in a mainstream environment.

In Chapter 5, Ann Pemberton and Robert Zenhausern explore how CMC can be used as a rehabilitation technique by providing basic computer literacy, motivational reading, writing, and thinking activities, and an introduction to the world to adolescents with educational disabilities. The authors summarize actual classroom situations that have arisen over the past two years as a result of their CMC activities, and at the same time show how special education teachers can use CMC to address their own professional needs. They draw their examples from the archives of a series of listserv discussion groups located at St. John's University in New York City and transcripts of the online experiences of learning disabled adolescents in a high school in rural Virginia. The chapter concludes with tips for teachers and a list of available online resources specific to the needs of those involved in special education.

Linda S. Fowler and Daniel D. Wheeler (Chapter 6) conducted a nationwide survey of 25 Kindergarten-Grade 12 teachers actively using computer-mediated communications in their classrooms and found that these teachers were pleased with their successes. The teachers reported that their use of CMC contributed to the development of a cooperative learning environment in which their students worked not only with each other, but also with peers around the world. They also noted an increase in cultural understanding and an improvement in writing skills. These teachers, all enthusiastic pioneers of CMC, overcame considerable difficulties to achieve their successes, but noted that better institutional support will be necessary if CMC is to become widespread in K-12 classrooms.

·In Chapter 8, Katy Silberger examines changes in the traditional role and structure of libraries in higher education as they face the technological opportunities and pressures stemming from increased use of new electronic information formats, such as electronic journals and monographs, and electronic publishing networks. In forecasting the role of the library of the future, Silberger notes that the proliferation of electronic text will add to, rather than replace, paper-based library holdings. Not all libraries will choose to archive electronic text, but instead will provide local, national, and international access and retrieval services for their patrons. Silberger believes libraries will remain the scholarly information centers of universities, but increasingly, their added role will be to facilitate research and communication within the global scholarly community.

George D. Baldwin's chapter (Chapter 9) opens with a discussion of the implicit conflict between Indian cultural values and beliefs and the English language used in most CMC. Indian students can adapt to the features of CMC that promote cooperative, active learning; however, the text-based nature of the medium is problematic, especially when students are required to participate before they have ascertained the relative ranking of other correspondents. But as long as students are allowed to watch, "listen in," and reflect prior to active participation, CMC can help them learn some of the skills necessary for success in the information society. Baldwin also reports on a number of Native American educational computer conferencing networks, providing access information and addresses.

John J. Saraille and Thomas A. Gentry (Chapter 10) present the Fractal Factory, a virtual laboratory for teaching and research that is evolving from a combination of computer networks, new analytical programs, digital image compression technology, and the expanding resources of the Internet. The model and core concept for the Fractal Factory come from the process of computing fractal dimensions, a process that has applications in many subject areas and provides a new cognitive linkage between the quantitative methods used in teaching science and real-world problems. The authors discuss the current status of the Fractal Factory in the hope that their example will help others gain access to collaboration in this CMC venue. They suggest that the study of fractals provides both a rich source of new insight on the natural world and a subject matter with broad applications for CMC-based instruction.

Raleigh C. Muns, in Chapter 11, suggests a continuity in scholarly communication from the Socratic dialog to the computer-mediated scholarly discussion groups typically found on the Internet. He describes and contrasts the Internet's e-mail-based communication channels, listserv discussion groups, and Usenet newsgroups, and offers two possible ways to evaluate online discussions: forum analysis and a methodology he developed for his own electronic publication, the *List Review Service*. Muns briefly reviews five existing online discussion forums that he has found useful for both learning about online communication and uncovering Internet resources: PACS-L, Comserve, IPCT-L, VPIEJ-L, and LIBREF-L.

Michael Szabo's chapter (Chapter 12) has two purposes: to provide a brief historical overview of PLATO and to examine several of PLATO's features that support and promote a wide range of communication for student learning. In developing one of the most powerful systems for the computer-assisted instruction form of computer-human interaction, PLATO's creators pioneered new methods of conferencing, messaging, and database management. Examining these new methods should give educators ideas about how they might develop their own communications applications using evolving network systems such as PLATO.

In the 13th and final chapter, Fay Sudweeks, Mauri Collins and John December introduce and explain several other important resources for those interested in computer networks, networking, and the Internet. They describe the basic navigation tools (FTP and Telnet) and give instructions on how to use these tools to search for, discover, and retrieve needed information. The authors compare and contrast various interactive conferencing systems, with an eye toward their potential uses in education. December's CMC list offers readers a compact but comprehensive guide to a broad range of resources concerning computer-mediated communication available in several media.

Chapter One

What is Computer-Mediated Communication

Gerald M. Santoro
Pennsylvania State University

WHAT IS COMPUTER-MEDIATED COMMUNICATION?

Computer-Mediated Communication (CMC) is the name given to a large set of functions in which computers are used to support human communication. CMC can be defined narrowly or broadly, depending on how one defines human communication. At its narrowest, CMC refers to computer applications for direct human-to-human communication. This includes electronic mail, group conferencing systems, and interactive 'chat' systems. At its broadest, CMC can encompass virtually all computer uses.

The broad interpretation derives from the recognition that computer systems were developed to receive data from humans (or from the environment in a way that mimics or extends human senses) and eventually return some form of that data to humans for some human purpose. Seen this way, such diverse applications as statistical analysis programs, remote-sensing systems, and financial modeling programs all fit within the concept of human communication. The meaning of CMC for the purpose of this book will be a compromise between these two extremes. The focus is on the use of computer systems and networks for the transfer, storage, and retrieval of information among humans. In this definition, the computer/network system is a primarily a mediator rather than a processor of the information.

11

A special focus of this book is on the use of CMC as a tool for instructional support. That support can range from simply providing students with electronic mail in an otherwise traditional class, to actually delivering instruction and supporting student-to-student and student-to-teacher interaction at a distance.

Who Uses CMC?

Let us first examine a few numbers that are descriptive of the extent to which information technologies pervade our world. Between 1977 and 1987 it is estimated that some 20% to 25% of American households adopted and began to extensively use personal computers (Chesebro & Bonsall, 1989).

Clearly some of this growth in the home use of computers stems from the evolution of the American economy from an agricultural and industrial base to an information base. Analyses by Porat (1974, 1977) and Ehrenhalt (1986) indicate that 28% of the U.S. labor force is employed in the primary information sector of the economy, with an additional 24% working as information processors in the industrial sector.

The increasing use of computers in primary, secondary, postsecondary, and continuing education is also a factor stimulating growth in the use of information technologies. Computer laboratories, once viewed as a luxury, are now considered to be as essential to education as libraries. Campuswide networks and the connection of these networks to the Internet are strategic goals at virtually every college and university worldwide.

The importance of information technology to education and to the U.S. economy was reflected in the theme of the Net '91 conference in Washington, DC: "Towards a National Information Infrastructure." This conference drew over 400 representatives from higher education, industry, and government concerned with the future of national educational and research networking (MERIT, 1991). Also in 1991, Senator Al Gore (then D-Tenn) introduced Senate Bill 272, which authorized the National Education and Research Network (NREN). This bill demonstrated recognition of a national telecommunication infrastructure as being as important to the U.S. economy as the interstate highway system.

So who uses CMC? Although there is no "typical" user of CMC, it might be helpful in defining CMC to consider the work and technical environments of three representative types of users. The examples given are by no means comprehensive. In fact, the variety of uses and applications of CMC are as diverse as the variety of human users.

Persons working in information-intensive professions. As mentioned earlier, a large segment of the U.S. labor force directly or indirectly uses

computer-based information systems in their work. Many of these professionals have access to microcomputers or terminals in their offices.
Most of these systems are connected to local networks (LANs), many of
which are then connected to wide-area networks (WANs), and many of
these are then gatewayed to the Internet.

These users access databases, specialized hardware/software,
electronic mail, and (possibly) group conferencing systems to support
their profession. A large number of these professionals use home computers (or portable computers) and modems to access information
sources while at home or traveling.

The functionality of these systems, taken to a logical extreme, is
reflected in the growing practice of "telecommuting" (Schneier, 1992).
Telecommuting is a practice in which employees work partially or primarily from home, using microcomputers and modems to access information systems, and perform their daily duties without regard to their
actual physical location.

Students. The dramatic drop in cost and increase in power of
microcomputers and modems have made it desirable for many students
to own personal computers, which they may use in support of their educational goals. Such uses include word processing, programming, database development, courseware, and access to electronic mail and group
conferencing systems.

The equally dramatic increase in the number of campus-based
computer stores and computer industry discounts on computer systems
for resale to students reflects the recognition of the value of students
having such systems. So, too, does the increased emphasis on the use of
CMC as an instructional delivery system for persons who cannot otherwise attend "traditional" classroom-based courses.

Individuals, families, or hobbyist. The personal computer was originally developed in the 1970s as a home system for entertainment or
hobby use. During the 1980s and early 1990s, the evolution of the personal computer and the development of commercial information systems such as CompuServe, PRODIGY, and America On-Line has pro-
pelled the personal computer from being an oddity to being a home
appliance as essential as VCRs, microwave ovens, and stereos.

At the same time, thousands of public bulletin-board systems
and free or low-cost software packages (FREEWARE/SHAREWARE)
have been developed to provide the home user with access to information technology once available only to those with access to industrial or
educational computer systems.

Commonalities Among These Users.

Three major common threads can be seen in the computer use of these different types of information system users. First, human computer users typically have access to a personal computer, which acts as a devoted workstation for local processing and access to remote host computers.

Second, most of these personal computers utilize modems or computer networks to access information, software, or specialized computer hardware at remote locations. In most cases the human computer users need not know the actual location of the remote host computer; access is attained through the use of a telephone number or network address.

Third, human computer users are increasingly using these systems to manage information transfer with other humans. In addition to work-oriented communication, much human communication through computer systems is social. Many friendships and deeper social relationships have begun on, and are supported by, CMC. In a survey of heavy computer users, Hellerstein (1986) found that social activity is regarded as a major application of computer systems. This is supported by an examination of the dramatic growth of transactions on bulletin board systems and group conferencing systems such as Usenet news (NETNEWS).

THREE CATEGORIES OF CMC

Following the middle-of-the-road definition of CMC, just provided, one can discern three broad categories of CMC functions. These categories are distinguished by the nature of the human-computer interaction and by the role taken by the computer in mediating the human communication process.

Although these categories are described and explained separately, it is most important to note that they are not mutually exclusive. In fact, it is both likely and desirable that functions from each of these categories be combined in a way that meets the specific needs of the human computer users—as well as the capabilities of the computer/network resources available to these users.

I describe these three categories briefly, with more in-depth descriptions to follow. The first category of CMC involves direct human-human communication, with the computer acting simply as a transaction router, or providing simple storage and retrieval functions. I refer to this category as *computer-based conferencing* or simply as *conferencing*. This category includes such functions as electronic mail, interactive messaging, and group conference support systems such as Listserv, Usenet NETNEWS, bulletin board systems, and so on.

The second category of CMC is one in which the computer has a more active role as the repository or maintainer of organized information, which originates with human contributors and is utilized by human retrievers. I refer to this category as *informatics*. Part of the current explosion of interest in the Internet is a result in the rapid growth of Internet-accessible informatics resources, including online public-access library catalogs (OPACs), interactive remote databases, and program/data archive sites.

The third category of CMC includes the computer structuring and managing of both the presentation of information and the possible choices available to the human user. The computer is programmed to take a more active role toward the human user in this category as opposed to the other two categories, in which the computer more passively carries out commands. This is the realm of computers as teachers or guides. I use the fairly generic term *computer-assisted instruction* (CAI) to refer to this category.

The differences in types of human interaction with the computer and in the different roles played by the computer in each of these three categories are quite significant. With conferencing it might appear that the computer is doing nothing more than playing telephone or postal delivery person. In fact, the messages, destinations, and purpose of communication are entirely provided by the human users. However, the computer, although operating primarily in the background, does have a major influence on the effectiveness of the communication process—particularly in ongoing group communication.

Because of this influence, it is important that design considerations for conferencing systems take into account what is known (or more importantly not known) about the nature of human communication interpersonally, in groups, and in organizations.

The roles of human and computer with informatics are more involved than with conferencing. In this category a true interaction takes place between the human, who is seeking information, and one or more networked computer systems, which potentially have the information being sought. Again, the design of the computer system is paramount to the successful location of needed information.

There are approaches being taken to the design of informatics resources. The first is to adopt standards (often rooted in technical evolution) that are then documented at great length to make them understandable. This is not an unreasonable approach because the effort is placed on training the human users in utilization of the resources. The second approach is to attempt to make the resources more "intuitive" or "user-friendly" by design. At first glance this would appear to be an obviously better approach, however, it suffers from two major hangups. The first is that "intuition" is a very fuzzy concept which varies considerably with cultural background and degree of prior computer experience. The second is that the human computer user can never be sure whether the requested information was not received because it was really not available, or because he or she just didn't formulate the inquiry properly.

With computer-assisted instruction the roles of human and computer are their most complex. The human is cast as student or apprentice and the computer is the teacher or guide. Although the information programmed into the computer originated with some other human, and quite possibly with a team of humans, it is the job of the computer to manage the instructional process within the limitations of its programming. Each of these three categories of CMC is evolving rapidly. The next three sections describe them in greater detail.

Computer-Based Conferencing

Computer-based conferencing takes three primary forms. The first is electronic mail, the second group conferencing systems, and the third interactive messaging systems. Each of these is designed for the support of direct human-human communication.

Numerous studies and analyses of human communication via CMC have shown that this method of communication incorporates aspects of written (literal) as well as spoken (oral) communication. An examination of "smilies" (Lewis, 1986) and the use of CHAT systems such as the Internet Relay Chat (IRC) show a communication form that is uniquely shaped by the medium, yet unquestionably human in nature.

Electronic Mail

Electronic mail (or e-mail) is unquestionably one of the most commonly used forms of CMC. In its most basic form it involves a human computer user composing and sending an online "letter" to another computer user. The recipient of this online 'letter' may then elect to read it, discard it, save it for later use, print it, reply to it, or send it to another computer user. This form of communication can be thought of as a "one-to-one" communication (Quarterman, 1990), although most e-mail programs permit mail to be sent to multiple recipients.

Electronic mail has been used on mainframe computers for at least two decades. Its current explosion in popularity derives from two factors. The first is the interconnection of hundreds of thousands of computers, ranging in size from giant supercomputers to inexpensive microcomputers, by electronic data-transfer networks such as the Internet,

BITnet, UUCP, and so on. (The nature and use of the networks are further explained in Sudweeks's chapter, this volume.) The second is the adoption of electronic mail standards that permit the transfer of electronic mail from one kind of computer system (and software) to another without loss of information.

The usefulness of electronic mail as a human communication medium stems partly from its ease of use. One can send an electronic mail letter to another computer user simply by knowing their electronic mail "address." This address encodes the actual physical location of the recipients' computer as well as their particular electronic "mailbox" on that computer. In function, this address operates much like a telephone number in the international telephone network.

Another reason for the growing use of electronic mail is that it provides for fast "asynchronous" human communication. This is communication in which the participants need not be online simultaneously. Human A composes and sends an electronic letter to human B. It sits in human B's electronic mailbox until human B (who is doing something else) gets to it. When convenient, human B responds to the letter by sending a reply back to human A. It waits in human A's electronic mailbox until human A is ready to deal with it, and so on.

This procedure is really no different than that of sending hardcopy letters through the postal system. However, there are a number of important additional features to electronic mail that make it advantageous for users. One of these is that electronic mail delivery may take mere seconds, even when the recipient's computer is located on the other side of the planet. This significantly reduces overall transaction time when people are working together via electronic mail over a long period of time.

Another useful feature is that local mailer programs often incorporate useful e-mail-management features such as automatic return addressing for e-mail replies, an ability to define group nicknames, an ability to store and selectively retrieve received e-mail, and automatic redirection of incoming electronic mail to another computer account.

A third useful feature of electronic mail is that it is an extremely convenient tool for managing communications when the user does a lot of other work on the computer as well. Many students, workers, and individuals have convenient access to personal computers. Why not use these systems to manage and support correspondence as well? It can be far easier to take a writing-in-progress from a word processor and transfer it to a colleague (for critical analysis, of course) via electronic mail rather than print it, address an envelope, and wait for days to make sure it reached its destination. Further, the information transferred via electronic mail is not limited to text. Pictures, sounds, and virtually any type of data that can be encoded onto a computer file is fair game for electronic mail transfer. (Although in fairness it must be added that with the current state of technology some pre- and posttransfer processing of the data file may be necessary.)

An interesting side note to electronic mail is the extent to which it is being used for social communication. Some early critics of electronic mail hinged their objection on what they perceived to be a "mechanical" approach. They felt it would be dehumanizing and limited strictly to task-oriented discussion. In fact, the opposite is actually true, and the range of orientation of electronic mail is truly as diverse as the range of human communication. Rice and Love (1987) observed that CMC systems can facilitate the exchange of socioemotional content. From this it can be noted that technology does not necessarily dehumanize; rather, technology can be humanized to meet everyone's needs.

Group Conferencing Systems

Group conferencing systems are essentially an extension of electronic mail. With electronic mail one can send an electronic "letter" to a group of persons as easily as to one person—provided that each of their electronic mail addresses is known. Group conferencing systems were developed to help manage special problems of group-oriented conferencing. These problems include managing large and changing group membership lists, providing efficient distribution of e-mail among group members, and providing for retrieval of prior, and perhaps related, transactions.

Group conferencing systems come in a variety of types. I mention three popular approaches here. The first is an electronic mail *exploder* system such as the Listserv program that originated on BITnet-connected IBM mainframes and was later copied (at least partially) to the unix platform.

An e-mail exploder handles two primary functions of group electronic mail. First, it manages the group subscription list. This allows (if the nature of the group warrants) computer users to join or leave the group at will. This way an individual group member does not have to keep track of the current status of all group members. This is a good thing because some Listserv groups have memberships in the thousands.

Second, the exploder takes any single group member's contribution to the conference and copies it to all other group members. This is the exploding function. Group members participate in the group by sending their contributions to the exploder. It makes sure that copies go to all other current group members. This long-lasting distribution method results in "one-to-many" communication (Quarterman, 1990).

The exploder typically also keeps an archive of all previous conference transactions. This allows a new group member to examine previous transactions to gain an understanding of the current context in which discussion is taking place.

A second popular approach to group conferencing systems is the *bulletin board system* or BBS. This approach simulates the bulletin board at a shopping center or the lunchroom of a company. With physical bulletin boards, messages are usually written on 3 x 5 cards and thumb-tacked to the board for all to see. If there are enough entries (and enough space), the board may have separate areas for announcements, items for sale, help wanted, and so on.

A computer bulletin board typically has a number of subject areas into which a user may post messages. Other users may read these messages and elect to respond to the group or to the individual who originated the posting. One example of BBS-type group conferencing is Usenet NEWS. This collection of newsgroups originated on the UUCP network. Individual conference "postings" are transferred through the Internet through a protocol named *nntp*. Users access Usenet NEWS through a local client newsreader, such as the NETNEWS program for VM/CMS operating systems.

Usenet NEWS originated with a fairly small group of unix-based computers connected via the UUCP network. It has since developed into a far more powerful system that runs over the Internet and BITnet in addition to UUCP. Hundreds of original topic groups (newsgroups) have exploded to the point that (when I last looked a few minutes ago) over 2,000 newsgroups are represented. These span the breadth of human experience from telecommunication protocols to alternative backrubs.

A third approach to group conferencing is what I call *conference management systems*. These are systems that support conference participants by imposing a structured approach on the conference. The structured approach allows certain features of database management systems to come into play. One example of this is thread management. In a conference, a *thread* is a particular line of discussion. It can often be difficult to follow threads properly when a conference has hundreds, or even thousands, of members. Sometimes there are multiple discussion threads happening at the same time. Thread management allows a given user to isolate only the thread of interest and track the evolution of that thread through various contributions.

Because of the structured approach, conference management systems can be fairly easy to learn and use. Examples of conference management systems are DEC VAXNotes, CoSy, Caucus, Confer, and EIES. The thread management capability, combined with other functions in support of group communications, results in a form of "many-to-many" communication. One of the growing uses of group conferencing systems is to support instructional communication. A number of universities utilize conference management systems such as VAXNotes for this purpose. At Penn State over 90 courses are taught incorporating private NETNEWS groups for course announcements, discourse, and other purposes.

It is tempting to think of instructional group conferencing as an obvious application of technology to instruction; however, various realities delayed its widespread use until the mid-1980s. Among the problems encountered were lack of convenient access to microcomputers/terminals, lack of centralized support for instructors/students, the reluctance of many faculty to explore new instructional approaches, and the reluctance of academic departments to give adequate recognition to those faculty who did successfully explore new instructional approaches.

These problems are being overcome in a number of ways. First, technology is increasing in power and decreasing in price. Although this trend may not be following the predictions of Moore's Law (Patterson, Kiser, & Smith, 1989),[1] it has nevertheless resulted in a situation in which $1,000 can purchase a quite usable personal workstation and modem for both local work and telecommunication. Second, large organizations are recognizing the need for both centralized and decentralized provision of training and support. In the 1960s and 1970s, the university computer center was a place where mainframe computer access was meted out to users. In the 1990s, the computer center is primarily a provider of training and expert support for distributed computing resources. Third, a growing body of literature is reporting on various approaches, strategies, and outcomes for instructional conferencing. Finally, there is a growing recognition by academic administrators of the value of technical innovation in instruction. This is partly because of hopes for greater efficiency and partly in recognition of the need to prepare students for an increasingly technical world.

One pioneer in the application of conferencing to instruction has noted that communication within a learning group often increases as a result of computer use (Hiltz, 1986). My own experience in seven years of using conferencing to support Liberal Arts courses shows that students embrace the technology and quickly adapt it to their own purposes (Santoro, 1989).

---

[1]Engineer Gordon Moore made the prediction that, beginning in 1965, the power of a silicon chip of the same price would double annually over the next 20 years.

Interactive Messaging

In addition to the asynchronous forms of computer conferencing discussed thus far, many computer systems have the capability for computer users to communicate in synchronous mode. Synchronous communication requires that all participants be online at the same time. As a result, the communication flows much like a telephone conversation. Because of the interaction that results, this form of conferencing is known as *interactive messaging*.

Early interactive messaging took place between people logged into the same computer system, even though they might be physically located far apart from one another. As computer networks were developed, some included the capability for interactive messaging between different computer hosts, and others omitted this capability. For example, the UUCP network does not support interactive messaging of any kind. The BITnet network supports unsolicited interactive messaging. This means that one computer user on BITnet can interrupt another computer user with a message. (Many systems do include commands for filtering or turning off such messages entirely.) The Internet supports interactive messaging, but not unsolicited messages. If a person on Internet wants to communicate interactively with another Internet user (assuming both have software permitting this), the initiator's software would send a request to the other person. That person would have to acknowledge that he or she is willing to communicate. If he or she does so, the software will then establish an interactive messaging session.

A simple example of interactive messaging is the unix "talk" program, which is covered in detail in Sudweek's chapter (this volume). A more robust example of interactive messaging is represented by the Internet Relay Chat (IRC) system. IRC follows the paradigm of a citizen's band radio in providing an environment for interactive messaging. A user first runs a local IRC client program, which then connects to one of a network of IRC servers on the Internet. The client program can be located on the user's PC or on a mainframe computer for which the user has an account. However, the PC or mainframe must have an Internet connection. The IRC servers manage traffic flow between IRC clients to ensure efficient network utilization.

The user selects a "nickname" and a 'channel' for communication. If the channel already exists, the user will be joined to it and will be able to communicate interactively with all other persons on that channel. If the channel does not exist, IRC will create it, and the user will be the owner (and initially the only resident) of that channel.

Once on an IRC channel, whatever a person types will be seen by all other channel members, and vice versa. The nicknames will be appended to each message, so each person knows who is saying what. IRC also provides other capabilities for managing interactive sessions, including maintaining a transcript on a computer file, private messaging, private/public channels, designation of channel topics, listing of available public channels, and preset option preferences.

HUMAN-COMPUTER-HUMAN CMC

The second major category of CMC is that in which the computer takes a more active role in storing and retrieving information for the human user. This form of CMC is often referred to as *informatics*. With informatics, the computer is programmed to act like an interactive library or database. People access the desired computer system through a variety of methods and issue a series of commands to locate and retrieve the desired information.

For informatics to work, the user must first establish a connection with the computer on which the desired information resides. In some cases this interaction is managed asynchronously by sending interactive or e-mail messages to the remote computer with the body of the message containing the command to be executed.

Users connected to the Internet have the more convenient option of using the 'Telnet' protocol to establish a real-time interactive link with the remote computer. Technically, Telnet is the Internet protocol for remote terminal access. This allows any Internet-connected user to log onto any Internet-connected host computer as if they had a local terminal connection to that computer. The growth in Internet-connected users has fueled a growth in the number and diversity of informatics applications. I describe a few of these below.

Online Databases

With an online database, the user establishes a connection to the remote host computer, issues any appropriate log-on sequences, and then issues the proper commands to locate and retrieve the desired information. Hundreds of online databases are currently available through the Internet, with at least a few of these also supporting some kind of asynchronous query mechanism.

Some examples of online databases include library catalog systems (OPACs), online medical/legal information servers, and weather information servers. Some specialized online databases include interactive game systems, NASA and FDA information servers, and a Ham

Radio Callsign database. Popular guides to online databases include "Accessing Online Bibliographic Databases" by Barron (n.d.), and "Special Internet Connections" by Yanoff (n.d.). (Both of these files may be found on the anonymous ftp archive ftp.cac.psu.edu in the /pub/internexus subdirectory. The Barron file is named LIBRARIE.TXT, and the Yanoff file is named INTERNET.SERVICES.)

Online file archives are network-accessible computers that store libraries of computer files for retrieval by users. The method of retrieval may vary depending on the exact setup of the archive. One of the most popular retrieval methods is the Internet file transfer protocol (FTP). Other retrieval methods include electronic mail and interactive messaging requests. With FTP retrieval, the file is immediately and interactively retrieved. With electronic mail and interactive messaging retrieval, the request is queued to a file server that sends the file to the requester via electronic mail. (The Listserv program supports queued file retrieval.)

The kinds of information that may be stored in online computer file archives is as varied as the nature of computer files themselves. Files may include programs (both in source and compiled form), data sets (raw and processed), pictures, sounds, text, and even animation and movies. There are only two requirements for the successful use of online file archives. The first requirement is that the user may have to possess a file decryptor or extractor program to process the file after transferring it. This is often necessary with binary programs because they are processed into encrypted or compressed form to ensure successful transfer. The second requirement is that the user possess whatever program necessary to utilize the computer file once it is retrieved. In many cases the necessary decryptor or extractor will be available from the same site as the binary programs. For example, if a user retrieves a weather satellite image from the archive vmd.cso.uiuc.edu (which are stored in GIF format), then the user must have the necessary software for displaying and manipulating the image.

Campus-Wide Information Systems

Expanding college/university networks and the ever-improving availability of network-accessible microcomputers/terminals has led to the development of campuswide information systems (CWIS). These are information servers that combine online database capabilities with menu-driven front-ends to other Telnet-accessible information servers.

Typically, the online database function provides users with campus information formerly available through publications or campus newspapers. This information may include the schedule of classes, the faculty/staff/student telephone directory, the policies/procedures manual, and other "official" information. It may also include a listing of campus events, the semester calendar, and announcements from various clubs and student organizations. In general, the idea is that the database component of a CWIS provides the most current information possible without the delays and waste associated with printed versions.

Two popular approaches to campuswide information systems are MIT's TECHINFO and Minnesota's Gopher. Both systems provide users with a hierarchy of menus. The user navigates through this set of menus searching for the desired information. In some cases the selection of a menu item will result in the display of information. In other cases the selection of a menu item will result in a Telnet session to some remote information server.

Both TECHINFO and Gopher are based on a client-server model. The user runs a client program on his or her local PC or a connected mainframe that provides the user interface and processes menu selections for the server. The server is typically located on another computer and accessed by the client program using Telnet. Client programs for both TECHINFO and Gopher are available for the Apple Macintosh, IBM-PS/2, various workstations, and various mainframe operating systems.

A slightly different approach to the problem of current information dissemination is found in the Wide-Area Information System (WAIS) developed by Thinking Machines Corporation. WAIS is also based on a client-server model, but in this case the user runs a local client to develop a number of query profiles that resemble problems. Each query profile contains two pieces of information. The first is a set of data that qualifies the kind of information being sought. For example, someone seeking information on computer-mediated communication might use the string "CMC." The second piece of information is the set of WAIS servers to be searched. These are in the form of Internet domain addresses, such as infomac@sumex.aim.edu (WAIS FAQ, 1993).

The WAIS approach is interesting in that a given user may develop a set of query profiles and issue them periodically to see if any new information has emerged. Such an approach can be extremely useful to persons who are interested in certain topics from online group conferences, but who are too busy to actively screen all conference transactions. If a WAIS server exists for the conference, it may be possible to create a query profile to elicit only relevant transactions from the complete set of conference transactions. On the other hand, WAIS suffers from the same major problem as other online databases. Namely, if a person does not find the desired information, it may be because the information does not exist, or it may be because they have not used the correct query profile to obtain it.

COMPUTER-ASSISTED INSTRUCTION

Computer-Assisted Instruction (CAI) refers to a broad category of computer use the purpose or which is to provide instruction to some human user. According to Burke (1982), the terms *computer-based instruction* (CBI) and *computer-managed instruction* (CMI) are also used to describe this category, although CMI also includes the notion of computerized testing, diagnosis, and record keeping.

The main idea behind CAI is that most instruction can be systematized into an algorithmic process. Once this has been done, it is possible to write a computer program to interactively deliver the instruction. In addition, the program will periodically test the student to ensure that the desired material is being learned. Such a CAI program is commonly referred to as *courseware*.

Two major advantages to CAI courseware are: (a) the ability of a student to learn at his or her own pace, and (b) the effective distribution of the instructional process to the student, reducing this load on a human teacher. In many cases the role of the human teacher is not eliminated, rather it is changed into that of a guide and mentor. In recent years, the principles and approaches of CAI are being combined with the functional capabilities of conferencing and informatics to form the emerging discipline of distance education (DE). One pioneer of distance education, Morton Flate Paulson (of the European SUPERNET project on Distance Learning), sums up the expected potential of this application of CMC: "My proposition is that it is possible to create a virtual school around a computer-based information system and that virtual schools will dominate the future of distance education" (Paulson, 1987, p. 72).

SUMMARY

The three major areas described in this overview chapter are different in their purpose and use, yet they are similar in that all three are essentially methods for information transfer between and among human computer users. This leads back to the original premise that computer systems— the grand symbol manipulators—are essentially tools for human communication. Just as communication activities permeate human existence, so will computer systems permeate human endeavor, whether in business, education, socialization, or leisure activities.

It is important to keep in mind that we are both the creator and the object of the creation of CMC. In the final analysis, the potential for benefit or harm stemming from CMC will be up to the humans who design, implement, and use it. On the plus side, CMC technology can permit the worldwide sharing of information in ways that seemed inconceivable only a few decades ago. On the negative side, the potential exists for a massive invasion of privacy and the creation of a two-tiered society comprised of those with network access and those without it.

As one participant in the development of CMC I wish to conclude this overview of CMC technology with the fervent hope that technical achievements can be paralleled by a dedication to its appropriate use and social responsibility.

REFERENCES

Barron, B. (n.d.). *Accessing online bibliographic databases*. Periodically updated and available from FTP archive ftp.cac.psu.edu in the subdirectory /pub/internexus as file LIBRARIE.TXT.

Burke, R.L. (1982). *CAI sourcebook*. Englewood Cliffs, NJ: Prentice-Hall.

Chesebro, J.W. & Bonsall, D.G. (1989). *Computer-mediated communication: Human relationships in a computerized world*. Tuscaloosa: University of Alabama Press.

Ehrenhalt, S.M. (1986, August 15). Work-force shifts in the 80's. *New York Times*, p. D2.

Hellerstein, L. (1986, May). *Electronic messaging and conferences with an emphasis on social use: An exploratory study*. Paper presented at the International Communication Association annual conference, Chicago, IL.

Hiltz, S.R. (1986) The virtual classroom: Using computer-mediated communication for university teaching. *Journal of Communication, 36*(2), 95-104.

Lewis, P.H. (1986, July 8). The summer break. *New York Times*, p. C5.

MERIT. (1991, March). LINK Letter—Electronic Newsletter of the MERIT/NSFNET Backbone Project (electronic publication delivered through Listserv).

Patterson, D.A., Kiser, D.S. & Smith, D.N. (1989). *Computing unbound: Using computers in the arts and sciences*. New York: W.W. Norton.

Paulson, M.F. (1987, December/January). In search of a virtual school. *THE Journal*, pp. 71-76

Porat, M.U. (1974). *Defining an information sector in the U.S. economy*. (Information Reports and Bibliographies, Vol. 5, No. 5). Stanford, CA: Institute for Communication Research, Stanford University.

Porat, M.U. (1977). *The information economy: Definition and measurement*. Washington, DC: Department of Commerce, Office of Telecommunications.

Quarterman, J.R. (1990). The matrix: Computer networks and conferencing systems worldwide. *Digital Press*, pp. 12-16.

Rice, R.E. & Love, G. (1987). Electronic emotion: Socioemotional content in a computer-mediated communication network. *Communication Research, 14*(1), pp. 85-108

Santoro, G.M. (1989). *Support of group problem-solving instruction through computer-mediated communication.* Unpublished doctoral dissertation, The Pennsylvania State University.

Schneier, B. (1992, October 12). Does telecommuting work? *MacWeek*, p. 8

Yanoff, S. (n.d.) *Special Internet connections.* Periodically updated and available from FTP archive site ftp.cac.psu.edu under subdirectory /pub/internexus as file INTERNET.SERVICES.

WAIS FAQ. (1993). Published on Usenet NEWS in newsgroup COMP.ANSWERS.

Chapter Two

Using Computer-Mediated Communication in Teaching University Courses

Jill H. Ellsworth
Southwest Texas State University

BACKGROUND

In the university, a limited range of teaching/learning methodologies are typically utilized. In the humanities the teaching will typically use the lecture method; in the sciences, there is the lecture/lab combination.

In an effort to provide expanded access, meet the needs of learners, and overcome some of the problems encountered by students who live and work at a distance from the university, I introduced Computer-Mediated Communication (CMC) into my undergraduate and graduate courses. The students frequently travel 1 to 2 hours to class, and CMC offered the hope of improved communication and enriched and improved instruction. CMC can provide communication access to persons, resources, and information, independent of time and distance. In some cases it is one-way, in others two-way, and in yet other cases it is interactive.

CMC can open up a new avenue for learning—it is not time-reliant, allowing for a certain interpersonal distance for those who desire it. It allows students to access information in an exploratory fashion, with fairly random access to information, or by using a structure that is useful to him or her, as opposed to one structured by the instructor.

Our CMC class activities were carried out with nontraditional undergraduates and graduate students at Southwest Texas State University. The students were enrolled in either an undergraduate Portfolio Assessment course, the initial course in the Bachelor of Applied Arts and Sciences degree (BAAS), or a graduate research methods course, for the Master of Science in Interdisciplinary Studies (MSIS).

The BAAS and the MSIS are both interdisciplinary degree programs designed for adults who desire and/or need individualized academic programs, and one that awards credit for nontraditional forms of learning. The individualized interdisciplinary program allows adult students, in conjunction with a faculty mentor, to cooperatively select educational goals and academic courses that are related to their career and life objectives.

These are intensive degree programs requiring extensive interaction between students and faculty. The mentoring activity is the key in the initial phases of the degree programs when the students are developing a prior extra-institutional learning assessment portfolio (in the case of both graduate and undergraduate students) and taking the research methods course (in the case of the graduate students). To meet the needs of working, less mobile, physically challenged, or older adults, the students have access to both a faculty-maintained computer-based BBS and a Digital Corporation VAX mainframe for information and assistance with course assignments.

Originally, it was anticipated that CMC would be an ancillary process or facilitative process to instruction, useful primarily for beta learning. As I progressed with CMC, I discovered that CMC was useful in both alpha and beta learning. *Alpha learning* is learning that is the major exposition of the concepts, ideas, facts, and processes. *Beta learning* is learning that could be called reinforcement or adjunct to the alpha learning. Alpha learning in my graduate research course, for example, would be a lecture on correlations and descriptive statistics, and beta learning would be the assignment of homework using a data set to make such correlations. I found that alpha learning using CMC was possible, even desirable, in meeting students' needs. I experimented with placing new concepts into the VAX Notes computer conference and found that it was effective in teaching these concept to the students.

PRINCIPLES

CMC in a course or, more generally, in a university setting, can take many forms. In this particular instance, it took a myriad of forms ranging from advisement to course-specific activities, using a variety of systems, including the use of a mainframe and the use of a departmental computer Bulletin Board System (BBS).

The teaching/learning process can involve a wide variety of CMC activities ranging from simple e-mail to rather sophisticated uses of computers for research activities, in which the interactions could be any combinations of student-to-student, student-to-faculty, faculty-to-student, faculty-to-faculty, student-to-others, others-to-student, and so forth.

The communication could be private, that is to say, only those who are communicating "see" and participate in the communication, or it could be public. In public CMC, all participants can "see" and participate in the communication activity if they choose. Some students preferred that their participation remain at a low level, or in the parlance of the students, they preferred to be "lurkers."

The communication format could also be didactic: in this case, communication flows from faculty to student, similar to read-only files.

PRAXIS

CMC principles and forms such as e-mail, computer conferencing, group computer conferencing, interactive messaging, and online database and archive searching were used in specific applications designed to achieve course and educational objectives, examples of which follow.

E-mail was used to provide a variety of kinds of interactions: student-to-student interaction, in which students could cooperatively complete assignments and communicate about class, processes, and content; or student-to-faculty and faculty-to-student interaction, encompassing a full range of communication ranging from advising, explanations, course content, evaluation, and the turning in of written assignments.

Conferencing via the mainframe involved a private computer conference (exclusive to class members) to provide shared, posted views, ideas, and collaborative writing activities, including peer-to-peer interactions. The computer conference allowed for this peer-to-peer communication to take on intellectual, or high-level content, without the influence of the teacher. Didactic postings, involving one-way communication, were used for making assignments. Postings in the computer conference were broad ranging in their purpose, level of formality, and intent. For example, one conference subsection dealt with locus of control research and was very scholarly in form and intent. Several of the graduate students had found this construct useful and were exploring it. Other topics included our new telephone registration (commentary ran 10:1 against), and more recently, the conference included a lot of discussion concerning the Clinton/Bush election campaigns and the activities of the Clinton administration as it settled in.

To extend the learning environment, students were encouraged to network more widely via various scholarly discussion lists using group conferencing and to extend their participation to include class-to-class communication with students from other institutions worldwide. The lists represented ranged from ERL-L (Education Research), RESEARCH, and QUALRS (focusing on forms of research) to INFO-NETS and HELP-NET, which recursively focus on using the nets themselves. Other lists explored included sociology, psychology, Spanish, and football.

An example of a specific undergraduate assignment involved the posting, to their class discussion group, of a section of the portfolio they were writing. The posting was read for discussion on the computer conference. Specifically, they were to upload a four-page piece of their writing, and each of the other students was responsible for posting at least one suggestion for improvement, a constructive comment, or a reaction. The first student was then to revise the passage by the next class and repost it. Additionally, the professor would offer a critique privately via e-mail to the student, and finally, assign a letter grade on the revised assignment.

The undergraduate students were also required to use references from at least one online database for a fairly traditional term paper. Specifically, they were to use a Telnet connection to the Washington and Lee Law Library, or utilize Bureau of Labor Statistics information in order to complete the assignment.

An example of a graduate-course CMC assignment involved locating and employing specific online research tools utilizing the Internet. The students utilized both Telnet and FTP to access databases and documents. They were to post a summary of it to the subsection of our class computer conference on resources. They were required to identify several useful tools, critique them, and give very specific directions for accessing the information. The resource file was then available to all students. The resources accessed ranged from ERIC to NAFTA (North American Free Trade Agreement), using Gopher, the Maastricht Treaty on European Union (Cornell), Sports Schedules (NHL), plus many others.

Both graduate and undergraduate students used the Internet Relay Chat (IRC) mode for interactive messaging. In most cases, IRC was used to communicate with each other, although from time to time it was used to communicate interactively with the professor.

The majority of the time, CMC was used in communication regarding course content, both in gaining content—alpha learning, and in reinforcement such as asking questions—beta learning. CMC was used, however, for other academic activities: It was used in problem solving, both in course-related and non-course-related material. And CMC was used to advise students on academic matters covering the usual topics, including degree planning. These were generally carried out via e-mail and IRC on the campus computer, and as such was interactive. Occasionally, it took the form of a broadcast message to all students via e-mail or computer conference. It could be simultaneous or time-independent in nature, synchronous or asynchronous.

Assessment and evaluation activities were carried out via CMC on a variety of levels. Specific assignments were critiqued and evaluated using CMC, as well as providing a forum for less formal assessment activities. CMC provided for "on-the-fly" opportunities for networking and mentoring as well. With the exception of the final portfolio or research proposal, which had to contain original signatures, I allowed any assignment to be submitted electronically. This meant that students did not have to be on campus in order to turn in papers.

In addition to the more serious teaching and learning activities, CMC was used as relief from stress, sometimes expressing itself as humor. In almost all cases, sometime during the semester, students began some form of a humor sub-topic or thread.

Early on during courses, I attempt to be more available via e-mail than by telephone, in order to encourage the use of CMC and reinforce procedural learning. This synthetic availability followed the initial training on the use of e-mail.

One problem encountered with CMC was that of access to the hardware and software needed to interface. Some students did not have access to a computer with a modem or a mainframe terminal. For some students, this necessitated coming to campus to use the technology, or in some cases, borrowing, or renting collaboratively needed items.

As a professor, I find that the systems set-up and preparation of materials require considerably more frontloading of my time and energy. Also, when a system breaks down, I must solve the problem on a tight timetable. However, I regain much of that time as CMC provides support for the teaching enterprise.

OUTCOMES

After using CMC in a broad spectrum of ways in support of diverse educational objectives, I discovered that there are developmental learning tasks that will make for a more successful integration of CMC in the teaching activity. The successful use of CMC in university courses depends on the utilization of tiers of developmental teaching and learning. Each plane of such learning requires mastery of the previous level. Tier 1 teaching and learning involves the exposition and mastery of the general context for the other learning tasks, answering such questions as "What are the general objectives of this course learning? What is expected, and how does CMC fit into the overall course?" Essentially, this tier lays the groundwork for the entire course; the student must have a matrix or context for the more specific learning and must understand the role and value of CMC in that learning. In effect, they must see the connection between what is being taught (the content) and the vehicles (methods and media) for that teaching.

Tier 2 teaching and learning builds on Tier 1 and involves introductory hands-on learning of the technical access and process information that students must acquire in order to start using the various technologies and tools. These are the skills or "how to" operational-level tasks: the rules of interaction. Typically, this will entail learning how to use a terminal and/or PC in order to access the mainframe or the BBS, covering such questions as "How do I sign on? and How do I use this communication program?" This involves using the hardware and learning the various software and protocols involved in the course, such as the Internet, e-mail, up- and downloading, using the computer conference, and in the case of the graduate students, using the various online tools such as ERIC. Each of these tools was used by students to communicate with each other, to communicate with the instructor, to retrieve information, and to turn in assignments.

Tier 3 teaching and learning necessitates gaining proficiency and mastery of the tools to the extent that they become second nature. Both teacher and learner must have sufficient facility with the tools of CMC, so that the tools themselves are not a communication barrier. This level results in the actual utilization of CMC in problem solving, information gathering, negotiating, and turning in assignments.

The teaching of these Tier 1, 2 ,and 3 skills must become part of the course, which may mean in-class time or formal adjunct lab instruction. Also, all too often, when faculty want to use CMC as an enhancement or as a major delivery system, they overlook the need to provide Tier 2 technical "how to" information. They will, for example, ask students to sign on to a mainframe and use the course notes conference to discuss their reading. The student has no clue as to how to do this, does not dare to reveal this, and does not know from whom to get the answer—and they do not complete the assignment.

Students have a variety of learning and personality needs that are especially well addressed by CMC options. Some fairly introverted students (as assessed by the Myers Briggs personality inventory: Myers, 1984) found that interactions with peers and professors were facilitated using CMC. They found it easier to communicate via CMC than in face-to-face situations. Also, students with certain learning styles as identified by the Learning Styles Inventory (Kolb, 1985) found that CMC enhanced their learning, especially those with learning styles in the domains of Reflective Observer and Active Experimentation. The individual with a learning style in the Reflective Observer domain prefers to learn in a situation that permits little personal interaction and allows for observation versus interaction; those with a learning style in Active Experimentation prefer learning situations that emphasize new approaches or the ability to control some of the learning situations themselves.

Access to information and ideas was enhanced using CMC and allowed for a less hierarchical approach, again meeting certain learning-style needs. The information was available when the student preferred to use it as opposed to being structured by faculty. In traditional information exchanges, faculty decide when information is imparted and in what order. CMC allows for more lateral exploration access as structured by the student, developing path-oriented and self-directed learning. CMC provides additional feedback paths and mechanisms, surprising responses, and yet another way to support flexibility in learning.

CMC has some unique characteristics that can enhance the teaching/learning enterprise. It is quick and can provide group interaction without requiring all persons to be in one location in order to meet. Because so many of our students are professionals; we often had one or more individuals participating in discussions from distant locations.

CMC provides for both synchronous and asynchronous communications. Communication that is not time-dependent allows students to participate at times most convenient for them. It crosses time barriers, providing great flexibility for teacher and learners. Students can leave communications of all kinds and homework when they wish, send large or small text files, formal papers, informal feedback, carry out ideation/brainstorming, offer critiques, and so forth. The IRC mode provided synchronous communication on similar content. Interaction that is not time-specific is increasingly important as students are not as campus-based as they once were and often work a variety of schedules. Quick feedback on homework and other assignments is more easily accomplished, allowing for faster turnaround because courses for adults frequently meet just once a week making feedback on written work difficult.

CMC allows for interpersonal distance simply not possible in a traditional classroom: Students did not have to see other students or the professor, nor did they have to interact. A few students began to take on outside-of-class CMC "personae" that were in some cases subtly different from their in-class personae. In some cases, the personae were quite different: for example, a student who was reserved and shy in the regular classroom became more vocal, even using humor to make her points. We allowed for anonymous postings, which although risky, appeared to break barriers associated with status, ethnicity, race, sex, and other characteristics. The students who were vocal in class were not the same students who were "vocal" in CMC.

SUMMARY

CMC has many implications for the teaching/learning enterprise, and in balance, the positive far outweighs the negative. On the positive side, there are many advantages to using the approach: It meets numerous learning and personality needs; provides access in a variety of modes; and ideation and brainstorming can be less inhibited, promoting active thinking. CMC approaches have great value to working individuals, especially those who are less mobile or shy. For students who find traditional approaches difficult, interpersonal transactions "cost" less.

CMC presents a few problematic issues for the student. These include requiring the frontloading of considerable information and skills (Tier 1 and 2 learning), necessitating the expenditure of time and energy. From the professor's point of view, it can cost instructional time, which means either outside-of-class requirements or the truncation of some other content. Additionally, individuals and institutions must provide access to hardware and systems, the cost of which may be considerable.

I found that the use of CMC very much enhanced the teaching and learning activity. Students, too, found it valuable. Although commentary on my course and teaching evaluations did reveal that the necessary frontloading of skills before they were operational was frustrating. This frustration faded, but was nonetheless a factor for a few students. Overall, comparing my teaching evaluations for similar courses revealed significantly higher ratings in many areas regarding feedback and accessibility outside of class, and in content acquisition. Overall, I will continue to use CMC broadly and encourage others to do the same.

REFERENCES

Kolb, D.A. (1985). *Learning style inventory.* Boston: McBer & Co.
Myers, I.B. (1984) *Myers Briggs type indicator.* Palo Alto, CA: Consulting Psychologists Press.

Chapter Three

CMC and Writing Instruction: A Future Scenario

James N. Shimabukuro
University of Hawaii
Kapiolani Community College

Today, if we in the discipline were to draw a line separating the innovative from the traditional and the new from the old, teaching students to use word processors to compose and revise drafts would fall to the right of center. For most of us, the personal computer (PC) is an integral part of composition instruction, as much a fixture as the handbook.

For the past decade, the computer·has invigorated the review phase in process-oriented approaches. Until the PC became accessible to students, the approach was a great idea. It made all the sense in the world to ask students to revise their drafts umpteen times "because that's what successful writers do." Practically speaking, however, rewriting an entire draft on a typewriter was, at best, tedious, and at worst, impossible. The PC transformed the idea into a viable option. The word processor allows a student to edit specific portions of a text and, with a press of a key, send the file to the printer. The result is a revised draft—quick and clean.

Text production, however, as important as it is, is still peripheral to the writing process. Planning, translating, and reviewing—the major phases—have been resistant to the instructor's direct control; activities designed to stimulate and inform students struggling through the process are difficult to implement, evaluate, and monitor. The problem is time and space: Given 50 minutes in a classroom, an instructor cannot confer with all 20 students. Teachers have been imaginative in their efforts to overcome this natural barrier: They have students collaborating in small groups, and some have tutors working with groups and individuals. These strategies work, but they are unwieldy and inefficient.

Teachers have turned to computers, looking for ways to adapt its power to their needs. Again, they have been innovative. They have improvised online heuristics to aid invention and made available spell, word choice, and grammar checkers to help in the revising process. The craft has been revitalized by these strategies, but much of the writing process remains inaccessible.

To more directly intervene in and thus guide the student's composing process, some teachers have experimented with computer mediated communication (CMC). In 1987, Troll described the system she used at Carnegie-Mellon University:

> The computers we used were IBM RT's, advanced function workstations that allow users to run many processes simultaneously. For example, students can revise a paper, study an on-line glossary of critical terms, review teacher and student comments on their drafts, read bulletin board posts on a paper topic, and send mail to the teacher or a classmate for clarification. All of these chores appear simultaneously in different "windows" on the high resolution monitor. (p. 22)

The stations ran off a mainframe, on network software. Considering where we are today, six years later, Troll's working model is surprisingly advanced. The software and hardware features she describes comprise a standard that is still out of reach for most teachers who are experimenting with networked computers in the teaching of writing.

From the outset, she found that the new technology had a positive impact on students. The new medium encouraged them to put more effort into their online messages and papers. Students often wrote better peer review comments. "[In] the EditText files that my students produced in commenting on one another's papers," she says, "many students produced full-sentence comments and short paragraphs covering everything from style to the cogency of the argument" (pp. 25-26). Perhaps, as Meeks (1987) states, students feel "increased motivation to work hard on assignments because they will be viewable by other students as well as by the instructor(s)" (p. 187).

One of the most important outcomes of CMC, however, is increased participation in the activities that make up the writing process.

Troll observes that "students who were shy in class asked questions or made comments on the computer, using either electronic mail or the bulletin board. The technology seemed to make communication easier" (p. 26). She finds that "increased interaction with the audience during the reading and writing processes makes the context more social, recursive, and dynamic" (p. 30). Thus, she concludes "that the quality and quantity of the discussions merit continued use of the electronic bulletin board as a vehicle for critical thinking and socialization of the writing process" (p. 27).

Recently, the networked computer classroom has really taken off. Programs such as *Daedalus*, written specifically for popular PC (Macintosh and MS-DOS) environments, have been the catalyst. By linking computers in a classroom, teachers are learning what Troll discovered, that they can overcome many of the real-time barriers imposed by the face-to-face environment. Everyone can talk at once in a class discussion. Students are able to form conferences of four to five members for in-depth exchanges, including problem solving, brainstorming, and draft review, and they can correspond with one another via e-mail. The beauty of computer-mediated communication is that students and teachers can move among conferences, participating as required or at their discretion, and the messages are stored as they are sent, providing a permanent, sequenced record that can be accessed, then or at a later time, by one, some, or all. Students are able to review discussions after the class is over and comment on or respond to others' ideas and questions via e-mail or uploaded public files. They are able to capture or download message files to their disks, from which they can later copy and paste text.

Reports on networked classrooms are beginning to appear in greater numbers. Teachers are learning that information is distributed and exchanged much more efficiently, and the quality of class and group discussions is improved (Beals, 1990; Henri, 1988; Hiltz, 1988; Kaye, 1990; Kuehn, 1988; Phillips & Santoro, 1989;). CMC helps to improve thinking (Phillips & Pease, 1985) and collaborative skills (Davis, Scriven, & Thomas, 1987; Kubota, 1991; Smith, 1990). There is tentative evidence that CMC has a positive effect on student writing (Casey, 1990; DiMatteo, 1990; Holvig, 1989; Miller-Souviney & Souviney, 1987; Murray, 1988; Phillips & Santoro, 1989; Roberts, 1987).

What networked computers can do for process-oriented writing instruction in the next decade or two is perhaps best examined by illustration. The following narrative is fictional, but it presents features that will probably become part of the virtual classroom.

THE SCENARIO

It is Saturday, 19:00, Hawaii time. Maria is at home, in her bedroom. She turns on her laptop computer, which has a built-in modem connected via a standard cable to the phone jack on the wall, calls up the communication program on her hard drive, logs on to the University of Hawaii UNIX system (UHUNIX), and goes to her mailbox. She had completed a draft of her essay the night before, sending it through the built-in spell- and grammar-checker and making a few last-minute revisions. She had composed the entire paper on her laptop, using a popular word-processing program. She had gotten up at 05:00 this Saturday morning, reread it once more, decided it was ready, and uploaded the file. She is in the final phase of this assignment, the third in her English 100 class.

The file was saved in her class's UHUNIX subdirectory, an area which had been set aside for up- and downloading text files. The assignment, which had been posted as e-mail to all members of the class by Dr. Chan, the English 100 professor, was to observe, describe, analyze, and discuss a specific human behavior. The deadline for the final draft is midnight, Monday. For her subject, she had chosen her boyfriend; she observed him as he watched a recent live telecast of a UH versus Brigham Young University football game. She thinks the draft is quite good, but she knows it could be better.

She had downloaded, read, commented on, and uploaded her three c-mates', or conference mates', drafts during the week, making sure to use the unique filename extension they had worked out earlier in the semester to differentiate among versions of the same file. All three were excellent. For Ebasa's and Cam-Tu's, she had commented on a few surface problems: run-ons, fragments, word choice; the descriptions and analyses had been excellent. For Ayako's, she had pointed out the need for a stronger thesis. Maria had grown into the role of the group's expert on focus and mechanics.

At the mailbox prompt, she types the command that lists all her mail. She has received over 70 separate messages from many different sources. This evening, she is interested in mail from her c-mates. Ayako, Ebasa, Cam-Tu, and Maria form an online c-group; there are four c-groups in her class with four students each. She is relieved to find that Ayako and Salevaa have left messages for her; she is a bit concerned that Ebasa and Cam-Tu have not. Salevaa is one of two student facilitators in her English 100 class. She reads the mail from Ayako first.

Ayako says that she appreciates Maria's feedback on her draft. She also feels that Maria's draft is "terrific." However, she suggests that Maria revise the introductory paragraph: It "doesn't grab" Ayako. Maria sends a reply to Ayako, thanking her for the compliment and the suggestion and asking for advice on how to strengthen the opening.

Next, Maria reads Salevaa's message. He, too, likes Maria's draft and seconds Ayako's comment. As usual, he is impressed with her skill at describing people, places, things, action, and so on. Her images are always vivid. He suggests a deeper analysis of the social causes for her subject's behavior: "Why does he behave so aggressively? Assuming that this is a learned behavior, who or what are the sources of his 'education'?" To generate ideas, he suggests a live online chat with members of her group. In closing, he commends her for her excellent reviews of her c-mates' drafts.

Maria isn't surprised. Salevaa, like Dr. Chan, always pushes for deeper analyses. She has read their messages to her and other students. In her c-group, she and the others have come to rely on Ebasa for advice on how to dig deeper. Ebasa has developed a reputation among his c-mates, as well as other classmates, for giving expert advice on meeting Salevaa's "deeper" requirements. Salevaa, too, has openly recognized Ebasa for providing his peers with help in massaging and milking their subject matter for insightful, significant ideas. Salevaa, in fact, is planning to recommend Ebasa to Dr. Chan to serve as a paid online facilitator after he completes the course.

Maria sends Salevaa a reply. She says she will try to set up a chat for Sunday afternoon, but given the short notice, she may need to settle for e-mail responses. She composes a message to the members of her group, asking them if they would be willing to help with her analysis for a half hour on Sunday, starting at 14:00. If not, she asks that they send suggestions to her. She logs off UHUNIX, exits the communication program, and turns off the computer.

On Sunday morning, 08:00, she logs on to UHUNIX and lists her mail. Ayako has posted a suggestion for improving Maria's introduction; she also says that she is looking forward to the chat at 14:00 HST. Ayako asks if they could spend a few minutes chatting about her thesis. Maria sends a reply, thanking Ayako for her help. She says that they should definitely spend a few minutes discussing Ayako's thesis. Maria finds brief messages from Ebasa and Cam-Tu. They, too, will be able to chat that afternoon. Maria is relieved.

At 14:00, all four are logged on and in the live-chat mode. Maria sends a greeting to the others. She composes the message in the lower portion of the split screen and sends it to the public area, the top portion of the screen. Immediately, the top screen begins to scroll with messages. All four have posted their initial greetings.

Ebasa gets the ball rolling. He, as well as the others, has read Maria's draft and all the comments related to it, including Salevaa's request for further analysis. He asks about her boyfriend's family background. Maria reports that Bobby, her boyfriend, had been raised in a family of jocks. Cam-Tu and Ayako immediately follow up with questions: "What sort of person is the father?" "Is Bobby the oldest child?" "Has Bobby been successful in sports?" In responding to these and other questions, she quickly emerges with possible explanations for his aggressiveness. She has captured the session to a file on her hard disk and plans to review the material later when she is revising her paper. She thanks her friends.

Maria then suggests that they discuss Ayako's thesis. After a few minutes, they are able to pinpoint the problem. Ayako needs to be much more specific about the main contrasting idea that she is developing. It is too broad. Ayako agrees. She quickly types and posts a revised statement. After additional feedback and revisions, Ayako is satisfied with the sentence that captures the essential point she is trying to make. She thanks her peers.

Before exiting chat, they talk about their social lives, families, friends, cultures, and so on. As usual, they talk about someday getting together, face to face. They thank each other for the help they have received and end the session.

Maria revises the analytical portion of her draft, based on the input she received online. At 17:00 on Sunday, she is done. On Monday morning, she will take a last look at the essay before uploading it as a final draft. She goes downstairs and joins the other members of her family who are setting up a barbecue on the outdoor lanai.

Maria is a freshman at a community college in Hawaii, on the island of Maui; Ebasa is a sophomore at a university in Ethiopia; Ayako is a freshman at a major public university in Osaka, Japan; Cam-Tu is a freshman at an ivy league college in Massachusetts; Salevaa, who lives in American Samoa, is a junior marketing major at UH-Manoa; and Dr. Chan, who lives in Macao, is a professor of composition at a community college in Honolulu.

THE NETWORKED CLASSROOM

The networked classroom will take many forms. This scenario presents one—albeit one that maximizes the virtual capacity of computers that are globally networked. This version will not appear overnight. As CMC is increasingly embraced, a developmental range will emerge, and this model will be at one extreme.

Generational schemes are often used (e.g., Marcus, 1984) to describe developments in computers. They provide a useful way to differentiate among the various CMC models for the teaching of composition. The future scenario, which links students and instructors at international sites, is based on what I am referring to as a fourth-generation model. The purpose of this scheme is to form a clearer perception of the possibilities, not to judge the quality or worth of individual programs.

Pre-Network

This network is a pre-area-network (PAN), computer-equipped classroom or lab. Computers are available to composition students in a classroom or at different sites on campus. The machines are not networked; each is an independent station or a stand-alone system. They are not hardware linked via cables through serial ports or network cards, and students and instructors cannot communicate electronically with one another. The computers are viewed as sophisticated word-processing machines or independent computer-assisted instruction (CAI) stations. A message is composed on a machine and captured to disk or printed on paper. The disk or hardcopy is then hand carried or mailed to the intended receiver. The system aids in the development of the message, but not in its transmission.

An example of a PAN setup is North Carolina State University's computer classroom. The writing instructors began with dual floppy, stand-alone Tandy IBM/compatibles. They installed hard drives on the computers in Summer 1992. Word processing is the primary function. Some of the teachers use Norton Textra Writer with their classes, but most use Word Perfect 5.1. Only 10 of the approximately 130 freshman composition classes are scheduled in the classroom (Fletcher, 1992).

Michigan Technological University's 1982 version of Wordsworth II is an example of a program designed for a PAN classroom. It consists of supplementary computer modules for process-based, interactive CAI in the composition classroom (Selfe & Wahlstrom, 1982).

First-Generation Network

This network is an isolated local-area network (LAN) classroom or lab. The computers at a particular location are networked on a server; however, the server is restricted to the site and isolated from systems in other areas, on and off campus. Students and instructors must meet at the site at scheduled times, and generally, applications and files are available at that location only. Besides enjoying the advantages of the PAN model, students are, during class, able to exchange messages, engage in live chat, share uploaded files for peer review, and so on.

The computer writing classrooms at Kapiolani Community College (KCC) are first-generation LAN models. Presently, the campus has two: one is equipped with approximately 22 Macintosh computers; the other with the same number of IBM-compatibles. The individual PCs are networked through Daedalus. The servers are a beefed-up Macintosh and an 80486 MSDOS machine. Both are located in the classroom. As LANs, they are not connected via communication lines to networks outside the classroom. Thus, they are not accessible to users after they leave the classroom, and users in the room cannot communicate with systems on the outside.

Despite the limitations, this setup has tremendous advantages over the PAN. Students are able to view assignments, instructions, and information files; participate in live chats; receive and send public and private messages; up- and download files; and engage in standard word-processing activities—much as the students in the future scenario. The major difference, however, is that all the work must be done in the classroom at the appointed time. The first-generation classrooms at KCC are popular, and they are scheduled for classes, back-to-back, all day, every day, from morning to night. A major drawback is that the files generated during live-chat sessions are not immediately accessible to students online once they leave the room.

To get around this limitation, students send the text to the printer for a hard copy (to keep costs down, this practice is discouraged) or take notes off the screen with paper and pencil. Those with access to Macintosh computers outside of class copy files to disk. However, the chat data files cannot be directly transferred from screen to disk without first being compacted by the instructor. These alternatives are extremely awkward and time-consuming. In a LAN setup, the network is, for all practical purposes, inaccessible to instructors and students after the scheduled class.

In a few years, the college is hoping to move up to a wide-area network (WAN) configuration, with students and teachers having access to classroom servers from other sites on campus. The communications infrastructure is in place for fiber optics, which will make multiple links feasible and affordable.

Second-Generation Network

This network is a site-limited, WAN (Weber, 1992) classroom or lab. Individual computers and servers are linked throughout much of the campus, but they are not accessible from off-campus sites. Students and instructors have all the advantages of the first two models, as well as access to relevant applications and files from various sites on campus throughout the school day. Troll's setup at Carnegie-Mellon is a WAN. MIT's Project Athena is another example of a second-generation network, a "campus-wide computing system which is available to *all* undergraduates and graduate students" (P.S. Huang, personal communication, February 4, 1993). The writing labs at the University of Massachusetts and the University of Idaho are further examples. At Massachusetts, one of the lab computers is linked to the university's mainframe. "Students with email accounts use that to load and mail their work back and forth rather than transporting a disk" (Carbone, e-mail, 1992). At Idaho, the lab is considering purchase of *Daedalus* or a similar integrated writing environment, which could be connected to the "campus backbone," allowing users access to programs from other servers on the WAN (Thomas, 1993).

At the University of California, Berkeley, Keeling (e-mail, 1992) will be "teaching a section of freshman composition making use of [a WAN] BBS for journal entries (which will enable students to respond more freely to each other[']s thinking and writing), group presentations, peer review workshops, bibliographies, and student conferences." He is also planning to "post model essays and university calendar events." His "students will be responsible for 2-3 writing tasks per week on the Bulletin Board, and the computer-mediated writing will account for 30% of their grade." He is "using a software package called PCBoard which will run on a multi-user host computer dedicated to this pilot project." His students will be "able to logon to the BBS from their dorm room computers or from one of the university computer labs." The CMC portion of the course "will augment [and] not replace classroom instruction."

The approach at the heart of the June 1992 Cornell [University] Learning Technologies' CMC workshop for writing faculty in Ithaca, NY, had elements of both second- and third-generation models. As advertised, it was to be taught by Nancy Kaplan, University of Texas at Dallas, and Stuart Moulthrop, Georgia Institute of Technology. The promotional electronic post highlighted the mutually beneficial relationship between CMC and process-oriented strategies: It makes "the writing process both more visible and more malleable." The ad further stated that "the benefits of electronic technology for writing pedagogy do not stop with word processing." WANs with e-mail capabilities "enable writers to collaborate and exchange ideas during formative stages of their work . . . transforming oral class discussion into simultaneous on-line discussion." Other announced activities included ways "to create a virtual classroom using a network" and strategies on conducting "classroom discussion as real-time writing" (L. Holmes, personal communication, February 17, 1993).

Third-Generation Network

This network is a site-focused, remote-access network (RAN) classroom that is accessible from on- and off-campus locations. Judging from the literature on instructional CMC in e-mail conferences—which tends to emphasize cutting-edge technology and current trends and issues—the third-generation RAN model is by far the most popular. Instructors and students are able to log on from a distance, but the college as a specific geographical location is still the hub for the management and delivery of instruction. Teachers work out of offices on campus, and many classes continue to meet, physically, in classrooms. In this setup, students and instructors enjoy all of the advantages of the first three models, in addition to off-campus access. A student could log on to the RAN from home with his or her laptop computer on Saturday evening, or early Tuesday morning, before classes begin.

The major advantage of moving from a second- to a third-generation CMC format is accessibility. S.N. Dunbar, in response to a teacher who complained that evening and part-time students don't spend enough time on campus to take advantage of computer labs, says that "using a modem from home and calling into the university mainframe is the answer to this." She explained that "there are programs, such as Participate, that allow students to interact with instructors at the times that are most convenient to all" (personal communication, February 4, 1993). This exchange underscores the importance of access in a teacher's decision to use or not use CMC. The RAN model allows all students, including night and part time, the option of logging on to instructional networks from home through modems and personal computers.

The University of Michigan has one of the most comprehensive RANs. CMC "has been in widespread use . . . for at least a decade, and is nearly universal now. Every student, staff member, and faculty member has access to EMail and computer conferencing. . . . Faculty use it to give out class assignments. Staff use it to run the university. Students use it for everything, including getting dates" (M. Alexander, personal communication, August 10, 1992). Some teachers, such as Condon (e-mail, 1992), provide Internet access to all their students. Users are able to access the network "from almost anywhere. All of the dorm rooms are wired into the network . . . . All of the systems commonly used for EMail are also accessible from the major national and international networks (the Internet, SprintNet, Tymnet, etc.)." They "are also . . . connected to the Merit Computer network which provides extensive coverage of the state of Michigan." The RAN messaging system "is available 24 hours a day, except from midnight to 8AM Saturday morning. It is reasonably busy from about 7AM to after midnight and very busy during the day" (M. Alexander, personal communication, August 10, 1992).

Students with personal computers at the University of Colorado, which is primarily a commuter campus, "quickly acquire modems and are very happy for the convenience" (L. Brodsky, personal communication, September 8, 1992) of being able to access their RAN from home and other off-campus sites.

Today, in the third-generation configuration, CMC is used primarily as one of a number of learning activities in courses in which students meet face to face periodically with their instructors. Out of class, they are expected to read material that is stored online and to participate in e-mail and/or live-chat conferences. The frequency, quantity, and quality of participation is usually spelled out in course syllabi. An example of this mixture of traditional and CMC methods, although in a field other than composition, is Management 670, as taught by Morton Cotlar, professor of professional management and industrial relations at the University of Hawaii-Manoa. The course, International Management and Industrial Relations, focuses on topics such as the international management and transfer of technology. In the latest rendition of the course, Cotlar designed a unique CMC activity. He invited a number of prominent professors from major universities across the country to serve as online guest lecturers. He asked his students to actively participate in the sessions and to enter into public and private e-mail discussions with professors and classmates on topics generated in, or as a result of, the lectures.

Another example is a course, Speech Communication 350, Group Discussion, taught by Gerald M. Phillips (1992), professor emeritus in speech communication at Pennsylvania State University. A good part of the course objectives are accomplished online. Students attend face-to-face meetings with an instructor who works directly with Professor Phillips; they also view videotaped lectures by the professor; however, rarely do they meet with him in person. Most of the information that is usually exchanged on paper or in conferences between professor and students are managed via CMC. Students signing up for the course receive a syllabus and instructions that include a description of the course, a detailed schedule of activities, and explanations of procedures. The course is innovative and unique, a radical departure from the traditional class in which the teacher and students meet, face to face, in a room or lecture hall, so many times a week, every week. Much of the material for the future scenario is based on Professor Phillips's course design.

Fourth-Generation Network

This network is a virtual, global-access network (GAN) classroom. Instructors and students are electronically linked around the world, and they seldom if ever meet face to face. The college campus as we know it is no longer the focal point. Offices do not have to be grouped at a single geographical location; instructors are able to work out of home offices, often far removed from the physical campus. The campus may house conferencing facilities, and so on, but traditional classrooms have all but disappeared. The campus is primarily the geographical base for the mainframe or system that functions as the network server. The future scenario is based on this last model.

Given the projection of a campus, classes, student body, and faculty that exist on the edge of virtual reality, teachers need to be aware of its significance for the profession. When the medium of instruction, the very fabric of their art, undergoes such drastic transformation, the collective approach must also change. In all likelihood, the roles of teachers, as well as students' roles as learners, will be redefined. Practices, too, will either be adapted to the new medium or discarded; new ones will undoubtedly have to be adopted or invented. In the following section, a few of the major implications are identified and discussed so that teachers might learn from tomorrow what they need to know today.

IMPLICATIONS

Time and Space

Students are able to access their class on any day, at any time, from anywhere. Maria, the student in the scenario, is at home on a Saturday evening, logging on to UHUNIX. Her professor, facilitator, and c-mates are scattered around the globe. The college is online seven days a week, 24 hours a day; services are, for all practical purposes, virtual. The notion of a college as a geographical entity may become obsolete. Entire institutions could exist in virtual reality, defined by an electronic address. The implications could be that: (a) the student must learn to manage his or her own time, and the instructor must learn to construct time frames that are appropriate for online classes; and (b) teachers and students must be able to develop working personal relationships without ever meeting face to face.

International, Multicultural Education

The virtual university will gather students and faculty from locations around the world. Classes with international, multicultural students will proliferate. The implications could be that: (a) students and teachers need to become sensitized to the different ethnic groups represented in the classroom; and (b) participants may need to learn a universal CMC patois, which will be defined in part by the technical jargon that work with computers seems to require. To some extent, the primary language of instruction, presumably determined by the national origin of the institution's leaders, will be flavored with words and expressions from the nations represented in the classroom.

Access to Computers

Participants, teachers, and students will rely on small, lightweight, modem-equipped, relatively full-featured notebook systems. They are flexible, allowing users to plug in to phone or communication lines at various sites on campus (including classrooms, labs, and study areas), in the community (e.g., libraries), or at home. The implications could be that: (a) colleges may need to require students to own laptops that are suitable for connection to networks as well as to communication and phone lines, (b) institutions, through bookstores, may need to provide students with hardware and software at low cost, allowing students to pay in installments with low or no interest—payments could be deferred until after graduation, or made in small increments over one to three years; and (c) computer classrooms, labs, libraries, and so on, may not need a terminal for each student. The student could create an instant station by simply plugging his or her personal laptop into appropriate outlets on the desk. After plugging in, he or she uses the necessary software in the computer to log on to the network.

Student Access

All faculty and most if not all students will be online. The implications could be that: (a) computing centers must expand the number of lines available to dial-up callers; and (b) the resulting cost could be monumental; however, it could be offset by network fees and by the reduced demand for on-campus facilities such as classrooms, parking stalls, study areas, and so on.

CMC Knowledge

CMC is complex and requires technical facility. The implications could be that: (a) faculty and students must learn to function in the network environment, (b) knowledge levels may need to be set for certain classes; and (c) CMC competence may be a criterion for faculty hiring and promotion.

CMC Curriculum and Instruction

Students will be expected to manage much of their own learning. The implications could be that: (a) students must become knowledgeable about how to learn, both independently and collaboratively, in a given discipline, and teachers must know how to empower them, (b) training programs for teachers must include strategies designed for computer-mediated instruction; and (c) CMC workshops must be provided for inservice faculty.

Writing Skills

Students and teachers will communicate primarily through the written word. This could imply that: (a) writing across the curriculum programs must be emphasized, as it is on most campuses; and (b) researchers must examine the medium and assess the impact of CMC on the writing process and its outcomes—Are there constraints or advantages that are unique to computer-mediated writing instruction? What are they? What are the characteristics of effective electronic writing? How are they achieved by successful writers?

Instructional Roles in the CMC Classroom

The teacher will not be able to monitor and guide all the students on his or her class rosters. This could mean that: (a) lead teachers will need to work with student group facilitators and section instructors (Professor Phillips' strategy could serve as a model); and (b) institutions and departments must develop programs to train student facilitators and section instructors.

These are only some of the implications. There are many more. In the next few years, others will surface, presenting new and exciting challenges.

CONCLUSION

Six years ago, Meeks (1987) saw the natural relationship between CMC and education: "It is this concept of communications being the fundamental benefit of the classroom environment that underlies the premise . . . that computerized conferencing provides one of the first opportunities to create a true 'virtual classroom'" (p. 186). Needless to say, writing skills will play a prominent role in this new environment. Currently, the virtual classroom is still more an opportunity than an established practice, but it has arrived. A growing number of teachers are incorporating features of this electronic medium into their curricula, allowing them to transcend, even for just a moment, the limits of scheduled, real-time, face-to-face meetings at on-campus sites. In the months and years to come, many more will follow, and the globally networked classroom will soon become commonplace.

REFERENCES

Beals, D.E. (1990, April). *Computer networks as a new data base*. Paper presented at the annual meeting of the American Educational Research Association, Boston, MA. (ERIC Document Reproduction Service No. ED 322 880).

Carbone, N. (1992, September 29). Reply to campus-wide e-mail.

Electronic message posted to Megabyte University (Computers & Writing) discussion list. MBU-L@TTUVM1.BITNET.

Casey, J.M. (1990, May). *Literature comes alive with kidlink computer conferencing: Telecommunications a key link to literacy and literature.* Paper presented at the annual meeting of the International Reading Association, Atlanta, GA. (ERIC Document Reproduction Service No. ED 320 158).

Condon, B. (1992, June 4). (Fwd: *C&CD*) IDS World Network Educational BBS (10) (4). Electronic message posted to Megabyte University (Computers & Writing) discussion list. MBU-L@TTUVM1.BITNET.

Davis, B.G., Scriven, M., & Thomas, S. (1987). *The evaluation of composition instruction* (2nd ed.). New York: Teachers College Press.

DiMatteo, A. (1990). Under erasure: A theory for interactive writing in real time. *Computers and Composition, 7,* 71-84.

Fletcher, J. (1992, October 11). To teachers of computer-assisted writing classes. Electronic message posted to Megabyte University (Computers & Writing) discussion list. MBU-L@TTUVM1.BITNET.

Henri, F. (1988). Distance education and computer-assisted communication. *Prospects, 18,* 85-90.

Hiltz, S.R. (1988, June). *Collaborative learning in a virtual classroom: Highlights of findings.* Paper presented at the Computer Supported Cooperative Work Conference. (ERIC Document Reproduction Service No. ED 305 895).

Holmes, L. (1993, February 17). Info request [re Cornell Learning Technologies Program's electronic announcement of "A workshop for faculty and their instructional technologies partners: Special focus on collaborative writing," June 14-17, 1992]. Electronic message sent to the writer at UHUNIX.UHCC.HAWAII.EDU.

Holvig, K.C. (1989). Jamming the phone lines: Pencils, notebooks, and modems. *English Journal, 78*(8), 68-70.

Kaye, A.R. (1990). *Computer conferencing and mass distance education* (CITE Report No. 98). Walton, Bletchley, Bucks, England: Open University. (ERIC Document Reproduction Service No. ED 328 221).

Keeling, J. (1992, August 12). Need resources. Electronic message posted to Megabyte University (Computers & Writing) discussion list. MBU-L@TTUVM1.BITNET.

Kubota, K. (1991, February). *Applying a collaborative learning model to a course development project.* Paper presented at the annual convention of the Association for Educational Communications and Technology, Orlando, FL. (ERIC Document Reproduction Service No. ED 331 490)

Kuehn, S.A. (1988, April-May). *Discovering all the available means for computer assisted instruction: Adapting available university facilities for the small to medium-sized course*. Paper presented at the annual meeting of the Eastern Communication Association, Baltimore, MD. (ERIC Document Reproduction Service No. ED 294 284).

Marcus, S. (1984). *Computers and the teaching of writing: Variations on a theme*. Report submitted to ERIC by Marcus, University of California at Santa Barbara. (ERIC Document Reproduction Service No. ED 254 843).

Meeks, B.N. (1987, February). The quiet revolution: On-line education becomes a real alternative. *Byte*, pp. 183-190.

Miller-Souviney, B., & Souviney, R. (1987). *Recognition: The engine that drives the writing process* (Report No. 17). (La Jolla: California University, Center for Human Information Processing. (ERIC Document Reproduction Service No. ED 307 627)

Murray, D. E. (1988). Computer-mediated communication: Implications for ESP [English for Specific Purposes]. *English for Specific Purposes, 7*, 3-18.

Phillips, A.F., & Pease, P.S. (1985, May). *Computer conferencing and education: Complementary or contradictory concepts?* Paper presented at the annual meeting of the International Communication Association, Honolulu, HI. (ERIC Document Reproduction Service No. ED 261 428).

Phillips, G.M. (1992). *Spring 1992 [Speech Communication 350] course syllabus*. Unpublished manuscript.

Phillips, G.M., & Santoro, G.M. (1989). Teaching group discussion via computer-mediated communication. *Communication Education, 38*, 151-161.

Roberts, L. (1987, May). *The electronic seminar: Distance education by computer conferencing*. Paper presented at the annual conference on Non-Traditional and Interdisciplinary Programs, Fairfax, VA. (ERIC Document Reproduction Service No. ED 291 358).

Selfe, C.L., & Wahlstrom, B.J. (1982). *The benevolent beast: Computer-assisted instruction for the teaching of writing*. Report submitted to ERIC by Selfe, Michigan Technological University, Houghton, MI. (ERIC Document Reproduction Service No. ED 234 398).

Smith, K.L. (1990). Collaborative and interactive writing for increasing communication skills. *Hispania, 73*, 77-87.

Thomas, G. (1993, February 10). Daedalus network at Idaho. Electronic message posted to Megabyte University (Computers & Writing) discussion list. MBU-L@TTUVM1.BITNET.

Troll, D.A. (1987). Encouraging a computer-intensive life style: Integrating reading and writing with the advanced function workstation. *The Computer-Assisted Composition Journal, 2*(1), 21-33.

Weber, J. (1992, September). Photonics: Revolution or evolution? *Byte*, pp. 169-178.

Chapter Four

Computer Access for Students with Special Needs

Joseph Kinner
Gallaudet University

Norman Coombs
Rochester Institute of Technology

Computer telecommunications, when enhanced by special, adaptive hardware and software, can drastically reduce barriers for persons with various physical and learning disabilities, and it can also facilitate interaction among those who are, for whatever reasons, inhibited in face-to-face settings. Both of these equalizing factors of computer-mediated communications (CMC) were noticed by students in a course taught by Professor Norman Coombs at Rochester Institute of Technology (RIT). One student in an African-American history class that met both in the classroom and through a computer conference system recognized this phenomenon and commented on it, "I also agree with everyone else about what a good idea using this conference is. By using the computer as somewhat of a 'universal medium', the everyday communication barriers are avoided." Differences, such as "being hearing impaired, being Black, White, or Green, being shy or not a good speaker," all vanished. This RIT course consisted of students from several ethnic backgrounds and also included both hearing students and hearing-impaired students. The teacher, Coombs, was blind.

Hearing-impaired students in a classroom require either that the teacher be proficient with American Sign Language or that an interpreter be present to facilitate the deaf student's class participation. When class discussion occurs in a computer conference, the hearing-impaired person does not require any special assistance to become part of a mainstream educational setting. One deaf woman in an American history course at RIT sent e-mail to the professor, "I really enjoyed having class this way because it allowed me to participate in a hearing class." She explained further that she was able to get everyone's views first hand without an interpreter in the middle of the communication. "I have felt so left out of it in other classes," she added. Hearing-impaired students may still have a problem with this format because, for those who have been deaf since birth, English is their second language. This woman lost her hearing as a young adult, and the computer conference was well suited to her situation.

Persons with other physical disabilities may require special software and hardware adaptations before the computer becomes a new communication medium for them. Visually impaired students may need either a screen-enlarging program to permit their "seeing" the screen or a speech synthesizer that will speak what is on the screen. Motor-impaired students often have problems in using the keyboard. Depending on the particular disability, there are various software and hardware devices that provide alternative input systems. Once appropriate access has been provided to the computer, these students function as equals in the computer classroom, and their disability vanishes. Everyone interacts on the basis of their ideas rather than having the communication shaped by stereotypes based on people's appearances.

Similarly, students who are inhibited in group discussion find that their stage fright is greatly diminished. One shy student confessed that with the CMC classroom, "you can say whatever you think or feel and not have to worry about somebody giving you a crazy look or something like that. I'm not a great speaker, so the (computer) conference helps me put my thoughts together and allows me to express them better without having my tongue twisted."

RIT/GALLAUDET PILOT PROJECT VIA THE INTERNET

The unique ability of CMC to reduce many communication barriers inspired a pilot project in 1991 between Gallaudet University and the Rochester Institute of Technology. Gallaudet is a liberal arts university for the hearing impaired in Washington, DC, and RIT has, as one of its colleges, the National Technical Institute for the Deaf. The pilot was to use CMC to include students from both campuses in the same class and to include in that class both hearing and hearing-impaired learners. There were two teachers, one on each campus, and one of them was visually impaired. The pilot included two courses: Mass Media and Deaf Culture taught by Professor J. S. Schuchman from Gallaudet, and Black Civil Rights in the Twentieth Century taught by Professor Norman Coombs from RIT with Professor Joseph Kinner from Gallaudet serving as a liaison person. The remainder of this chapter focuses on the Coombs/Kinner course and generalizations about the uses of CMC with the physically disabled learner.

The course content was delivered through a captioned version of the video series, *Eyes on the Prize*, produced by Blackside Inc. and originally broadcast on Public Television. The text was *Voices of Freedom* by Henry Hampton. The class discussion was held on a computer conference system—VAX Notes—produced by the Digital Equipment Corporation and running on a DEC VAX computer at RIT. VAX Notes is essentially a computer bulletin board. It is structured like a two-dimensional matrix with a set of topic notes on various subjects. Replies to each topic get attached to each topic note. Topics are numbered 1, 2, 3, and so on. Replies to topic 3 would be numbered 3.1, 3.2, and so on. It permits having several different discussions simultaneously. It also saves all topics and replies, permitting readers to connect at any time even several days late and still catch up on the entire transaction.

RIT students connected to the discussion in VAX Notes either by a DEC terminal in a campus lab or with a PC and modem from home. The Gallaudet students connected to a computer at Gallaudet and reached RIT over the Internet. Personal contacts between students and between student and teacher use VAX Mail. Only rarely did a student appear in person at the office of either professor. Coombs had previously taught several classes online, including some hearing-impaired students. He has also taught many deaf students in the classroom at RIT with an interpreter handling the communication with the deaf students. These students were mainstreamed in regular RIT classes. For Kinner, this was his first experience with CMC, which gave him a fresh perspective, and in teaching deaf students at Gallaudet, he did his own signing in classes that normally contained all-deaf students. The pilot class had 18 students who finished the course. Three quit during the course. Two found they had taken on more than they could handle, and one developed carpel tunnel syndrome, which prevented his using the keyboard. Eleven students were on the RIT campus; five of these were hearing impaired. Seven logged in from Gallaudet with one of them being a hearing student. RIT held a 1-hour, face-to-face orientation meeting to familiarize students with the computer system. About half of the students came. RIT students are frequently at home with computers because of their technical background, and many did not feel in need of such orientation.

With few exceptions, the Gallaudet students who signed up for the course did feel the need for a face-to-face orientation, and all of them showed up for the first meeting. Having earlier introduced himself and his role in the course as the on-site liaison support person to the students via a letter delivered through campus mail, Kinner used the orientation to guide students through the use of the computer, to hand out materials explaining the course, and to emphasize the unique features of CMC. He then went on to demonstrate how to log on to the VAX and then supervised the students as they practiced. During the hour or so of orientation, all of the Gallaudet students except one successfully logged on to RIT; the student who was having difficulty met with Kinner the following day and did successfully learn how to use the computer. One of the important features of this course, even though students rarely availed themselves of the opportunity, was having the chance to meet face to face with Kinner. This was particularly true during the early stages when students were adjusting to the new technology. Once these skills were mastered, students learned to depend more on themselves and to seek their own answers to the problems they encountered. This emphasis on developing self discipline and individualized learning were what helped bring Gallaudet into this pilot project in the first place.

After viewing, in the African-American history class, a video that portrayed the killing of a young boy and reading related materials from the text, the students were asked to comment on the following questions posted on VAX Notes by the professor:

> Between 1890 and 1910, there were over 4,000 Blacks lynched, which is over 200 a year or something like 2 every 3 days! Although the number had dropped significantly by the 1950s, Till's lynching was not the only one which occurred. Why did Till's death make such national news? What aspects of Till's murder and of the trial were most surprising to you?
>
> The 1950s seem like a long time ago to you. It wasn't so long ago! I received my BS in 1955! Did any of you have relatives, still alive, who lived anywhere in the South at that time? Have they told you any shocking stories from their youth? These questions are only to start a discussion. Comment on anything related to Till and lynchings.

The first reply was from a hearing-impaired RIT student who answered some of the questions and added some interesting family information:

Emmett Till's death made the national news since it was such a brutal murder and many Black people across the United States felt that it was the last straw to those nonsense killings of Blacks in the South. . . . Two men were arrested and brought before the court for killing Emmett Till. There was enough evidence to find those two White men guilty for murdering Emmett but a White jury found them not guilty. Till's uncle was a witness and he had the courage to point his finger to the White men in court for bringing grief to his family. . . . My grandmother lives in Queens, New York, and I remember her telling me about her visit to the South in the 1950's. She remembers a lot of tension going on in the South and there were a lot of protests for equal rights for Black people.

The next reply was a question from a hearing student at RIT: "I was a bit unclear after watching the video if the individuals that had murdered the boy had come right out and admitted that they had done it or just implied it. . . . My next question is can that individual not be tried again even if he has the nerve to come right out and admit he murdered the boy?" At this point the professor pointed out that American law does not permit a person to be tried twice for the same crime. Next, a hearing-impaired student logging in over the Internet from Gallaudet added: "I totally agree about the jury being so bigoted and I was surprised that the two men were found not guilty even though the evidence was there. And not only that, they totally disfigured Emmett, I will never forget his face." He went on to connect the video to contemporary events from the news, "And for some reason, it made me think of the Rodney King beating in California. This clearly shows that racism is still around today. It's real sad." Another Gallaudet student said, "TILL'S DEATH MAKE SUCH NATIONAL NEWS BECAUSE, THIS VICTIM OF FOURTEEN YEAR OLD WAS MUTILATED AND IT NEVER HAPPEN TO BE SO GRUELING AND ALSO TO A MERE CHILD. WHAT I FOUND MYSELF ANGRY NOT SURPRISING ABOUT THE TRIAL IS THAT THE DEFENDANT WAS FOUND NOT GUILTY, WITH ALL THOSE OBVIOUS EVIDENCES AGAINST THE DEFENDANTS." In spite of the apparent language problem in the previous reply, the student was not inhibited from participating, and no one had a problem understanding the intent of the remark. The faculty encouraged uninhibited, relaxed discussion, rather than pushing to get proper grammar and spelling.

After two further replies from Gallaudet participants, another RIT hearing-impaired student commented on how she was emotionally moved by the pictures in the video. Then she went on to add some stories from her family:

> I spoke to my father last night on the phone and asked him questions about that trial. He grew up in a county in Louisiana where there were lot of people that are racist. I asked what people there thought of it. (He was a year older than Emmett when that happened.) He said he heard a lot of talk about the men what they 'd do if a black man had flirted with their wives. They said they'd shoot him. Despite the fact Emmett was only 14, some thought he was grown up! I'd like to share my father's experience relating to this case. In his neighborhood, a young black man had flirted with a wife of a man who was away in Marines in Korea. That man's brother-in-law found out and wanted my father's brothers to help him take the black man to the woods to beat him up. But Dad's brothers refused to help. Dad doesn't remember what the white man did to him, but doubts he did anything cuz he was afraid to do it alone.

The teacher again stepped into the discussion flow to reinforce the personal sharing that was taking place, "Thanks, for sharing those stories. It helps us realize that history isn't always so far away and doesn't always relate to other people. It sometimes is closer to home than is comfortable." Believing that connecting past history to personal and family happenings makes the history more real and facilitates learning and understanding, the teacher wanted to encourage this kind of sharing.

This is only a sampling of the 23 replies to this topic, but it demonstrates the ability of CMC over a data network to facilitate a discussion by people separated by physical distance, physical disabilities, and also by time. The course lasted 10 weeks. Students viewed 14 hours of documentary television, read the textbook, and shared in the computer discussion. Students were asked to respond to 58 sets of questions, and the 18 students made an average of 21 replies. During the course, students averaged 227 lines of discussion each. (Actually, as there were a couple of students whose participation was minimal, the average for those who genuinely participated was even higher.) Students also had to write two take-home essay exams and to submit one written paper. These assignments were also submitted on the computer. This much writing was important for the development of those students with English deficiencies. Although this was not one of the course objectives, it was an expected byproduct, and more than one student said that it did help their writing abilities.

The final discussion topic in the computer conference asked the class to express their views on the electronic classroom. "At first it was weird for me," one young man from Gallaudet confessed, "because I am so used to being in a classroom instead of using the VAX as a way to receive and send messages from me and the teacher and to students too. But as the weeks went by I got the hang of it. . . . I find it enjoyable and it is a unique experience I will never forget." Another Gallaudet student said that she enjoyed the class because, though she was African American, she had never learned much about the civil rights movement, and she appreci-ated the opportunity. "Anyway, Dr. Coombs," she continued, "I think you did a marvelous job considering the fact that you haven't met any of us here (at Gally)." A woman from RIT also shared her original anxiety, but said that "it turned out to be not as hard as I anticipated. I enjoyed the material—it was interesting and it wasn't a class that puts you to sleep." Another RIT student shared that the course enabled him to work at his own pace and still participate in discussion with others. He concluded that "it put the responsibility on the students to learn themselves."

Another Gallaudet student said, "Watching the videos made me feel like I was really there watching it happen. I saw so much anger and other emotions in blacks and whites, it helped me see how they really felt." Another Gallaudet student commented that the course helped her develop more self-responsibility and also inspired her to take an intern-ship at the King center in Atlanta. A hearing Gallaudet student said that, even though she did not particularly like the electronic delivery system, she did participate more than in the classroom. She also liked the flex learning system which let her schedule her own time. Similarly, a hear-ing-impaired Gallaudet woman shared how much she liked controlling her time. "I really enjoyed this experiment. . . . This way of going to class has taught me how to be responsible for my own work."

Some students who did not participate much also shared their successes and frustrations. One Gallaudet student who had difficulty with English admitted that she was anxious about taking a course on the com-puter, but she specifically thanked Professor Kinner for encouraging her to take it. She said the computer wasn't that hard, but she also hoped to meet the RIT professor in person some day. She seemed to miss the face-to-face interaction, but she also seemed to lack self-motivation. A RIT stu-dent said that "even though I do not get to participate much, I still find it enjoyable reading other students' feedback. I think I would be a better participant in a classroom than on the VAX because I never seem to be able to get to the computer and type." Another RIT student liked being able to compare ideas with his deaf peers from Gallaudet, but he found his outside activities interfered with his getting to the computer. He con-fessed, "I find it a valuable learning experience since I have to be motivat-ed enough to learn it myself and make myself face it." The final comment from a Gallaudet student said, "It taught me some responsibility. Every time I finish my classes and can find time to do VAX, I really enjoyed it."

The other complaint listed by several of the Gallaudet students was that, when they were connected to the RIT VAX system over the Internet, sometimes the screen would "freeze" for seconds or minutes between key-strokes. This was due to heavy line traffic, and it was one of the complaints that spurred an upgrade of the connection with the Internet system.

RESEARCH EVALUATION REPORT

The course was also evaluated through questionnaires and interviews. These were conducted after the exam and grading in order to protect student anonymity and encourage an honest response. Although the picture that emerged was quite similar to that provided by student comments in the computer conference, some negative comments were stated a bit more strongly. Though the responses were anonymous, they were also voluntary and only about one-quarter of the students participated. This might have skewed the results in a more negative direction.

The formative evaluation was done by Barbara G. McKee and Marcia J. Scherer from Instructional Development at the National Technical Institute of the Deaf (NTID) at RIT. Students were requested both to fill out a questionnaire and to participate in a personal interview. The interviews were conducted by a graduate student who was in an educational specialist program at NTID and who was also proficient in American Sign Language. The study combined the input from students in the two courses into one set of results. Separate data are not available for this course as the intent was to evaluate the delivery systems rather than the courses themselves. A total of 51 students from the two campuses registered for the classes. Twenty-six were from RIT, and 25 from Gallaudet. Six dropped out (two from RIT and four from Gallaudet), and the researcher was not able to determine the reasons for their decision. Of the 45 participants—24 from RIT and 21 from Gallaudet—who finished the course, 8 voluntarily filled out questionnaires, and 10 came to a personal interview. Once the courses were concluded, the members moved on to busy schedules and were difficult to reach. It is also possible that those who were hearing impaired, which was about three-quarters of the group, may have been resistant to being objects of study. Even though the goal may have been to study the system, filling out questionnaires and submitting to a personal interview may have felt as if the person was the object of the evaluation.

The questionnaire asked a series of questions about the students' opinions of various aspects of the course and had them rate their answers on a 5-point scale. The interview also tried to probe the same issues, but in more depth and with better opportunity to include subjective responses. The report also included evaluations by the interviewer and by the faculty who taught the courses.

The report noted that "students divided themselves into two basic groups: (a) those who enjoyed and were satisfied with the delivery system and stated they would be happy to enroll in another teleconferencing course, and (b) those who were not satisfied and stated they had no intention of enrolling in another such course." Aside from the complaints about the periodic slowness of the Internet connection, negative comments were all psychosocial: either they missed the face-to-face social contact, or else they had trouble motivating themselves to do the work when there was no schedule to provide that discipline. None of the dissatisfaction indicated that using the technology was too difficult or that the technology was inadequate to deliver the content. (Both courses were history courses, and therefore this does not indicate whether the technology would be adequate for other content areas.) None of the hearing-impaired students who were accustomed to American Sign Language indicated that the computer provided any problems in conveying course content. None of the hearing students commented on problems arising from the class containing physically handicapped participants. Sometimes a reader might guess by the use of awkward English that a student was hearing impaired, but other times this fact would be indistinguishable. Apparently, CMC functions well as a mainstreaming mechanism.

When asked if they felt comfortable communicating through the computer, 50% either agreed or strongly agreed, and only 37% disagreed or disagreed strongly. One told the interviewer that "I feel more comfortable [with discussions through the VAX]," and "It helped my English skills." Another confessed to being shy in a classroom and said, "I prefer discussions through the VAX because I do not have to worry about people looking at me. I feel more comfortable." Another who also felt that people were less inhibited on the computer, at the same time thought that the discussions were less spontaneous. Others said it gave them time to think and express themselves better.

Eighty-seven percent said they did miss "seeing" their fellow students. When asked if this left them feeling isolated, half said yes, and half said no. Several told the interviewer that they missed seeing facial expressions and body gestures. One wrote on the questionnaire that "deaf people need to depend on eyes and hands." This statement may partly explain the strong emphasis on the need for visual cues in communication stated by members of this class. Previous classes I have taught with CMC did not express the need for visual feedback this strongly. It may be a special function of the communication habits and needs of the hearing impaired. Interacting through the use of sign language is not only a visual means of interaction, but the participants' entire body becomes involved in the exchange.

Participants were asked how they would compare these courses with traditional classes. Twenty-five percent said they found it easier to communicate using CMC, whereas 62% disagreed. When asked about the frequency of communicating with the professor, the group split with 37% agreeing or strongly agreeing that there was more frequent interaction, and the same percent disagreeing. Thirty-seven percent indicated that they had more interaction with their peers using the computer than in a traditional classroom, and 50% said they did not. Two questions on the evaluation asked about how this delivery system impacted their personal work habits. Seventy-five percent indicated that this system put more responsibility on them to manage their own time, whereas 12% disagreed. "I can do the work when it is convenient for me," one commented, but then added, "I can get lazy. I can put it off too easily. I have to have good disciplinary skills." Another liked the ability to access the system any time, which meant that one didn't have to wait until the next class to ask a question. Several claimed that they did learn better time management and independence. Several among those who were the most dissatisfied said that the course required discipline, which they lacked. Fifty percent said it was harder for them to keep up with the work, and 25% disagreed.

When asked for a general rating of the courses, 50% agreed or strongly agreed that they were excellent. Twenty-five percent disagreed. Fifty percent said they would recommend such a course to a friend and 25% would not. Thirty-seven percent further said that they would like to take another course in such a format. Twenty-five percent were uncertain, and another 25% said they would not. However, of the 10 students interviewed personally, 6 said they would take another computer-delivered course, which was a much higher percentage than that which resulted from the written questionnaire.

The report concluded that the slowness and inefficiencies of the Internet connection between the two campuses caused frustration. Even those students who most appreciated the delivery system complained strongly on this point. It should be noted that this problem is not necessarily inherent in the Internet but resulted from the particular grade connection being used by these institutions at that time. Since then, RIT has upgraded its connectivity, and this problem would be reduced in future online courses.

The second widely expressed complaint was the lack of regular face-to-face interaction. Students who came to enjoy computer-mediated interaction did not seem bothered by this. Not surprisingly, different students have different social and learning styles and hence have varying needs. Some students have more need for a face-to-face contact, whereas others can find CMC interaction useful for learning.

Further, the report noted that almost none of the students had been aware that these courses would be delivered using CMC. Some noted considerable confusion about why it was not being given in a "normal" format. Whereas CMC is most frequently used as a distance delivery system, on-campus students were recruited for these two courses because they were easy to identify and because the quality of their work was already known. The report noted that the experimental nature of these courses had not been adequately communicated. Students selected the courses because of their content, without any regard to the delivery system.

Undoubtedly, if students had realized the CMC component, many of those who most felt the need for face-to-face social contact would have self-selected themselves out of the project.

Finally, the report did find the CMC classroom facilitated genuine discussion and learning. Further, it provided students with a "flex" learning environment that encouraged development of self-discipline and taught students how to work better independently. Several students commented favorably on this feature both in the questionnaires and in the personal interviews. Some seemed to appreciate it because they were already self-starters and enjoyed the opportunity to work within such a context. Others recognized their need for self-discipline and felt that working independently without a schedule assisted them in developing such personal habits. Most of those who found CMC frustrating also commented that they were not self-starters and that they wanted and needed more structure.

For some of the hearing-impaired learners, the daily writing practice helped them to improve their English language skills. Shy students were less inhibited, and it pulled them more actively into group discussion. This was true for shy hearing students as well as for shy hearing-impaired learners. The report cautions against drawing sweeping conclusions from its data because they were based on a small number of respondents.

FACULTY EVALUATION

Faculty perceptions of the course, although recognizing some weaknesses mentioned in the report that needed to be addressed, were more positive than the evaluations by students who participated in the formative evaluation. The small sample on which the report was based may partly account for the difference. Also, faculty had understood the nature of the course's delivery system, and they approached it with expectations based on that fact. Therefore, they tended to look more abstractly at the nature of the communication that occurred, whereas students were more likely to evaluate it by their feelings, highlighted by their expectation of a face-to-face interaction. As the discussions were mediated through a computer, the instructors have a written record against which to compare their views.

This record shows free and open sharing about the course content as well as demonstrates how the participants connected the content to events out of the lives of their families. Reading it gives the clear impression that the content had become internalized and that it engaged the students at a personal and vital level. Faculty felt that these discussions were of a higher quality than was typical in a traditional classroom. This enhanced discussion was expected by faculty with experience in computer conferencing, but this expectation was not conveyed to the students. It was feared that announcing the ability of CMC to induce more open sharing might make students self-conscious and be counterproductive.

As mentioned previously, the unique ability of CMC to reduce many communication barriers inspired this pilot project between Gallaudet and RIT/NTID. For the first time students on both campuses, deaf and hearing, were able to take courses together using CMC. Time and distance between the campuses and the students were irrelevant, and varying modes of sign communication, crucial factors in the courses taught at Gallaudet, no longer were so important. Removing this barrier had an immediate impact on one of Kinner's former Gallaudet students who had taken courses from him the year before. In one of Kinner's upper division courses for majors, for example, he observed the reluctance this student had to participate in any of the class discussions, primarily because the student had very weak signing skills. This student never overcame his feeling that his signing was not on a level equal to the others in the class, and he often expressed his anxiety to the instructor about his inability to communicate his thoughts and ideas effectively in sign language. When this same student took the course using CMC delivery, however, it was a completely different matter. He felt totally at ease, he communicated openly and honestly—and more frequently than any other student from Gallaudet. This student loved the course and found it intellectually and emotionally challenging, and at the same time he felt it was liberating and empowering in the most positive ways.

Most of the students from Gallaudet, in talking with Kinner, responded to the course in much the same way as did the student just mentioned. However, there were a couple who had some problems adjusting to the method of delivery and the self-motivation demands of the course.

Those who already possessed or who quickly developed computer skills tended to overcome whatever shyness they had at the beginning and participated in discussions often. They responded positively to the insistence on self-discipline and managed their time responsibly, completed their assignments ahead of or on time, and depended entirely on themselves to get the work done. The quality of their work improved steadily throughout the course. One or two students did have difficulty getting started on the computer and remained reluctant to engage in discussions as often as the others. These students were never able to develop meaningful strategies to enable them to cope with the responsibilities and demands of the course, and they frequently desired to meet with the instructor face to face. Kinner's previous experience with these students in his other courses, in which they consistently demonstrated weak study habits and a lack of self-discipline, indicates that they were not as well prepared as the others in the class.

Was this pilot project successful? From Kinner's perspective the answer is unequivocally "Yes." Some students encountered problems getting started, a couple never did feel entirely comfortable with the computer, but virtually all the students enjoyed the course immensely and recommended that it be taught again in the same way. Kinner, for whom this was his first experience with a CMC classroom, was tremendously impressed by the skillful ways Gallaudet students embraced computer technology and by the frequency and eagerness with which most of them participated in the class discussions and communicated their thoughts and feelings with their deaf and hearing peers at RIT. Many years of teaching at Gallaudet have made Kinner aware of how difficult it is to integrate many different modes of communication into a coherent class discussion, especially when many of the students are shy and hesitant to give their views and thoughts about the issues being discussed. He observed a very different and, in many ways, much more promising process of communication in this project.

He saw students develop a strong sense of self-discipline and assume more responsibility for their own learning. Shy students and those with weak sign skills felt increasingly comfortable in this unique learning environment and learned to communicate honestly and openly with the other students. Future CMC projects may benefit some deaf students by incorporating some face-to-face interaction between students and instructor, but based on Kinner's observations of, and participation in, this project, including his follow-up discussions with students, he is convinced the course was a great success and that more like it can, and should be, developed in the future.

Coombs also felt the pilot project was successful. Combining students from two geographically separated campuses was no real problem. The benefits of the CMC classroom that he had observed previously carried over into this project. One RIT hearing-impaired student added the comment that communication by CMC was helpful because it required no interpreter as a communication intermediary. At RIT few faculty sign for themselves, and interpreters are common in most classes.

Coombs was surprised at how many students had motivation problems and how many complained about the lack of face-to-face contact. He noted that, among those struggling over self-discipline, there were both hearing and hearing-impaired learners. The problem was not connected with any physical impairment. In previous CMC courses taught by Coombs, the audience was usually distance learners who were usually older and much more mature. Whether hearing-impaired persons have more need for visual feedback in communication is not clear, but Coombs noted that this group did not expect a CMC format. His previous computer conference classes did have a more realistic picture of what the delivery medium would be like. This would suggest that student expectations and levels of maturity are important factors in a successful CMC classroom.

CONCLUSIONS

CMC in the form of e-mail and computer conferencing can serve both as a replacement for the traditional classroom and as an extension for such a classroom. This has been documented previously in other places and has been confirmed in this volume. CMC offers some unique features of its own. Because it is time and place independent, it facilitates and encourages learner independence. The student can set his own work schedule and pace his or her work to accommodate personal needs. Educational strategies that help students become self-starters and more self-disciplined will provide them with important work skills for the information age.

CMC also facilitates and encourages an open and free sharing of ideas and experiences. Furthermore, it tends to equalize participants in a discussion. Shy students participate more readily, and students who normally dominate a discussion find it does not work in a CMC setting. No one person can control others by controlling the debate. Others are free to skip or ignore their contributions.

The ability of CMC to create more open and equal interaction is the feature that helps to integrate disabled learners into a mainstream class. Physical disabilities vanish from sight, and participants interact on the basis of their contributions.

Although both RIT and Gallaudet are uniquely equipped to assist hearing-impaired learners, the members in this project needed no special help beyond a brief orientation period. This would indicate that the successes of the RIT/Gallaudet project can be replicated elsewhere with very little special preparation. Visually impaired and motor-impaired students may require adaptive hardware and software, and they may require some special training to use it. However, students will frequently have mastered those skills before becoming involved in the

CMC course. At that point, these students should need little more than encouragement to become part of a CMC classroom.

However, this project did alert the faculty to three important considerations. These qualifications are largely true for all students, whether physically impaired or not. First, some students feel a need for regular face-to-face interaction. These persons should be steered toward other learning methods. If, however, CMC is being used for students residing on the campus with the teacher, such courses should integrate classroom contact with the computer component. The teacher also has the responsibility to set an open and interactive tone for the discussions. CMC is a highly interactive technology, but, by itself, it will not yet make a nonresponsive teacher into an interactive moderator. The faculty member needs to recognize and exploit its strengths.

Second, student expectations significantly influence their response to a CMC class. When those registering for such a course realize it will be delivered by CMC, they accept the technology with few complaints. When they expect a traditional delivery method, some adjust readily, whereas others become frustrated and dissatisfied.

Third, this particular CMC classroom was run on an asynchronous basis. Students could "go to class" at any time. They could "talk to the teacher in his office" at any time. Both the VAX Notes conference used for the classroom, and VAX Mail used for office-type communication are available at any time and on any day. Students with poor self-discipline procrastinated and fell further and further behind. A time-independent class format demands more maturity than some younger students have developed. The system works well with adult learners. For less mature participants, the course should build in requirements for regular, scheduled participation. Keeping these qualifications in mind, mainstreaming disabled learners via CMC is a possibility that can be adapted in almost any setting.

SOURCES OF RELEVANT INFORMATION

EASI: Equal Access to Software and Information, is a project of Educom and is concerned with computer access for the disabled primarily, in higher education. It can be contacted by e-mail on the Internet: easi@educom.edu or by paper mail at: EASI, Care of Educom, 1112 16th St. NW, Suite 600, Washington, DC 20036.

The Trace Research and Development Center is an extremely valuable source for adaptive technologies for handicapped persons, and it can be reached by paper mail or phone at: Trace Research and Development Center, S-151 Waisman Center, 1500 Highland Ave., Madison, WI 53705. Phone: (608) 262-6966, TDD (608) 263-5408.

To obtain copies of the unpublished formative evaluation report mentioned above, write to: Barbara G. McKee, National Technical Institute for the Deaf, Rochester Institute of Technology, One Lomb Memorial Dr., Rochester NY 14623.

Coombs has written several articles on the use of CMC with disabled students. Two of these are:

Coombs, N. (1989). Using CMC to overcome physical disabilities. In R. Mason & A. Kaye (Eds.). *Mindweave: Communication, computers, and distance education* (pp. 180-185). New York: Pergamon Press.

Coombs, N. (1992). Teaching in the information age. *Educom Review, 41*(2), 28.

Chapter Five

CMC and the Educationally Disabled Student

Anne Pemberton
Nottoway High School
Nottoway, VA
Robert Zenhausern
St. John's University

The Americans with Disability Act was initiated to ensure the rights of the handicapped with respect to access, employment, education, and all those amenities less-challenged individuals take for granted. People with physical or sensory impairment have made substantial gains both in terms of the physical environment and accommodations in employment and, most pointedly, in education. The child with visual problems, for example, is given a rehabilitation approach to problems involving vision; alternative sensory input are provided (braille, talking books, etc.). This is in marked contrast to services provided to children with educational disabilities. *Educational disabilities* is a broad term that encompasses children who are labeled mentally retarded, learning disabled, emotionally disturbed, autistic, and all those myriads of disorders that fall under the name "developmental disability". Individuals with educational disabilities are unfortunately often treated as though they were responsible for the disability. They are told to: "Work harder," "Pay attention," "Stop being lazy." Blind children are not given drills in how to see, but the child with an educational disability is given practice in precisely what he or she cannot do, which is called "remediation."

This chapter explores the use of computer networking as a rehabilitation technique for children with educational disabilities. The initial use of computers for students with special needs focused on drill and practice. The game formats, graphics, song and dance, and the novelty of the computer were all used to disguise the fact that the students were getting electronic ditto worksheets. The goal of such software was to improve basic skills through repetition with the hope that it generalized to other situations, such as tests. This is the inherent structure of remediation.

The rehabilitation aspects of computers began with the introduction of word processing, spell- and grammar-checkers, and speech synthesizers. Educationally disabled students can depend on the computer for basic techniques so they are free to concentrate on the content. Computer-mediated communication (CMC) becomes the natural next step, opening a wide variety of content to students. Students are not just learning computer literacy but are becoming truly computer literate.

The chapter contains three sections. The first section shows how CMC can be used with educationally disabled adolescents to provide basic computer literacy, motivational reading, writing, and thinking activities, and an introduction to the world. Actual classroom situations that have arisen over the past two years as a result of CMC activities are summarized. The second section shows how the special education teacher can use CMC to address professional needs. Experiences are drawn from the archives of a series of Listserv discussion groups located at St. John's University in New York City and the online experiences of educationally disabled adolescents in a high school in rural Virginia. The final section includes tips for teachers and lists of available online resources specific to the needs of special education.

STUDENTS AND E-MAIL

Class starts on an exciting note when one of the young men in my class bursts into the room bearing a treasured missive from the most beautiful girl in the school. Whatever the planned lesson, it won't begin until the whole gang helps decode each and every precious word.

E-mail correspondence has the same sense of reality as a note from a pretty girl. The following e-mail anecdotes were saved from the correspondence generated by several classes of students identified as "learning disabled" (LD) or "mildly mentally retarded" (MMR). Several students with sensory or physical impairments, in addition to the educational disability, also participated. These students attend a small high school nestled among the tobacco fields and dairy farms in southside Virginia.

Students were given class accounts on Virginia's PEN network and access through a single computer with modem in their classroom early in 1992, and one day a week was set aside in their English classes for the online activities. The following gives a flavor of the interactions that arose from this correspondence. E-mail correspondence was successful in broadening the horizons for these students, but one unique type of interaction involved a group exchange with an interesting "expert" that allowed the whole class to contribute to a single reply.

One class corresponded with an educational philosophy PhD candidate, J.C., who wondered if emotions could be transmitted in such a coldly technical medium. It happened that he had to have surgery and the following notes were sent before and after that occasion.

Date: Thu, 24 Sep 92 12:19:10 EDT
Dear John
I hope you come out good with your surgery. Tell if it hurt? Tell us about it when you get out. Are you scared? T said don't worry it will only hurt for a little while. Im sorry to hear that you are going into the hospital I hope everything will come out all right. I will say a prayer for you tonight. Please write us to let us know how things came out. We all love you so take care and keep in touch.
Love ya!
Mrs Pemberton's class.

Date: Fri, 25 Sep 92 12:26:26 EDT
Dear John
We are glad to hear from you. Im glad things worked out for you. My brother is going to have the same thing when he gets older. I asked my mom what operation it is and she told me. I'm really glad things came out great for you. I'm looking forward to hearing from you again.
Take care and keep in touch. WE LOVE YOU!
M and class.

Students who participate in these correspondences have become proficient in keeping up with their e-mail. At first, messages were stiff, barely answering direct questions with single words and simple sentences. Over time, not only has the complexity of text increased, but a certain writing style has also developed as the students pooled their knowledge of the mechanics of CMC and tried to apply it all to whichever one of them was writing for all at the keyboard.

CMC provides a variation on the Pen-Pal theme in which the

delays between messages can be measured in days rather than weeks. One unique forum for PenPals is the BITnet discussion list BICOM-PAL@sjuvm.bitnet (Big Computer Pals), which is an international project linking disabled individuals through computer networking. The goal of BICOMPAL is to develop student-mentor relationships between individuals with various disabilities. It serves as the "personals" file in which potential Pals can leave messages about themselves and describe the characteristics of those with whom they would like to communicate.

One of the earliest stories on the list involved N.N. who was described as a 16-year-old part-Cherokee LD student good with his hands and already in trouble with the law. For a few months CMC caught his imagination, and he enjoyed reading and writing and took pride in doing it well. He wrote to a shop teacher in Australia:

> The weather here is cloudy today. We have all kinds of weather here. Do you have any favorite singer? How long have you been teaching? Why did you decide to teach? I am making picnic tables in the shop class. What are you making in your shop? Well I have to go now.

Getting a bit braver, he decided to send a picture of himself to an interesting young woman in grad school who went skiing on weekends.

> I am 16 years old. I do like snow but we dont get much here. What does your name mean? I like to work. What do you look like?

```
        | | | | | | | | | | | | |
        /------------ₑ_- - - \
        |                     |
        |                |→|
        |                |→|
      ┌─|   0    0 →|_|┌ |
      ┐ →/\-╗   |→₂|
      |  _____/  |·
        |_____|
```

For emotionally disturbed fourth graders in New York City, the improvements began after a mere two weeks of computer networking. Students improved word spacing, spelling, punctuation, and format; and students changed their perceptions of themselves. One child wrote that he had hit his teacher. The responses to this were sympathetic, and the child responded that he felt bad that he did it. This did not seem unusual until his teacher told everyone that this was the first time the child had expressed any remorse for his actions.

In addition to these general e-mail messages, some very special relationships emerged that were very close to the concept of a resident tutor. Dr. Zenhausern corresponded with a class who called themselves "The Computer Heads." He helped them explore their own thinking styles and taught them some neuropsychological generalities. The following illustrates how these learning disabled students applied what he had taught:

> Date: Thu, 19 Mar 92 13:12:40 EST
> dear dr.z,
> In class on Tuesday we wrote directions off of maps. Mrs. P gave us 2 cities in VA and the map of VA told us to write the directions to go from one to the other. Then she told us to give left brain directions to go from one to the other. She read us your left brain directions as an example. L. has the best left brain directions and O. has the worst. We decided that because L. has the most words in hers and O. has the least.
> bye for now
> The computer heads.

The CHATBACK List initiated a resident tutor program under the name Far Star. The Far Star Project spun the tale that a spaceship of curious but friendly aliens had tapped into the Internet and wanted the participant students to describe themselves, where they lived, and some aspects of their society. Some of the postings were individual responses to all the questions, and some were class group responses to a single question.

A small group of learning disabled and mildly retarded seniors attempted to explain to the aliens the significance of the colors of Earth seen from the spaceship in the flyover. After a few false starts, and lots of discussion on what the aliens would already know, the group posted the following:

> When you fly by the planet across the top that we call the north pole, you will see two pieces of land that we call continents one is big and one is small. The small one is called North America. We live on North America. At the top of North America you will see white. You are looking at Canada which is white because it is winter and it is cold. Below the white you will see green that is the United States. That is the color of the trees, and grass. Half way down the United States you will see Virginia. Look to your right until the green touches the blue of the water, and you will be looking at Virginia. Nottoway County is about 130 miles from the water among the trees.

A class of 11th graders, who called their class group "The Educated Brains" in their online signature, replied to the question of how we are "programmed":

> You wanted to know if we are all equally intelligent. And how we are programmed, and who decides what our program will be. We are not all equally intelligent. Some people can think better than others. Some people can talk better than others. Some people can remember better than others. Some people can read better than others. Some people can write better than others. Some people go to college and some people can't go to college. Some people can learn better than others.
>
> We decide ourselves what we learn. Some people help us decide what we learn. Those people are teachers, parents, friends, guidance counselors help some times, governments, principal, and the man up stairs.

A class of 10th graders with notoriety as rebels chose to answer the question of whether there is "violence" on our planet. Only the opportunity to think about and explain such an "irreverent" topic induced them to get into the discussion and writing of this reply:

> We are answering question number five. You want to know why we have violence on this planet. We have violence on this planet because we don`t like each other. We fight over property, we fight over girls, we fight for peace, we fight for freedom, and some of us don`t fight.
>
> We stop fighting when someone wins or someone dies or someone gets hurt or we blow up the earth. We might stop fighting if people could learn to keep their big mouths shut.

The youngest participants accepted that the aliens were real, and the adolescents wrote tongue-in-cheek, but kids in the upper elementary/middle school grades were undecided. Toward the end of the project one such group from Ohio shared their disbelief with a similar group in Germany. They explored whether or not their teachers were writing the "alien" posts and whether one of the aliens would actually appear in their school when summoned. Enter Zman, Student of the Aliens, with an assignment from his teachers to find out if the children were "real." If the children would just explain to him how they think, he could determine if they were real or made up by *his* teachers!! After Zman finished his assignment, with the help of his curious friends, the spaceship flew out of the range of communications. Yet, well into the next school year, every few weeks, a short message appears on TALK-

BACK with a student asking if Sherose and Ali-Enn and Zman have returned to earth orbit.

STUDENTS AND PROJECTS

Far Star was one of many projects that have emerged from CHAT-BACK@sjuvm.stjohns.edu. The Chatback Trust is an organization that was created five years ago in the United Kingdom by Tom Holloway under the aegis of IBM. The purpose of the project is to utilize computer technology in the education of students with special needs. Initially, CHATBACK was limited to Dialcom, an isolated network developed by British Telecommunications with no outlet to the Internet. In 1991, CHATBACK was imported to the United States with the creation of the BITnet Lists CHATBACK@SJUVM and TALKBACK@SJUVM.

The CHATBACK List is reserved for the planners and teachers who use it to develop and evaluate the projects for the children. TALK-BACK is the List in which the students post their results for the projects.

The Projects on CHATBACK are many and varied. In addition to Far Star, the Projects during the 1991-1992 school year included Breakfast Game, in which students described what they had for breakfast that day. In the Christmas Food Game, students described what they were going to eat on Christmas (or another December holiday) Day.

Because the participants on CHATBACK are international, activities that require students to write descriptions of their daily life tend to gently raise the cultural consciousness of the students involved. Students in Special Ed English classes in rural Virginia read about half the postings to Christmas Food Game before composing and posting their own anticipated feasts. Several commented on the fact that European children were more likely to mention drinking alcohol than American children. But no one missed the line from Tom Holloway, Director of Chatback, who promised that his Christmas Breakfast would include: "Spotted Dick with Custard Of Course." The first anticipation for an e-mail response accompanied the wait—to learn that "spotted dick" is a steamed pudding with raisins, in a traditional yule log shape, served with custard.

The school year 1992-1993 brought new CHATBACK projects. Steel, Beans, Games, and Rivers were new BITnet lists that gave a growing number of students an easy way to participate in these creative projects.

Steel is an actual around-the-world yacht race that began in late September 1992 and ended in May 1993 and which was sponsored by the manufacturer of the 10 identical yachts that were competing. Daily postings of latitude and longitude coordinates encouraged students to plot the progress of the race either on printed maps, or on Geoclock, a shareware program of world maps.

One school in Ohio explained how it was using the Steel project in the classroom:

> This is what our 5th and 7th are doing with the Steel race. Each person created a tiny ship with the graphic editor of Print Shop. The other grades voted on the 10 best. These 10 were christened with the 10 Steel Race names. The class was divided into 10 groups with each drawing a boat, and each time a posting comes in one of the members of a boat moves that boat to the correct latitude and longitude. The 7th choose to use a globe and the 5th choose to use a World Map.

Many student's first posts had word-spacing difficulties, frequent spelling errors, little punctuation, incorrect capitalization, and consisted of short, stiff sentences. As replies came in, and students realized there were *real* people out there, they developed pride in their work—enough pride to conquer mechanics. As time and development continued, students developed individual writing styles for their online correspondence.

PROFESSIONAL NEEDS

The computer networks are not only valuable for the education of the students, but they provide an impetus to professional growth that then can be reflected in the classroom. One advantage of CMC to the special ed teacher as a professional educator is access to the experience and ideas of others in the field. Unlike professional journals, discussion lists and newsgroup participation bring together one teacher with other teachers and with academics.

The ALTLEARN BITnet list features a discussion among the professionals who work with the learning disabled and those with similar educational disabilities. ALTLEARN discusses alternative approaches to learning, particularly those that adapt instruction to the learning style needs of the student. ALTLEARN brings together academics and practitioners in discussions and resource sharing that benefit the students as well as the professionals.

The LD-reading list on the province-wide network in Saskatchewan is one of many online courses available to professionals. Ld-reading pairs a discussion list and a weekly electronic conference to provide technical support for introducing the Direct Access Reading Technique (DART) to teachers at a remote school in central Canada. DART is a reading technique that works for the kids who fall through the cracks in phonics instruction.

Information on specific disabilities is often gleaned through interaction with parents and the adult disabled in a support group. There are several electronic support groups for persons with various disabilities that would be of interest to special educators.

AUTISM List at SJUVM is an electronic support group for children with autism, their parent, and teachers. The list has also become the domain of high-functioning autistic adults who bring their unique and experiential insights to those who now work with children with autism.

The following messages were exchanged by a mother who is autistic and has an autistic daughter and the father of a girl who is autistic. The mother and daughter live in Australia, and the father and daughter live in New York State. This interaction shows the advantage of sharing experiences halfway around the world. The mother wrote about her daughter's difficulties with social interactions:

> When we went on that school excursion to Blackbutt Nature Reserve, during the lunch break the teachers took a small group of children each to play games. As each group followed its teacher to a corner of the playground, H was left standing in the middle of the field on her own. From where I was sitting I could see what the problem was . . . . no one had said "Come with us!" She stood there for about a minute and I was just about to get up and go to her when she turned and came running back to me and buried her head in my shoulder. It turned out that she was convinced that nobody wanted to play with her. I took her over near the group on the pretense that I was going to play with her but as we got close the teacher spotted us and asked H to join in. Without a moment's hesitation she ran up to the other children and joined in their circle.

The father was able to apply this to his own case:

> I think I see the point that you're trying to make: Helen was not being rejected, just thought she was because no one explicitly asked her to join in. I see that in S too, although there are times she will go over and try to join in. Unfortunately her actions and methods of joining in are different and other people (grownups and kids) don't understand it and kind of get estranged by it and walk away, assuming my daughter won't understand, they fail to see she was trying to join in with what they are doing even if it wasn't the same.

A major topic of discussion on the AUTISM List has been the effectiveness of facilitated communication as a technique of communication for people with autism. (In facilitated communication, a facilitator puts his or her hand on the shoulder, arm, hand, etc., of an autistic person who is answering questions by typing on a keyboard.) The use of facilitated communication was considered from a variety of perspectives, including its effectiveness from an empirical standpoint, the possibilities for abuse, and the almost mystical nature proposed by those from the more extreme fringes.

The computer networks and facilitated communication have been combined at PS 177 in New York City, a school for children with developmental disorders. By means of a grant from NYSERNet (New York State Education and Research Network), a private, not for profit corporation, PS 177 has been given access to the Internet. The children will be able to use facilitated communication techniques in sending messages around the world with the expectation that CMC will serve to amplify the effects of facilitated communication. The project began in January 1993.

INFORMATION RETRIEVAL

Sometimes the special educator needs to locate information on a specific topic in a hurry, perhaps to develop an effective program for a student returning to school after an accident, or for a student transferring from another school with an uncommon disability. The teacher needs access to current information without trips across town or across the state to the libraries that may store it. Electronic retrieval tools give teachers access to information stored in libraries around the world. There are more than 4,000 BITnet discussion lists and 2,000 Usenet groups, most of which maintain archives of past postings. A list of some BITnet lists of most interest to special educators is shown in Figure 5.1.

Figure 5.1. Lists on Bitnet of interest to special ed teachers

Altlearn	alternative approaches to learning
	listserv@sjuvm.bitnet
ASLING-L	American Sign Language list
	listserv@yalevm.bitnet
AutismSJU	Autism and developmental disabilities
	listserv@sjuvm.bitnet
Behavior	Behavioral & emotional disorders in children
	listserv@asuacad.bitnet
Bicompal	Big Computer Pals
	listserv@sjuvm.bitnet
Blind-L	computer use by and for the blind
	listserv@uafsysb.bitnet

Blindnws	Blind News Digest
	listserv@ndsuvm1.bitnet
Braille	discussion list for blind
	listserv@searn
Chatback	discussion list for Chatback projects
	listserv@sjuvm.stjohns.edu
Commdis	speech disorders
	listserv@rpiecs.bitnet
DDFind-L	forum for networking on disabilities
	listserv@gitvm1.bitnet
Deaf-L	deaf list
	listserv@siucvmb.bitnet
Disres-L	disability research list
	listserv@ryerson.bitnet
Eyemov-L	Eye Movement network
	listserv@spcvxa.bitnet
L-HCAP	Handicapped people in education
	listserv@ndsuvm1.bitnet
Mobility	SJU mobility disabilities list
	listserv@sjuvm.bitnet
SCR-L	study of cognitive rehabilitation
	listserv@mizzou1.bitnet
SPCeds-L	special education students list - SUNY Buffalo
	listserv@ubvm.bitnet
Stutt-L	Stuttering Research & clinical practice
	listserv@templevm.bitnet
Talkback	student reply list for Chatback projects
	listserv@sjuvm.stjohns.edu

The BITnet lists have a very simple and effective information retrieval system that will allow searches of the archives of any BITnet list, providing an index of the entries or their actual copies. The search can be by key word, author, date, and topic, as well as by any boolean combination. For example, there were two major discussions on attentional deficit disorders on the ALTLEARN list in 1992 and as an example, the following command was sent to listserv@sjuvm.stohns.edu:

```
//Scan JOB Echo=Yes
DATABASE SEARCH DD=Data Outlim=5000 Cpulim=999
//Data DD *
Select add or adhd in ALTLEARN since 92/01/01
index
/end
/*
```

A sampling of the 390 entries received is shown in Figure 5.2.

Figure 5.2. Postings to the list ALTLEARN that contain the keyword phrases "ADD" or "ADHD" (excerpted)

> index				
Item #	Date	Time	Recs	Subject
000677	92/01/01	14:21	27	Learning to chew
000682	92/01/25	12:02	254	EW Conf, Moscow
000689	92/02/06	15:15	72	Re: Testing for learning styles
000693	92/02/07	14:15	45	Re: Need some information, please
000696	92/02/07	14:25	159	Autism Advocacy Update

Universities are storing dissertations and papers in electronic form. K-12 networks are building archives of curricular and instructional materials. Software, books, and movie reviews are available in electronic form. A satellite TV network publishes its programming in electronic form. Lots of public domain, shareware, and software samples are available electronically. Even the most revered and sacred of paper documents, such as the U.S. Constitution, the laws of the land, the Bible, the Koran, and other religious and secular texts, are available in electronic form. During the 1992 presidential election, the position papers and many of the speeches of the candidates were available in full, in electronic form. Locating this information is as easy as using a word in the document title in a keyword search using the ARCHIE program to find out where the document is stored. The FTP program can then be used to bring the file to the teacher's computer. (More information on these information management tools can be found in Sudweeks's chapter, this volume).

Another means of accessing electronic information is with VERONICA and Gopher. Gopher is a menu driven, Internet information and retrieval service developed by the University of Minnesota and named for their mascot, the gopher. VERONICA is a refinement to Gopher and was developed at the University of Nevada, Reno. Like ARCHIE, VERONICA is a keyword search program that searches through the information cataloged on the electronic Gophers and creates a custom menu on the users screen to aid in the retrieval of the desired information. The Gophers are menus of documents, files, and such related to a specific topic. In January 1993, there were about 300 registered Gophers and many more under development. One of interest to special educators is the Cornucopia of Disability Information (CODI).

SUGGESTIONS FOR TEACHERS

The most important consideration is the teacher. A teacher must be an accomplished networker before he or she can run an effective electronic classroom. It is critical to provide the training, time, equipment, and support that the teacher needs to become accomplished. The following suggestions might be useful in initiating your own CMC project.

Standard Security Precautions
- Do not let students use your account.
- Never give a student your password (type it in for them if necessary).
- Always keep the passwords for all student accounts on file.
- Monitor student accounts frequently. Set accounts to save all outgoing and incoming mail.
- Maintain a professional correspondence with anyone your students correspond with (or their teachers).
- Read all incoming and outgoing mail from strangers with students.
- Discuss Netiquette before getting online the first time.
- Remind students that rude, racist, sexist, demeaning, abusive, and scatological language or remarks could result in loss of access.

Preparations for the First Experience
- Activate the student account, set up the password, and set any parameters to make use easier for students.
- Forward some exciting/interesting mail to the student account so they will discover something there and have a reason to write their first e-mail.
- Provide a seatwork assignment for any students who aren't interested in the first session. Permit them to change their mind.
- If available, project the first few session onto a large screen. Point out to students how to read the headers, where to find the body of a message, and the role of the signature file.
- Put the most hyperactive student at the keyboard for the first session. Tell this student what keys to press, and let the other students watch the results on the screen.

Day-to-Day Activity
- Rotate the person at the keyboard among all students. Each student should have the opportunity to logon, read incoming mail, and reply or write messages. Don't let a single student monopolize the keyboard.

- Students who are shy of the computer should be given very short sessions at the keyboard until they become more comfortable.
- Provide students with enough class time to keep up with e-mail responses.
- Always schedule more time (days per week, especially) for network activities than you expect to need.
- Always keep an alternate assignment available for times when nets are down.

Choosing Online Projects
- Start looking for projects before students get online for the first time. Pick some topics that will appeal to the interests and experiences of the students.
- Study the project thoroughly. Make sure that students will have access to the information to be collected and posted. Make arrangements for any field trips, visitors, and so on, necessary for the project.
- Forward to the students' account a description of the project and directions on how to become involved.
- Let students make the final decision to participate in any online project.
- Let students read the contributions of others to a project both before and after they upload theirs.
- Encourage students to keep a hardcopy of their project experiences. This can be as simple as a printout of a log of all related files, or as complex as a slick desktop publishing product.

Chapter Six

Online from the K-12 Classroom*

Linda S. Fowler
Daniel D. Wheeler
University of Cincinnati

The use of computers in both elementary and high school classrooms has increased dramatically during the last decade. One facet of this growth has been the use of computers for Computer-Mediated Communications (CMC). Students and teachers can now communicate with those in other classrooms across town or across the world. The utilization of telecommunications in classrooms opens another dimension for students and teachers to broaden the study of science and history, improving writing skills, and investigate other communities (Levin, Riel, Miyake, & Cohen, 1987). The use of telecommunications also increases information sharing, collaborative learning, and reduces the isolation sometimes experienced by teachers and students (O'Shea, Kimmel, & Novemsky, 1990).

Participation in CMC is still fairly low among K-12 classrooms. The percentage of U.S. schools having modems has certainly increased

*This chapter is based on Linda Fowler's dissertation. Dan Wheeler was a member of the dissertation committee. We have used first person plural ("we") to report positions that we both take or decisions that were made jointly. We have used first-person singular ("I") to report actions taken to conduct this research by Linda Fowler.

from the 7% found in 1988 (Office of Technology Assessment, 1988, footnote 11). But, according to Hadley and Sheingold (1993), only a small percentage of those schools were using them for CMC.

In spite of the current low level, CMC activities are growing rapidly. Inexpensive microcomputer bulletin board systems are being operated by many schools. Several states have acted to provide statewide networks for teachers to use. FreeNet systems have appeared in several cities. These provide access for members of the public as well as for educators.

Because CMC is just beginning to be used, very few studies describing computer-mediated communications are reported in the literature. Most of the available studies focus on teachers using only one type of computer network for one particular project or activity. These have been very valuable, but it is now time for a broader look.

Our study focuses on the ways teachers use electronic networking with students. The results are based on interviews with 25 teachers who have used telecommunications to connect their classrooms with other classrooms around the country and, in some instances, around the world. The categories of CMC utilized by the teachers and students in this study functioned with the first two categories described in Chapter 1 (this volume): computer-based conferencing, and informatics.

For our study, we chose to do telephone interviews so that we could get richer and more detailed reports about what teachers were actually experiencing with CMC. We were particularly interested in what they had to say about how CMC changed the educational context for their students. We also paid close attention to the factors that they identified as contributing to their successes and failures.

CONDUCTING THE STUDY

We wanted to interview a sample of teachers who were actively using CMC in their classrooms. We also wanted to get a diverse sample covering a range of grade levels, geographical locations, and kinds of computer systems used. We started by asking network representatives from the AT&T Learning Network, TERC (Technology Education Research Centers), LABnet, National Geographic KidsNetwork, and FrEdmail (Free Educational Electronic Mail) for names of teachers who used their systems. Additional contacts came from reading messages on the KIDSNET mailing list (kidsnet@pittvms), and a few teachers were recommended by teachers I was interviewing.

Seventy names were received. These individuals were contacted by telephone or e-mail. I explained that I was working on a dissertation and asked if they would be willing to be interviewed by telephone and recorded. The interviews were not conducted at the time initial contact was made. If the teacher agreed to participate, a mutually agreeable time was established when the teacher would be available for at least an hour. Of the 70 potential interviewees, some could not be reached, some were not willing to be interviewed, and some could not find the time for an interview. Successful arrangements were made with 26 teachers.

The interviews followed a script consisting primarily of open-ended questions. The use of open-ended questions in the interviews allowed the teachers to explain the things they felt were most important. Some direct questions were used during the interview to assure that similar background information was obtained from all the teachers, but they were minimized because they tend to narrowly focus the interview and some of the teachers' ideas would not be captured.

The interviews began with an open-ended request: "First, I would like you to describe the things you and your students have done with telecommunications this past year." The interviews all ended with the following: "I'd like to close by asking you two questions: What was the biggest problem you encountered? What was your biggest success?"

The telephone interviews were conducted from October 1991 through April 1992. Each interview was recorded with the teacher's permission. The taped interviews were then transcribed and checked for accuracy. One recording was lost, so the results reported here are based on interviews with 25 teachers. In order to preserve the anonymity of the teachers, they are identified in this report by first names. These are not the true first names of the teachers, but gender identification was maintained.

The final sample included 10 elementary school teachers, 5 middle school teachers, and 10 high school teachers.

RESULTS

The first very strong impression from the interviews is that these teachers have been successful with CMC. They talked about their experiences enthusiastically and described in great detail what they and their students had accomplished.

Here are some of their general statements about the impact of CMC:

Ira: But what I would say is that the computer was the initiator. I think it opened up a whole new world.
Bill: Just the dynamics of using telecommunications, I think is more of an affective thing than cognitive. . . . Just the excitement of being able to correspond with somebody.

Meg: I don't notice that in a regular classroom, not to that extent to try to learn something about a different culture. It WAS so impersonal. This is much more meaningful and they've got a lot of friends over there. It makes a big difference.

Dave: Students kept a log of their reactions to interactions. A couple said that they really got deeper insight into what response is about and the idea of how different people respond. They really felt that they had grown in their ability to respond.

June: It's a totally broadening experience. Kids are able to express themselves on the computer that may be a bit inhibited in doing it in person.

Nan: I have one young man, in our school, who is very gifted, but who is so socially inept, actually handles and carries himself . . . and if you saw the child you would think he was very retarded. He's getting on computer now. I mean he doesn't speak with people, he doesn't look you in the eye. But he's getting on computer and getting a friend and will probably be his first friend.

Cara: They have certainly become more thoughtful The ones that participated in the network and it just amazes them when they can relate to someone from a different country or even a different state. . . . They start trying; they start thinking about issues. . . . They will more readily solve problems given to them over the network then they will in a textbook.

Meg: The obvious social implications for us has (sic) been awareness of differences and respect for those differences. . . . I've noticed too, a caring. . . . It's a personal level of awareness, rather than just a general statement of a cultural difference.

It is clear from the interviews that the teachers in this study are not typical of teachers in general. They are the ones who volunteer, seek out better ways, experiment, and dedicate many extra hours to their profession. The majority of the teachers in this study are ones who habitually go beyond the defined environment, whether it be the traditional four walls of the classroom or the prescribed curriculum for that class. Listening to their stories, it is evident that these people do not take "No" for an answer.

Uses of Telecommunications

When I asked the teachers what goals they had for their students in using telecommunications, they all answered in general terms and not with specific instructional objectives. The most common goal, stated by nine teachers, was to have their students learn and appreciate cultural differences and to have them become comfortable in a larger, diverse world. Improvement in writing skills was another common general academic goal. Several wanted their students to have experience with technology, in some cases, as preparation for entry into the job market.

The variety of e-mail connections provided teachers with flexibility in choosing projects or curricula that fit existing instructional objectives for their classes. For example, Barb was asked to coordinate a project as part of her class's involvement with the AT&T Learning Network. Because one of her school requirements for the fourth grade was to do a recycling project, she chose to use the topic of recycling. By expanding the study to all the schools in her learning circle, her students not only completed the project, they were able to bring a larger perspective by comparing results to schools across the country and in Canada.

Several short mathematics projects were described by teachers. Bob described a statistical project with M & M candies. He had the students sort by color and build a statistical model. Twenty schools nationwide joined his class in this project

Jan described a statistics project using baseball cards. Each group of teachers and students who signed up got 150 baseball cards. A whole series of activities was done with the data on the back of the baseball cards. Two industrial statisticians served as mentors for that project.

Several short projects were described. Meg was very excited when she described her fifth-grade class's involvement in a countrywide picnic. Fourteen different classes across the country compared grocery prices on a list of items that might appear on a picnic menu. A central location received lists from each of the schools. Then a cumulative list was sent back to each of the participating schools so that the students could compare their prices with the other schools. Many of the schools concluded the project with a real picnic all on the same day.

Rob sent out an e-mail message asking students to watch and report on a meteor shower. The students had to learn how to pinpoint a meteor and describe the location and time. They had to figure out how to write up their results so they could send them over telecommunications. When all of the reports came in, the students found out that people saw the same thing at the same time in different parts of the world.

Success Was Not Easy

In spite of the success these teachers had with telecommunications, it did not come easily. The teachers reported a continuing struggle with the technology. The computers are NOT easy to use. Many of the teachers encountered difficult problems getting their computer, modem, and software to work smoothly with the host system that provided the connection for telecommunications.

About half of them reported considerable difficulties with the technical aspects of telecommunications. Cara's report is an example:

> (It) is really complicated to call into the state mainframe. (I would) send mail to other states and wouldn't get stuff back, I wouldn't put the right code at the end. I couldn't tell the difference between Internet and Bitnet. Manuals are coming out. . . . Yesterday, I got a message that they were going to send (them). . . . Some days I don't know why I stayed with it. It's frustrating. (I spent) two weeks trying to figure out how to get it to print and then I found out there was no way, because that was one of the bugs in the system. You know how one of these things with the computer, you get involved in it and it takes you two days to figure it out and then it takes two seconds.

One of the continuing refrains was the difficulty of getting access to telephone lines. Most of the teachers had succeeded (eventually) in getting a telephone line into their classrooms, but there were many reports of having to go to the office, library, or remote computer lab in order to do telecommunications. Yet, teachers put up with this inconvenience. Hal's response was typical: "You don't need a dedicated phone line to get started. Just use what's available in the school and show the administration. The result will sell the concept and process."

Teachers Used Several Systems

Most of the teachers in the sample had used more than one CMC system. Several had used as many as five different systems. Table 6.1 shows the distribution of system use for all the teachers in the sample.

The telecomputing systems used by the teachers in this study can be divided into four categories that we call structured projects, activity connections, online services, and generic connections. The structured projects that teachers in our sample were involved in were National Geographic KidsNetwork, LabNet, Star Schools Project, GlobalLab, and AT&T Learning Network. These projects typically provide curriculum

Table 6.1. Telecommunications Systems Used by Teachers

Name	Structured Projects					Activity Connections		Online Services			Generic Connections	
	Kids Net	Lab Net	TERC Star	GLab	ATT	Iris	Fred	AOL	Pro	Dia	Bit/Int	BBS
Ann					X							X
Barb					X							
Carl					X		X		X			
Dave												X
Earl						X		X	X		X	X
Fran	X				X							
Gay					X						X	X
Hal	X							X	X		X	X
Ira	X											X
June	X											X
Ken							X					
Lee	X				X				X			X
Mary		X								X	X	X
Nan										X	X	X
Pat					X							
Stan		X										X
Sam		X	X								X	
Sue	X											
Rob		X		X			X				X	X
Al						X	X				X	X
Bob							X				X	
Cara					X						X	
May	X	X				X					X	
Meg							X					X
Jan										X	X	X
	7	5	1	1	8	3	6	2	4	3	12	15

key: GLab=GlobalLab; AOL=America Online; Pro=Prodigy; DIa=Dialog; BBS=bulletin boards; Bit/int=BITnet and Internet guides that specify in considerable detail the classroom activities and kinds of telecommunications that will be sent. They also provide telecommunications software and access to a network that will work smoothly with that software. Technical support is also available. All this comes at a price; the cost of these projects prevents many teachers from participating.

Iris and FrEdmail are examples of what we call activity connections. These systems provide access to online, curricular based projects. Some are provided by the system organizers, and others are offered by the teachers who connect. There is considerable variation among the projects. Much of the structure comes from the teachers who volunteer to organize activities on the system.

Several of the teachers used commercial online services that are intended for a much wider audience than just classroom educators. These included America Online and Prodigy. These provide e-mail, encyclopedia services, educational programs, access to databases, electronic bulletin boards, news and weather, and live conferencing. They usually include specific software for connecting into the service. As with the structured projects, the match between the provided software and the telecommunication system reduced the technical problems the teachers had.

Most of the teachers had used systems that provided what we call generic connections. These come in two kinds. Twelve of the teachers had used systems that were connected to the high-speed international networks, such as Internet and BITnet. Fifteen of the teachers had used microcomputer-based bulletin board systems (BBS). In addition to the local offerings, many of the BBS systems were connected together by dial-modem links. There are a number of educational activities available through each of these kinds of systems.

The teachers who used more than one system were asked to compare the connections. The two teachers who use both the AT&T Learning Network and NGS KidsNetwork, Fran and Lee, shared enthusiasm for both. As Lee said, "(They are) both wonderful but different. The AT&T curriculum interfaces better. National Geographic provides much more structure in that everyone is doing the same experiment and sharing the same results." Lee stressed the importance of a coordinator in comparing these two structured connections:

> An AT&T difference that I like is that they encourage (you) to be more professional. The communication circle coordinator tends to get things going and maintains it; (coordination is) not done with National Geographic. There is a lot more interaction over and above what is in the manual through AT&T.

Carl compared FrEdmail to the AT&T Learning Network this way: FrEdmail's more wide open. It's more dependent upon having a local node (system) within dialing access. Whereas with AT&T, you can be in the middle of Alaska. We've got several people, and all you have to do is call 1-800- and you're in. So, you can't compare the two because they both do different things. And they're both wonderful.

The consensus of the teachers is that it is easier to participate in the structured programs. The guidance they provide makes it easier. The other kinds of systems require more initiative on the part of the teachers but also provide them with more control to do it their way. Some teachers found this very rewarding. No matter which of the four categories of connectivity was used, the teachers were all excited about what the globalization of their classrooms accomplished.

Social Interactions and Cooperative Learning

One of the most consistent themes running through the interviews was the impact of the telecommunications activity on the social organization of the classroom. The use of CMC changed the way the classroom functioned. In many cases, patterns of cooperative learning developed.

The conceptual framework of Vygotskian theory provides a good basis for understanding the functioning of CMC in a classroom. One of the key concepts is the *zone of proximal development*. Vygotsky (1978, p. 86) defined this as:

the distance between the actual developmental level as determined by independent problem solving and the level of potential development as determined through problem solving under adult guidance or *in collaboration with more capable peers*. (emphasis added)

This definition expresses Vygotsky's notion that what children can do with the assistance of others might be in some sense even more indicative of their mental development than what they can do alone (Meichenbaum, Burland, Gruson, & Cameron, 1985). Their achievements in a supportive social environment make the largest contribution to their cognitive development (Fowler, 1994).

All of the teachers reported using group activities with CMC. Most of them thought that the use of CMC created a particularly favorable environment for cooperative learning. Only three of the teachers saw no difference between CMC and their other classroom activities. These some of the typical comments:

Ann: A lot of cooperativeness develops . . . we did not go about it
systematically to say, "O.K., we're going to do the AT&T
Learning Circle and we're going to use cooperative learning." But it evolved as part of the learning circle and using
telecommunications, where it was the logical progres-sion
for children, rather than sitting together doing, you know,
sitting alone doing work that it was so much easier to put
them together so that they could share ideas and work cooperatively on projects and we saw that evolve and that was
not the purpose initially, but that is what happened and it
was a very natural progression, it wasn't a created progres-
sion.

Hal: It promotes the use of groups. When you're working with
telecommunications, it gives a focus. It's an avenue that the
kids and their group, can move towards.

Ira: A lot of it is pairs or triads depending on the size of the class. And
that just fit perfectly . . . it makes a very nice vehicle.

June: It was group effort—it was more of a group and team effort. . . .
I do cooperative learning and group effort things . . . you saw
the minds working together, you saw them working in
groups.

Nan: The students work in partners or in groups because there's just
not enough time for the kids to do it individually. They
become helpers of each other. My procedure is to train two
or three kids to operate the software and they, in turn, train
others.

To effectively support the students' efforts with collaborative
learning, teachers need to serve more as facilitators rather than as direc-
tors or controllers. Collaboration among students supports the role of
teacher as facilitator. The teacher in the facilitator role is not usually
found in a traditional classroom environment. Collaboration improves
the effectiveness of learning by imposing peer evaluations on students'
products from around the world-not just a teacher's reaction to their
work. The reports from the teachers in this study support the results
found by previous researchers who looked directly at classroom interactions (Cohen & Riel, 1989; Riel, 1985; Riel & Levin, 1990; Weir, 1992;
Womble, 1985).

The use of small groups and peer teaching applies Vygotsky's
concept of the zone of proximal development. The small group arrangement used with all the teachers interviewed in this study incorporated
collaborative problem-solving methods to work with not just the other
students in a particular classroom, but with peers around the world to

find solutions to multiple social, economic, and ecological problems in national and international contexts. The experiences of the students in this study in problem solving in a collaborative way with other people in other locations provide conditions that hopefully will contribute to a new generation of people who will work collaboratively in solving world problems.

Cultural Awareness

One of the arguments often used to support the use of telecommunications is that interactions with distant partners will broaden the cultural horizons of the students. There is ample evidence to support this in the interviews. When I asked the teachers what goal they had for their students in using telecommunications, seven said it was having their students learn and appreciate cultural differences and to have them become comfortable in a larger, diverse world. This reply supports the response given by the teachers when they were asked to describe their biggest success. Eighteen of them made comments that indicated that cultural awareness was an overwhelming positive result of using e-mail. The use of CMC changed the isolated local classroom into part of a global classroom environment. This expansion of horizons has an even greater impact on, as Nan said, "the students who never go beyond the local mall."

The following are some of the specific comments the teachers made:

Ann: They felt connected to another culture because they had communicated with these children.

Cara: They have certainly become more thoughtful. . . . It just amazes them when they can relate to someone from a differ-ent country or even a different state. . . . They start trying; they start thinking about issues. . . . They will more readily solve problems given to them over the network then they will in a textbook.

Meg: The obvious social implications for us (have) been aware-ness of differences and respect for those differences. . . . I've noticed too, a caring. . . . It's personal level of awareness, rather than just a general statement of a cultural difference.

Many teachers want their students to become comfortable in a larger, diverse world. Several of the teachers, representing all grade levels, spoke at length in describing how the interclassroom interactions supported real experiences rather than dry information from a textbook.

Writing Skills

Writing assignments in school often have no real audience; they are written just for the teacher. Writing done for a telecommunications project does have a real audience: the kids at the other end. Participation in telecommunications gives students experience with writing in a meaningful context. A number of teachers commented on the change in their students' perspective on writing.

These were some typical comments:

Ann: I saw great improvement in writing skills; vocabulary.... I can see an improvement in what they did because they were challenged by the fact the quality of the work that was com-ing over the network was very high quality. And they were no longer satisfied with, "We live in (Our Town). We are happy."

Pat: Academically, the kids get a lot of practice with their own language, with writing letters, with writing communication, with formulating whole sentences, with putting their thoughts down.

Cara: It seems to me that students are more concerned about what they write. If they're writing . . . the message that they intend to send over the network . . . they're about 10 times more likely to ask me to read it first than if they were just writing it and then stuck it in the pile to turn in to me. There's a little bit more motivation there to come in the next day after they've gotten messages back and things like that.

Only a third of the teachers reported an impact on writing skills, but for these teachers, the opportunities for writing to a real audience was one of the major reasons for using CMC in their classrooms.

RECOMMENDATIONS

As a result of this study, several recommendations can be made to facilitate teachers who want to begin using CMC. We have found five categories of requirements for successful use of CMC: technical support, time, computer equipment, software, and network access.

Technical Support

Technical support is needed to establish and maintain the connections. Beginners may require the level of support provided by the structured projects if local technical support is not available. A "buddy" system was also suggested by some of the teachers. When a teacher begins this new medium there should be at least one other teacher in the school with whom he or she can team. Even when both are beginners, the sharing of the progress and the problems helps. This method is part of the collaborative learning that is an outgrowth of the use of telecomputing with students.

Time

CMC requires time. Teachers need the time to learn how to use the equipment. They require planning time to incorporate the new technology into an existing environment. Because uploading, downloading, and distributing messages is very time-consuming, some support is required, especially in the lower grades, as students do not have the ability to type their own responses.

Computer Equipment

CMC requires equipment. Up-to-date equipment in adequate amounts reduces the technical support and the time required for CMC. But teachers must often make do with whatever they can get. Several teachers reported scrounging for computers, either by asking for donations from local users groups or by hunting for computers in their schools that were not being used.

Software

The software provided by structured projects and online services is much better than the combination of standard terminal emulation software with a generic host. But even these are not as good as they could be. Better software is being developed, and it will be worth the effort to seek it out as it becomes available.

Network Access

The ideal situation is to have a group of computers for the students to use, all of which are capable of telecommunications. This can be done with a local area network (LAN) connected to a telecommunications link. None of the teachers in this study had such a system. The best that they had was a dedicated telephone line to one computer in the class-room. This is certainly workable.

All five of these kinds of resources are necessary for successful use of CMC in K-12 classrooms. It also helps to have dedicated teachers and interested students. Providing adequate levels of these five resources will help maintain the dedication of the teachers and the inter-est of the students.

Conclusions

The teachers in this study are an exceptional group of educators. They have been the pioneers in the use of CMC in K-12 classrooms. They have demonstrated that CMC can bring both excitement and solid learning experiences to their students. The links around the globe have extended the world of their students into a global classroom environment.

These teachers have shown that there are many benefits in the use of CMC in their classrooms. Many found that their students demon-strated cooperative learning and improved social interaction when activ-ities were done together using CMC. Cultural awareness was enhanced by contact with students in other locations via the medium of electronic mail. In addition to the general benefits of CMC, many teachers promot-ed the development of basic academic skills, such as writing and mathe-matics, using team projects. Typically, teachers did not know what use they would make of CMC when they began. They developed activities to support their academic goals for the students as they proceeded.

Can other teachers duplicate their success? Or does it require the uncommon initiative and dedication of these teachers? We believe that these teachers have shown the way and that (with adequate support) many more teachers will soon find their way into the world of telecom-munications. The isolated classrooms of today will give way to the glob-al classrooms of tomorrow.

REFERENCES

Cohen, M., & Riel, M. (1989). The effect of distance audiences on stu-dents' writing. *American Educational Research Journal, 26,* 143-159.
Fowler, L.S. (1994). Working together with technology. In E. Boschmann (Ed.), *The electronic classroom.* Medford: NJ: Learned Information.
Hadley, M., & Sheingold, K. (1993). Commonalties and distinctive pat-

terns in teacher's integration of computers. *American Journal of Education, 101,* 265-315.

Levin, J. A., Riel, M.M., Miyake, N., & Cohen, M. (1987). Education on the electronic frontier: Teleapprentices in globally distributed educational contexts. *Contemporary Educational Psychology, 12,* 254-260.

Meichenbaum. D., Burland, S., Gruson, L., & Cameron, R., (1985). Metacognitive assessment. In S.R. Yussen (Ed.), *The growth of reflection in children.* New York: Academic Press.

Office of Technology Assessment-SET-379. (1988). *Power On! New Tools for Teaching and Learning.* Washington, DC: U.S. Government Printing Office.

O'Shea, M.R., Kimmel, H., & Novemsky, L.F. (1990). Computer mediated telecommunication and pre-college education: A retrospect. *Journal of Educational Computing Research, 6*(1). 65-75.

Riel, M. (1985). The computer chronicles newswire. A functional learning environment for acquiring literacy skills. *Journal of Educational Computing Research, 1,* 317-337.

Riel, M.M., & Levin, J. A. (1990). Building electronic communities: Successes and failures in computer networking. *Instructional Science, 19,* 145-169.

Vygotsky, L.S. (1978). *Mind in society: The development of higher psychological processes.* Cambridge: MA, MIT Press.

Weir, S. (192). Electronic communities of learners: Fact or fiction. In R.F. Tinker & P. M. Kapisovsky (Eds.), *Prospects for educational telecomputing: Selected readings* (pp. 87-109). Cambridge, MA: The Technical Educational Research Center.

Womble, G. (1985). Revising and computing. In J. Collins & E. Sommers (Eds.), *Writing on-line: Using computers in the teaching of writing* (pp. 775-820). Upper Montclair, NJ: Boynton/Cook.

APPENDIX

This appendix contains information about the structured projects and activity connections that were used by teachers in this study. There are many other projects available.

The AT&T Learning Network

The AT&T Learning Network is a curriculum-based program that links together a community of educators and students using the AT&T worldwide telecommunications network. The AT&T Learning Network uses telecommunications by combining groups of culturally and geographically diverse students to exchange ideas and opinions and produce collections of works written by all the team members. The geographical diversity offers the students expanded perspectives and a wide peer group. The AT&T Learning Network links teachers who share common interests and helps each teacher by providing structured projects and technical support. It supports collaborative learning, develops team building, and provides workforce skills for the future.

AT&T Learning Network
PO Box 6391
Parsippany, NJ 07054-7391
US: 1-800-367-7225 ext 4158
Canada: 1-800-567-4671

National Geographic Kids Network (NGS Kids Network)
Developed by TERC with funding from the National Science Foundation and the National Geographic Society, the NGS Kids Network is a series of science units for grades 4-6. During each unit students read original research, use a computer to record and analyze data, and then share their findings, via a modem and telecommunications, with "research teammates"—a group of geographically diverse classes in the United States, Canada, and other countries. The elementary curriculum series includes the following units: Hello!, Acid Rain, Weather in Action, What's in Our Water, Too Much Trash?, What Are We Eating?, and Solar Energy. TERC is currently developing five units for the middle grades: What is Your Soil Good For, How Loud is Too Loud, How Does Your Body Get the Oxygen it Needs, What Are We Doing to Our Water, and a data inquiry module that develops data analysis and investigation skills. The National Geographic Society will also publish the middle grades curriculum. For more information about the elementary units contract:

National Geographic Society
Educational Services
PO Box 98018
Washington, DC 20090-8018
US: 1-800-368-2728
Outside the US: 1-301-921-1322

For more information about the NGS Kids Network/Middle Grades Curriculum contact:

TERC Communications
2067 Massachusetts Avenue
Cambridge, MA 02140
Phone: 617-547-0430
Fax: 617-349-3535
Internet: Communications@TERC.edu

The TERC Star Schools Project 1987-1990

The TERC Star Schools Project was funded by the U.S. Department of Education to provide math and science education in an environment that combined technology with engaging, hands-on experience. Using microcomputers and a telecommunications network, young scientists and mathematicians in grades 7-12 engaged in large-scale, cooperative investigations and shared findings with students and professional scientists across the country. Results were shared among students, professors, and scientists nationwide. With support from the network, teachers and students created an active learning environment that empowered students to design and conduct their own projects.

Global Laboratory

The Global Laboratory Project is a worldwide network of student scientists involved in collborative environmental investigations. United by telecommunications, shared technology, and common procedure, students from over 20 countries conduct original research on global and local environmental issues. Students collect data with low-cost, high-tech instrumentation developed by TERC and share their findings over the project's telecommunications network. Students then develop research plans, conduct collaborative inquiries, electronically publish their results, and conduct peer views. Funded by the National Science Foundation.

LabNet: The High School Science Network

LabNet is building a telecomputing network of the science teaching community. This LabNetwork provides a community of practice among teachers—teacher-to-teacher support for the improvement of science teaching and learning. It began in 1989 with 160 physics teachers and is expanding to include 1,300 teachers of high school physics, chemistry, biology, and other sciences, as well as educators who teach science to younger children. LabNet is committed to supporting the spread of project-enhanced science learning (PESL) in which students formulate their own questions, design their own research, and build their own experimental apparatus, guided by teachers as their mentors. Funded by the National Science Foundation. enhancement program that links high school physics teachers and students in grades 9-12 on a network to support the development of projects incorporating microcomputer-based laboratory tools.

For more information about the TERC Projects, contact:

TERC Communications
2067 Massachusetts Avenue
Cambridge MA 02140

Phone: 1-617-547-0430
Fax: 1-616-349-3535
Internet: Communications@TERC. edu

FrEdMail (now Global SchoolNet Foundation)
The Global SchoolNet provides several Internet related service. The FrEd Mail network fosters the development of a low-cost, community-based, distributed electronic data communications network to provide free or low-cost access. The network consists of over 250 electronic information servers located throughout the country and in some international locations. The projects on the system are developed and run by teachers and their students as well as the support staff of the Global SchoolNet Foundation. The popular FrEdMail content is also available on many Internet hosts through the Global SCHLnet Newsgroup Service. The goals of the Global SchoolNet Foundation include promoting the development of effective reading, writing, and communications skills in students at all grade levels as well as promoting understanding a global scale.

Global SchoolNet Foundation
PO Box 243
Bonita, CA 91908-0243
fred@acme.fred.org
1-619-475-4852

Iris
The Iris Network for Teachers and Schools is a "telecommunity" of, by, and for educators who come together electronically to promote excellence in education through new and effective uses of technology. Iris provides a rich source of educational information , a variety of online telecommunications projects that enhance the K-12 curriculum, and a forum for discussion of best teaching practices and issues of importance to educators. Iris offers electronic conferencing and email, databases, file libraries, and full access to the Internet (Telnet, Gopher, FTP, newsgroups, etc.). Iris is a nonprofit 501(c)(3) education organization.

Iris, Inc.
P.O. Box 29424
Richmond, VA 23242-0424
Voice: 703-243-6622
Voicemail (202) 298-0969
FAX: (703) 841-9798
Technical help line: 800-277-0414
Internet: iris@tmn.com

Chapter Seven

The Higher Education Electronic Infrastructure: The Impact on Libraries and Computer Centers

Katy Silberger
Marist College
Poughkeepsie, NY

INTRODUCTION

Higher education is witnessing a revolution in the manner in which scholarly communication occurs. This revolution involves how scholars communicate with known and unknown colleagues on a one-to-one, one-to-many, and many-to-many basis during research and prepublication and peer review in the generation of new scholarship. Exciting new electronic information formats are becoming available for the expression of ideas. Equally important are significant improvements in the way in which scholars can access, locate, and obtain information in and through the assistance of libraries. All these developments have significantly diminished geographic and disciplinary barriers to, and the time lag inherent in, the scholarly communication process.

Over the past decade there has been a proliferation of relatively

101

inexpensive microcomputer hardware and user-friendly software within higher education. Advances in telecommunications technology have enabled communication between computers of all sizes on a worldwide basis. This vast network links scholars with libraries and all their electronic resources, forming the foundation of an electronic infrastructure for global scholarly communication. The development of this infrastructure is occurring at a time when the United States is laboring under unprecedented debt due to the federal deficit, the massive trade imbalance, and the mammoth Savings and Loan bailout. The resulting economic pressure will put some constraints on the development of the electronic infrastructure, but it will also drive innovation to the extent that applications are developed that will save institutions money.

TRADITIONAL ROLE AND QUALITIES OF THE LIBRARY WITHIN HIGHER EDUCATION

Libraries have traditionally functioned as the scholarly information center of colleges and universities. For hundreds of years, libraries have been responsible for the selection, acquisition, arrangement, storage, retrieval, and loan of scholarly information in higher education.

For as long as they have been serving the information needs of the academic community, libraries have demonstrated technological flexibility and innovation. For example, the earliest of university libraries collected manuscripts. With the invention of books, periodicals, microforms, and audiovisual formats, libraries have expanded their operations to accommodate these new formats without abandoning their support of older ones. As the possibilities for electronic publishing are being explored by the scholarly community, libraries are experimenting with the electronic prototypes as they are generated.

Libraries traditionally have provided users with assistance in locating and obtaining the information resources they need. Reference librarians provide individual instruction to patrons in the use of specific information resources as they seek out help at the reference desk. On a more formal basis, librarians also provide group instruction, known as "bibliographic instruction," to undergraduate and graduate students. Librarians address classes with library-related assignments or offer classes in the use of a specific information resource to voluntary participants. As information resources become more sophisticated and complex, the demand for bibliographic instruction is growing.

ECONOMIC PRESSURES ON LIBRARIES

Economic pressures on libraries have been steadily increasing. Acquisitions budgets have been severely stressed by increases in the price of books and journals. The rate of journal price inflation has been almost twice that of the general rate of inflation. When faced with difficult decisions, libraries have been shifting funds away from the acquisition of monographs over to serials. In response to this crisis, librarians have been studying seriously the problems in order to devise innovative solutions.

The crisis in journal subscription prices has stimulated the library profession to explore alternatives to commercially distributed print journals as a means of scholarly communication. Institutions of higher education, as well as U.S. taxpayers through government grants, have been supporting research through faculty salaries, offices and laboratories, and research grants and stipends. They also motivate scholars to publish prolifically by making the number of publications a criteria for tenure and promotion. The bulk of the research generated is then given to commercial publishers. Authors turn over their copyright, and in many cases, even pay the publishers in the form of page costs to take ownership of their scholarship. The publishers turn around and sell the scholarship financed by higher education back to libraries at prices that steadily out-pace the rate of inflation. For economic reasons, publishers maintain limited back stock. The long-term availability of printed scholarship is guaranteed only by libraries that pay the bills to maintain the space and shelves on which the journals are stored, as well as finance the extensive interlibrary loan network that makes the scholarship available to the academic community (Okerson, 1991, p. 426).

Some of the commercially produced electronic information resources such as online remote database systems and scanned full-text image products carry such high price tags that libraries are unable to offer access to them without recovering some costs from the users. This breaks with the library tradition of not charging users directly for services.

TECHNOLOGICAL OPPORTUNITIES AND PRESSURES

There is great concern in the United States that our educational system is not preparing the workforce that is required for a postindustrial society. Our current educational system, based on the needs of a 19th-century agricultural society, is not able to produce the globally competitive workforce needed in the information age. Business and industry tell us that they need workers with greater mathematical and scientific knowl-

edge, better reasoning and problem-solving skills, social skills for working in cooperative teams, and basic computer literacy. Successful facto-
ries are automated, and businesses are linked together by sophisticated
telecommunications and computer networks. In response to this reality,
higher education must modernize their facilities and curricula to
address this very serious need. As teaching techniques diversify from
the lecture-based model to include guided discovery by the students,
individually and in groups, the use of the library in higher education
will increase considerably (Leonard, 1992).

Although technology enables library technical services to reduce
costs through networked resource sharing and automated processing,
and by enabling libraries to offer new, user-friendly services, it creates
increased demands on the reference department. The first microcomputer in many reference departments was used for searching remote online
bibliographic database systems such as DIALOG, BRS, and Orbit. CD-
ROM technology then became available, and some of the most popular
databases searched on the remote online systems became available on
CD-ROMs. CD-ROMs are quite attractive because their costs are fixed.
With relatively user-friendly interfaces, they proved to be very popular
with patrons. CD-ROMs certainly have stimulated much of the increase
in library use. Most libraries are replacing their traditional card catalogs
with OPACs (Online Public Access Catalogs), the electronic grandchil-
dren of the card catalog. In addition to being available on the local campus computer network, OPACs generally are also available for remote
log in by patrons with a microcomputer and modem. This development
has freed scholars from having to physically travel to the library to begin
research. At the same time, reference librarians have had to respond to
the needs of remote patrons by providing vehicles for communicating
with patrons outside the library. The future trend in this area is for
libraries to make other electronic information resources, such as periodical indexes and abstracts, available for remote access either on the
OPAC or through a CD-ROM network.

THE NETWORKS

Whereas the electronics revolution continues to maintain its pace at the
micro and personal level, another equally powerful revolution is occurring at the mainframe and networking level. Two major networks,
Internet and BITnet, are powerful new computer communication link-
ages providing the academic community with swift new vehicles of
communication.

Internet offers scholars the ability to use resources at a remote computer on an interactive basis, as well as the ability to transfer documents of a considerable size from a remote to a local computer.

The interactive use of computer resources on a remote computer is accomplished by a program known as "Telnet." Through the Telnet process a user can connect to a remote computer and use resources designated for public use. One of the more popular resources used on the Internet are library OPACS. Although few scholars would want to invest the time in learning the collection strengths of libraries and the searching software of different OPACS throughout the world, librarians are already doing so. By working with a librarian, a scholar can now learn about scholarship published in national and international areas. To some degree the availability of OPACs throughout the world is providing an alternative to the expensive, commercially produced remote online bibliographic database systems.

The program to transfer documents between computers is known as FTP (file transfer protocol). FTP allows a user to log in to a remote computer as an "anonymous user" and request the transfer of selected documents to her or his local computer. Scholars have been submitting documents to archives for retrieval by anonymous FTP in order to broaden the prepublication peer review process. The Merit Network Information Center has been making its official documents available in this same manner. Interesting experiments with FTP are occurring. For example, the GPO (Government Printing Office) is making the text of Supreme Court decisions available on a 48-hour turn-around basis through the FTP process. Project Gutenberg has been coordinating the conversion of hundreds of classic works in the public domain into machine-readable format, which are then made available for FTP.

E-mail has brought about several significant changes in the scholarly communication process. Discussion groups enable scholars of different disciplines and in distant geographic locations to become collaborators. They are able to exchange ideas in writing at a much quicker pace than when using conventional mail services. Through the medium of electronic mail they are able to submit documents for perusal and comment by any interested party, and through the medium of discussion groups they are able to announce their availability and solicit comment. Harnad (1991) characterized this process and designated it as "Scholarly Skywriting":

> There now exist numerous electronic networks such as Bitnet and Internet that link academic and research institutions globally. They not only make it possible to send electronic mail from individual to individual almost instantaneously, but they allow individuals to send multiple email to groups of individuals reciprocally, anywhere from a few collaborating colleagues, to all the experts in a given sub-

> specialty, to an entire discipline—all just as quickly as individual email, but with the emergent benefits of the interactive feedback. I have called this new medium "scholarly skywriting." (p. 342)

BITnet (Because Its Time Network) provides a very reliable, free, international email network. Participants can send messages to another individual or send the same message to several individuals. A very popular application of e-mail on BITnet is the discussion group. A listowner or moderator establishes a listserver on an institution's mainframe computer and defines the topic or topics of discussion for the group. (For further information see the Resources chapter at the end of this book). Participation in most discussion groups is open to everyone with access to BITnet. Some participants in discussion groups make contact with individuals on a one-to-one basis as a result of something posted to the list. Discussion lists facilitate the exchange of ideas transcending disciplinary and geographic boundaries.

A number of discussion groups are issuing electronic newsletters and electronic journals in addition to providing a discussion forum. At present there is considerable variety in format and quality among these newsletters and journals.

The communication possibilities opened up by the networks have led to so much collaborative work that some have nicknamed the network as "the collaboratory" (Yavarkovsky, 1990). Scholars are discovering colleagues with common interests within other disciplines and at other, distant institutions. The networks open up vast, almost overwhelming, possibilities to researchers, but at a certain price: There are commands and routines to be learned in order to avail oneself of these electronic riches. Consequently, another type of collaboration is also occurring as a result of the networks. Researchers are seeking out and forming collaborative teams with support personnel on their campus, particularly librarians and computer center personnel. Although the networks offer powerful possibilities, they require specialized knowledge of hardware, software, telecommunications, and information retrieval and manipulation techniques. It simply is impractical for someone with specialized knowledge in one area to spend the time to master these other specialities. Collaborative campus teams are the obvious answer.

NEW ELECTRONIC INFORMATION FORMATS AND LIBRARIES

Electronic Journals

A number of articles have been published describing potential alternatives to the current print journal setup. In 1989, Rogers and Hurt published an article in the *Chronicle of Higher Education* discussing the idea of a new scholarly electronic communication system: "We need to harness available technologies to reform the entire system of scholarly communication. The $500-million spent annually on journal subscriptions could finance a new system" (Rogers & Hurt, 1989, p.).

Such a new system was needed, they argued, to gain control of journal subscription prices, space and shelving demands made on the library, and to give them ownership of the results of the research financed by higher education. In their vision, documents would remain in electronic format until a patron specifically requested that the library make a printed copy for his or her use. Rogers and Hunt saw interesting interdisciplinary connections being made between scholars who would all be participating in the same network. They also envisioned format enhancements over print journals. Such new capabilities would include the ability to allow readers to tag notes and comments to articles and to log usage of a piece of work (Rogers, 1989).

Dougherty also explored the notion of developing an electronic publishing network in an article in the *Chronicle of Higher Education* in 1989. He asked the question:

> Why not marry the technological capabilities of computer centers with the expertise of university presses (as producers) and libraries (as retailers and distributors) to expand the university's role as producer and distributor of scholarly and scientific research? (p. A52)

Dougherty recognized the stability and cost-effectiveness of the printed scholarly journal and suggested that such a computerized system not set out to replace the print journal. Rather, he suggested that higher education explore alternative uses of its electronic infrastructure in search of a solution to the current journal price crisis.

Yavarkovsky offered his vision of a scholarly publishing network in the *Educom Review* (1990). Yavarkovsky suggested that higher education look at the network structure of radio and television broadcasting as a potential model for the higher education electronic publishing system:

> Broadcasters own their production and transmission infrastructure, just as computer centers and their parent institutions do. They develop programming of their own; they purchase programming from independent producers; they serve diverse audiences in independent markets; and they serve audiences with common interests in diverse markets. . . . The broadcasting analogy is not perfect, but it has some elements worth considering. An affiliate organizational arrangement, providing for some centralized services and oversight, would strengthen the electronic publishing network financially and administratively. (p. 16)

Editorial nodes could be established throughout the geographic area of the network, while many more nodes might hold copies of documents for Telnet viewing, FTP, or whatever protocols may be developed. The system would also need to address the design issue of subsequent upward compatibility, so that documents thus generated and stored would be available "in perpetuity," as paper documents on nonacidic paper and microforms appear to be.

The scholarly community is currently experimenting with electronic journals as a viable medium of scholarly publishing. At present there is concern that electronic journals are not accorded the same scholarly prestige for tenure and promotion as are print journals. Because Internet resources are at present being accessed by a small percentage of faculty, electronic journals are not yet a familiar medium. In order to obtain copies of articles and/or issues of many e-journals, the user must have a solid basic knowledge of commands commonly used on Internet. Such expertise will become more common with time. There is also concern about the long-term availability of issues and articles in e-journals.

OCLC, a non-profit library consortium, and the AAAS, the American Association for the Advancement of Science, are engaged in a joint endeavor—the Primary Journals Online (PJO) project—to develop and publish a peer-reviewed scientific electronic journal. They intend to publish this journal on a more timely basis than can be achieved in print and make the journal convenient and pleasant to use in electronic format. The project is also aware of the financial strains on libraries and intends "to help the academic library community with defining less costly alternatives to the subscription and storage of serials and journals" (Noreault & Kellar, 1992, p. 235) The electronic format envisioned by the PJO would be available for consultation online, but not retrievable by FPT for local storage and retrieval. Print copies of articles could be ordered at a fee and faxed if needed quickly. The subscription would pay for annual access to the journal.

At present, access to e-journals through indexes and abstracts affects their acceptance as bona fide scholarly vehicles. Many e-publishers are finding it difficult to persuade publishers of indexes and abstracts to include their publications in the list of journals indexed because it is a medium that has not yet been integrated into their workflow.

Electronic Monographs

Project Gutenberg has as its goal to make 10,000 e-texts available by the year 2000. Project Gutenberg receives minimal funding and relies heavily on the efforts of volunteers who type or scan in entire books. The works converted to machine-readable form are free of copyright, either because the copyright has expired, or because they were published in the public domain. These texts are available for FTP from Project Gutenberg at mrcnext.cso.uiuc.edu (between 6:00 p.m. and 9:00 a.m. Central Time only).

Other types of monographs are also being made available for unrestricted FTP. Some scholars are using the medium to obtain broad peer review. A number of well-written guides to using the Internet were placed for anonymous FTP in the first edition. The second edition, revised and improved as a result of voluntary peer critique, was then published commercially.

Another category of monograph is being made available for FTP at the same time that it is commercially printed and distributed. Generally the organizations publishing in the e-text/print combination are not-for-profit organizations interested in disseminating information rather than making a profit from the sale of information.

Imagining the Library of the Future

Electronic documents have already established themselves as a viable information format. Although there are those who predict a paperless library of the future, there is little to indicate that such a reality will come to pass. Within the world of information, formats find ideal niches. A format may occupy several niches but be replaced by ideal formats as they evolve. Rarely does a format lose all its niches. People still write letters by hand, and calligraphy remains a sought-after skill. Photographic portraits did not eliminate painted or sketched portraits, nor did video cassettes eliminate movie theaters, and so on.

Over the next few decades the niche to be filled by electronic documents gradually will become clearly defined. Certainly e-texts are much more flexible than printed texts. They can be searched for words and strings of words. Hypertext links can be made between portions of a document, allowing it to be read in a meaningful, although nonsequential order. The document can be transmitted very rapidly throughout the world via telephone lines. Printed versions can be generated on demand and customized in terms of fonts, size of paper, and so on. At the same time there are potential problems with the flexibility of the electronic format. Such documents can be changed easily, either intentionally or through computer malfunction, and this raises concerns about document security and integrity. Should such a change occur as a result of human corruption of a document, either by someone attempting to discredit an author, or by the author him- or herself attempting to correct an error discovered after publication, the ultimate acceptance of such publishing by the scholarly establishment would be imperiled. Thus, any electronic publishing system will require a network in which multiple hosts store read-only copies of a document.

There will still be many situations in which a bound printed work will be preferred. Books are extremely portable, can be used without any additional technology, and can be read by the light of the sun alone. The availability of electricity, computer/program capability, and so on, need not be addressed in order to read a book. Books are also energy efficient and tolerant of a wide range of environments, temperatures, and climates. They are extremely user-friendly to the eye as a result of centuries of refinement of typefaces and paper surfaces. Print text is a stable format, changes to which are detectable.

The library of the future will include a variety of successful formats: Printed books and journals will certainly retain a substantial niche. Microforms will be present as well, although they may lose some of their niche to scanned images stored on CD-ROM. Videotapes, audiotapes, and audio CDs will continue to serve some information needs. And electronic monographs and journals will certainly occupy a substantial niche as well.

E-journals will evolve as different groups find advantages in the different qualities of the format. The more timely publishing cycle will attract the scientific community. Other discipline areas will develop e-journals because of the flexibility of the format. For example, some will find attractive the ability to create hypertext links between references made in the body of the article and the cited document. Thus, when the reader comes across such a reference, a simple keystroke sequence could open a window containing the text of the document referenced. Authors would also be able to make revisions to articles and papers after initial publication. Such changes could be clearly identified in the document. Critiques of the article could also be appended directly or through a hypertext link as well. Other e-journals will be created because of the lower initial start-up costs of publishing in e-format.

In the "Library of the Future" one will find sophisticated computers connected to global telecommunications networks. These computers will have state-of-the art monitors for the display of various specialized electronic document formats and be able to accommodate downloading to all popular storage mediums. The library's high-speed, high-quality printers will have binding capabilities. Document reproduction and binding on demand will be done on a cost-recovery basis.

The OPAC will continue to provide physical descriptions of all items collected by the library, including a call number to guide the patron in retrieving those items. The system of call numbers can expand to accommodate documents stored in machine-readable format. The OPAC will also have indexing and abstracting for articles appearing in both print and electronic journals. It will also have a gateway into the "electronic stacks" of the library. The electronic stacks will provide access to electronic documents, regardless of their physical locations, which can be viewed easily from a single terminal. The electronic stacks will include monographs and e-journals. The library acquisitions department will select all documents in the library, be they print, microform, or electronic formats, according to the same conceptual criteria.

Electronic discussion groups will eventually become a new format of periodical publication. At present there is some discussion of how to cite specific postings from an electronic discussion group. Despite the variation in the quality of discussion, over time there will be enough worth quoting in the collective archives of the discussion groups that librarians will be called on to lend their expertise to organizing and describing (technically known as bibliographic control) those archives for subsequent retrieval.

The additional electronic capabilities of the library will make it possible for patrons to access the riches of the library from greater and greater distances. Librarians will communicate with some patrons via telecommunication and computer devices and, in some cases, never have face-to-face communication with the patron. Ironically, however, some of the new electronic formats will make it necessary for patrons to come to the library because the sophisticated computer equipment necessary to review and print will be found there. For example, some electronic documents may require more sophisticated video displays than common home computers will have. Patrons may also come to the library to borrow from and consult reference works from the considerable print collections.

The "Library of the Future" will have an even more complex structure of information than today's library, thus creating a proportionately greater need for librarian assistance and for bibliographic instruction. In addition to helping patrons use local information resources, they will help patrons navigate the vast and complex global networks in pursuit of necessary information. As we see happening already, libraries will provide directory information such as names, addresses, and telecommunications parameters for individuals, discussion groups, and other organizations communicating via networks. Libraries will continue to help scholars identify by subject area peers with similar or complementary areas of research interest. Despite the significant changes and enhancement which the electronic infrastructure will bring to the library, the "Library of the Future" will retain strong bonds in common with the first libraries of the Middle Ages. Libraries will continue to include various print formats within their collections, including manuscripts, both historic and modern. The printed book will still be found in the library, and new books will be acquired annually. Continuing its tradition of technological flexibility, the "Library of the Future" will collect information which meets the needs of its patrons in the most effective format. Most important, like its ancient ancestors, the "Library of the Future" will remain the scholarly information center of the university, facilitating research and communication within the global scholarly community.

REFERENCES

Dougherty, R.M. (1989, April 12). To meet the crisis in journal costs, universities must reassert their role in scholarly publishing. *Chronicle of Higher Education, 35*, A52.

Harnad, S. (1990, November). Scholarly skywriting and the prepublication continuum of scientific inquiry. *Psychological Science, 9*(6), 342-343.

Leonard, G. (1992, May). The end of school. *Atlantic Monthly*, pp. 24-32.

Okerson, A. (1991). With feathers: Effects of copyright and ownership on scholarly publishing. *College & Research Libraries, 52*(5), 425-438.

Noreault, T. & Kellar, L. (1992, May 5-7). The Primary Journals Online Project. *Proceedings of the 13th National Online Meeting*, pp. 235-239.

Rogers, S.J. & Hurt, C.S. (1989, October18). How scholarly communication should work in the 21st century. *Chronicle of Higher Education, 35*, A56

Yavarkovsky, J. (1990, Fall) A university based electronic publishing network. *Educom Review, 25*, 14-20.

Chapter Eight

Computer-Mediated Communication and American Indian Education*

George D. Baldwin
Henderson State University

Until the learning environment feels like a clan, the Indian student will not be engaged.
—a Red Lake Ojibwa (Charleston, 1990, p. 8)

INDIANS AND COMPUTERS

For readers who are familiar with American Indians and Alaskan Natives only through the narrow stereotypes portrayed in television and film, the tribal activities described in this chapter should be a surprising contrast. Rather·than thinking of Indians as they existed 100 or more years ago, readers must imagine Indian youth, academics, and scientists in locations all over the United States hovering over glowing terminals, while fingers fly on clicking keyboards. Many of the Indian people communicate in this

Parts of this chapter were written with the assistance of funding from the National Science Foundation's Science, Technology and Values Program Grant # SBE09212935.

manner for hours each week. Some are collaborating with research teams, others are receiving inservice training for college credit, many are simply chatting. Collectively, they have become active in an electronic "virtual ethnic community," which is worldwide in its membership.

Numerous listservs and bulletin board systems (BBS) have developed distinct ethnic biases, a fact fairly well understood by those who use computer networks. It is a well understood phenomenon in mass communications (Higgons, 1992). The emergence of Jewish, Hispanic, Latino, black, and most recently, American Indian and Alaskan Native computer networks was, in retrospect, inevitable. The borders of these growing "virtual communities" are defined not so much by their geography, but by the interests of the participants. Native networked communities include participants representing the children of the First Nations attending Canadian schools (Seaton & Valaskakis, 1984) and Alaskan Native and American Indian junior high school students who attend reservation boarding schools. Graduate and undergraduate Indian college students and their professors are also online , working with each other through the worldwide Internet. Remarkably, tribal members relocated in urban areas or even Europe are now communicating with their rural or reservation cousins.

The purpose of these computer networks is generally stated in the goals of the project or program that funded them: The networks manifestly support education, research, or are designed to improve access for the Indian public to specialized information useful for tribal development. Within the networks, the latent function is clear: They promote and defend native cultural beliefs and values. Both of these functions, latent and manifest, can be discerned from the content of the written conversations in which network participants engage. Within these conversations, the social life of the networks becomes visible to even the casual observer. The participants, as well as their audience, represent a fascinating component of pan-Indianism; the intertribal social movement which is described by one anthropologist as several tribes uniting, usually to confront an enemy such as the federal government (Schaefer, 1990). The enemy that the networked natives are confronting today is the incursion of the Western world view by the transmedia intertextual phenomena of television, radio, press, and video games (Kinder,1991).

To understand the impact of telecommunications on our people, 20 Indian leaders in communications recently attended a meeting funded by the National Science Foundation. "The Native American Telecommunication Forum" was attended by Indian leaders working in the communication field who worked together for two days discussing the issues related to new communication technologies. From these discussions a central theme emerged: There is a tremendous need to understand the sociocultural and socioeconomic impact of telecommunications and technology on native people (Americans for Indian Opportunity, 1994). The Native leaders who attended recognized that little is known about the use of the telephone, television, or radio by the Indian people of the United States. Nor do we know how it has impacted on our cultures or beliefs. We have assumed that the mass communication technologies of the 20th century have influenced our lifestyles in a multitude of ways similar to the impact of anglo educational systems. The more recent phenomena of computer-mediated communication (CMC), which has not been studied as much as other forms of mass media, offers similar challenges to the cultures and changing traditions of Native people.

Contrary to stereotypical images, American Indians and Alaskan Natives are not strangers to computer technology. Several social and economic forces have actually encouraged the growth of computer use in Indian populations. Perhaps the major force was the growth of an extensive government bureaucracy on reservations. On many reservations the government offices acquired an infrastructure of PCs (personal computers) and mainframes, and in turn these systems required trained clerks and managers to operate them. Federal funding supported both. As a result, tribes such as the Cherokee and Navajo have several mainframes each and dozens of PCs.

Recent surveys conducted at Indian boarding and reservation schools have demonstrated the significant investment in computer hardware by Indian educational institutions, primarily Apple IIs (Pilz & Resta, 1991). The 27 Indian colleges are similarly computer literate to varying degrees (American Indian Higher Education Consortium, 1992). These two studies tell us that the technological density (number of computers per person) is respectable in comparison to non-Indian schools. The pedagogical use of these systems by teachers and the success that they are having with their Indian students who use the technology is not reported. What we do know about computers and the education of American Indians is primarily anecdotal or found in the presentations of teachers at conferences such as the National Indian Education Association. The proceedings of such conferences suggest that the use of HyperCard on the Macintosh is being developed by independent Indian educators across the country. We can also see that language and cultural preservation via computer is expanding in a rapid manner, with educators working with as diverse populations as the Zuni, Ojibwa, and Lakota. Educators at our conferences are reporting remarkable gains in the use of computer-assisted education in the tribally controlled schools. Reports on the pioneering uses of distance learning technologies for Native education have not been as well documented. Papers are nonexistent, presentations are lacking, and for the few reports that are available, the educational value of the projects seem exaggerated.

Barnhart (1984) was the first to report the use of electronic mail to promote English literacy with Alaskan native secondary students. Modest goals and an effective evaluation procedure assisted in making this project successful. To this day the University of Alaska teleconferencing/computer network may serve more Native students than any network in the lower 40 (Office of Technology Assessment, 1989, p. 155).

The Transcontinental Classroom Project (funded by special legislation to Mansfield University) reportedly enabled 17 Indian community colleges to offer additional courses taught by nationally recognized experts and to share expertise and courses among institutions. The Mansfield Project, as it became known by the Indian institutions, proposed to utilize an audio/video/graphics interactive computer-based system. This equipment was purchased and delivered to several tribally controlled colleges, and it was a remarkable failure. Key individuals on those campuses chosen to participate were not involved in planning or implementation of the network. Mansfield, in a self-evaluation of the project that was based on two surveys returned from the 17 institutions that participated, found that all schools reported a positive success. Three years later, only one of the schools is using the equipment, primarily for word-processing (American Indian Higher Education Consortium, 1992).

LANGUAGE LITERACY, LEARNING STYLES, AND CMC FOR INDIAN STUDENTS

> I detest writing. The process itself epitomizes the European concept of "legitimate" thinking; what is written has an importance that is denied the spoken. My culture, the Lakota culture, has an oral tradition and so I ordinarily reject writing. It is one of the white world's ways of destroying the cultures of non-European peoples; the imposing of an abstraction over the spoken relationship of a people. (Means, n.d., p. 19)

CMC systems require that the user has some degree of skill in reading and writing. This may change in the future as systems become more dependent on voice mail, graphics, and video imagery, but in the systems reviewed in this chapter, there is a heavy dependence on the "ascii cage" of computer keyboard characters. For cultures that have historically transmitted their teaching through oral traditions, the use of English text introduces a huge disadvantage for the student. A review of the literature regarding American Indian student achievement in language arts indicates that this population ranks far below the norm in reading, language arts, and language arts-related categories (Brown, 1990). Reflected in these statistics is the reality that many Native Indian students cannot use the language necessary for success in school—English.

Part of this problem may be caused by the markedly different cognitive style adopted by American Indians (Brown, 1990; Cattey, 1980; Ross, 1982). These cognitive processes are structured by the Indian child's social environment that stresses cooperation and de-emphasizes competition. The traditional American school system, with its emphasis on competition, may be inimical to an Indian student, depending on his or her degree of acculturation. Teachers working with Indian students have discovered this, and curriculum designed to take advantage of cooperative style has appeared. These curriculum designs, such as positioning the teacher as a facilitator who orients the students to collectively solve problems, as described by Freire and Macedo (1987) and Kozol (1985), may be more culturally appropriate for Indian students. Curiously, similar findings on CMC and cooperative learning are reported by Harasim (1986, 1987), Hiltz (1986, 1988) and in an early report from Heffron (1984). Taken together, these findings suggest that teaching techniques that promote cooperative, active learning within the CMC environment are adaptable for effective teaching with Indian populations. Pedagogically, then, CMC may be quite effective with Indian students, if one can overcome the barrier of using written English. Furthermore, English writing in CMC is often used by the Indian student in electronic conversation with others, some of whom are strangers they have met or observed in undefined social relationships.

American Indians and Alaskan Natives, in common with other ethnic minorities, have their own peculiar grammatical qualities of oral communication (Bartelt, 1986; Leap, 1977; Leechman & Hall, 1955). Basso (1990) found that Indian people in several Arizona tribes—most notably the Western Apache, Navajo, and Papago—tend to remain silent in social situations in which the status of the focal participants is ambiguous, if role expectations are unclear, or if there is some unpredictability in social relations. These problems are reflected in the communication of Indian people online, particularly the secondary school students located in remote rural areas where socialization to Anglo norms may not be as complete as for those Indian students in urban areas or on college campuses.

This phenomenon is rarely seen as clearly as in a recent conversation between two teenagers communicating on ENAN, the Electronic Native American Network. An assignment was given to all of the children in a class at a boarding school in the southwest to send a message to someone on the network. In a message directed from one young man to a girl, he wrote, " I don't know you and I know I shouldn't talk to you, but if I don't I won't get the points for this assignment." American Indian and Alaskan Native people on the nation's Internet listservs may be lurking as well, passive consumers of conversations about themselves, hesitant to commit what they perceived to be the gross social infraction of interrupting and disagreeing with those whom they do not know or with whom they have no defined social relationship.

Thus, the English language problem is reflected in more than what Native people write, it may be found in what they do not write. For example, there is some evidence to support the hypothesis that the American Indian social convention of "appropriate silence" is reflected in the online behavior of Indians. For example, Native reactions to "flaming" on the FidoNet Native Affairs conference and Internet listservs are often those of silence (lurking) or retreating (unsubscribing). On the Electronic Native American Network (ENAN), Indian student participation appears to be at its lowest when the children are asked to initiate conversations with strangers, such as guest scientists or online lecturers, especially prestigious Indian leaders. This behavior denotes respect to the guest, but the lack of visual cues of encouragement to speak has made such pedagogical experiments fairly unproductive.

Indian students who transcribe their spoken word to the written format for computer conferencing may have other problems in communication as well. In an analysis of writing done by sixth to ninth graders using ENAN, this researcher found that most students were functioning at the second or third grade level of readability. Teachers who evaluate such writing have the difficult task of deciding if nonstandard grammatical forms in the writing are really "mistakes" that need correction, or if the writing is acceptable if the meaning of the communication is clear. Implicit in the evaluation of these written conversations are the values and beliefs of our traditional education system and its dependency on written English language skills. Educators have discussed this phenomenon in other contexts, finding that traditional education is text-book driven, and success in school requires mastery of cognitive academic language proficiency, which Native students do not achieve. Written communication can thus be used as an ideologically charged tool for either cultural domination or cultural survival (Aronowitz & Giroux, 1988; Bakhtin, 1986; Cook-Gumperz, 1986; Diessner, 1985; Freire & Macedo, 1987; McLaren, 1988; McLaughlin, 1991; O'Brien, 1990). None of the Indian CMC networks currently in operation use a Native language to any great extent. Although there have been a number of pedagogical experiments to teach writing to Indian students with computers (Hualapai Bilingual Academic Excellence Program, 1988; Hymer, 1988; Jacobi, 1985), the INDIANnet project is the only network project that has committed itself to the development of a graphics interface that supports

Indian fonts. The use of Native languages in the CMC environment has not progressed far beyond the experimental stage.

It is true that there are a number of successful multimedia educational projects underway (Donahue, 1990; Novelli, 1990; Souder, 1990; Turnbull & Hoebel, 1990) which may be a boost for indigenous language uses. First-Class and ResNova CMC software, based on the Macintosh System 7 operating system, allow multimedia communication via telephone and computer network. Nevertheless, the majority of the Internet domains and BBS communication systems are still text-based linear formats that operate like books and require cognitive academic language proficiency.

This leads us to conclude that CMC, as a pedagogical technique, is inappropriate at this time for Indian education if cultural preservation of the tribal languages is a goal of the curriculum. On the other hand, if one ignores the issue of language and its relationship to cultural values and beliefs, the active/group learning paradigm may be beneficial for Indian students. Moreover, if it is incorporated in a culturally sensitive manner into the CMC learning activities, it may become a vehicle for promoting English literacy in the native student.

Because CMC allows the Indian student to read the comments, tour the network as a "lurker," and contribute only after contemplation and becoming comfortable with their probable relationships to others on the system, CMC may work well for Indian students, if given extra time to "meet" everyone. Guest speakers and lecturers may wish to approach students directly through private personal mail and establish a rapport before attempting to teach in the online group setting. Several of the projects reported later in this chapter have students working in teams, cooperating to solve problems through effective communication with distant partners. Furthermore, given time, Indian students do develop personal relationships with others on the networks whom they have never personally met face-to-face. On ENAN, the desire to communicate with other individuals is a powerful motivator for writing. In fact, children using ENAN are well aware that adults are reading all of their conversations. As a result, many of them have resorted to communicating with each other in a remarkably primitive, yet private, manner. They send letters through the regular U.S. mail to each other!

There are a number of computer networks that have significant Indian populations. For convenience these ethnic communication networks can be organized into three domains: (a) listservs and newsgroups found on the Internet, (b) Bulletin Board systems linked to the Internet and/or FidoNet, and (c) singular BBS Systems that are not connected to other networks. Table 8.1 lists these systems and their access addresses as they existed at the time of publication.

Table 8.1. American Indian and Alaskan Native Computer-Mediated Communication Networks Internet Listservs and Newsgroups

INTERNET LISTSERVS, NEWSGROUPS, AND FTP SITES

Alt.Soc.Native
>A Usenet newsgroup.

AISESnet@selway.umt.edu
>American Indian Science and Engineering Network. Owned by Dr. Borries Demeler. E-mail: Demeler@selway.umt.edu. Montana State University, Bozeman, Mt. This is an Indian organization.

Indknow-L@UWAVM
>The Indigenous Knowledge list is for and about topics related to Indigenous people and their knowledge. This list has many conversations not related to the Native people of the Americas, but sometimes has information related to us. Non-native owned.

INDIANnet-L@spruce.hsu.edu
>This list is for American Indian and Alaskan Native nonprofit organizations, governments, and individuals. It links with the INDIANnet BBS network. INDIANnet-L is a project of Americans for Indian Opportunity and is managed by Dr. George Baldwin (Osage/Kaw). His e-mail address is Baldwin@holly.hsu.edu.

NativeLit-L@Cornell.Edu
>This Listserv is owned by (Dr.) Michael Wilson (Kiowa) See NativeProfs-L. Wilson is a Professor of English literature with area of specialization in American Indian Literature.

NativeProfs-L@Cornell.Edu
>Listserv for the Association of American Indian & Alaskan Native Professors. Not for general subscription. Owned by (Dr.) Michael Wilson, University of Wisconsin, Box 413, Milwaukee, WI 53200.

Native-Lit-L@Cornell.eEDUdu
>Listserv for those interested in American Indian literature. It is managed by Dr. Michael Wilson.

NativeNet: AN OVERLAPPING SET OF LISTSERVS
>These listservs have overlapping memberships and are organized by topic. Although they have co-owners, all of them are owned by Gary Trujillo.

NAT-1492@TAMVM1.tamu.edu
>Issues pertaining to aboriginal people and Columbus

NATIVE-L@TAMVM1.tamu.edu
Issues pertaining to aboriginal people

NAT-CHAT@TAMVM1.tamu.edu
American Indian chat listserv

NAT-EDU@TAMVM1.tamu.edu
Issues relating to Indian education

NIPRI-L@GWUVM.Gwu.Edu
The National Indian Policy and Research Institute. Owner: Bambi Krause, Asst. Director, National Indian Policy Center, The George Washington University, Washington, DC. E-mail: Krause@gwuvm.gwu.edu

FTP SITES

Henderson State University: INDIANnet Census Information Center
Census files: pines.hsu.edu or 198.16.16.10
Login: anonymous
Password: guest

Cornell University: ftp.cit.cornell.edu
directory: pub/special/nativprofs

Internet Gopher Service
Gopher csd4.csd.uwm.edu

BULLETIN BOARD SYSTEMS (NOT NETWORKED)

ENAN: The Electronic Native American Network.
800-548-2669 Must have approved access!
TBBS system w/ MS-DOS & INTERNET Connection for email.

IIDN: Iowa Indian Defense Network
319-335-9838
SystOp: Robert Clinton
TBBS system / MS-DOS

CAIED-BBS: Center for American Indian Economic Development BBS
602-523-7320
SystOp: Kate St. Germaine
TBBS system / MS-DOS

SciLink: The Kids from Kanata project. (Canada)
416-921-7868
SystOp: Jon Ord
CAUCUS system w/ Unix

IHS-BBS: Indian Health Service Bulletin Board
301-443-9517
SystOp: Bruce Chomsky

Zuni BBS :
505-782-5835
SystOp: Chris Carson

INDIANNET FIDONET BULLETIN BOARD NETWORK

INDIANnet BBS:
605-393-0468
Syst-Op Anne Fallis. Project Director, Dr. George Baldwin. Funding from Americans for Indian Opportunity. ResNova system with NAPLS Indian Art Graphics and INTERNET E-mail connectivity. Numerous tribal activities and government civic information for tribal planners and grant writers. Links to the Internet via INDIANnet-L.

1st Computers (NativeNet Hub)
813-521-3149

Cherokee BBS
704-497-5898

Freedom BBS (Wisconsin)
715-839-9842

Igloo Station (Canada)
514-632-5556

Messhall BBS (Canada)
403-258-7545

Native American BBS (Michigan)
517-485-2372 (great text book and photo files)

Necronomico (Texas)
210-675-4287

Monduno BBS
206-786-9629

NativeVoices BBS
918-660-0677   Syst-Op Al Webster, Tulsa Oklahoma

Quarto Mundista BBS (Washington)
206-786-9629

Rain Dance BBS (Ohio)
614-884-4350

The Reservation BBS System
203-742-7205

RUSSELL BBS (Montana)
406-423-5433 (Great NAPLS graphics Indian Art)

Spirit_Knife (New Mexico)
702-656-7654

Towers BBS
609-327-9133 / 609-825-7776

Because these networks have hundreds of subscribers who "talk" among themselves daily, there is a social life of sorts that has developed within and across the domains. The communicating individuals have evolved into "virtual communities" of Natives and non-Natives, drawn together by virtue of their shared interests in information of interest to Indian people. The section that follows describes several representative systems and the activities that occur on them.

INTERNET LISTSERVS AND USENET NEWSGROUPS

AISESnet

AISESnet is an Internet mail distribution list that provides communication between individual members of the American Indian Science and Engineering Society (AISES). Members are generally found on college campuses, high schools, and several private sector companies that have Internet access. The list's topics include AISES organization issues, Native American issues, engineering and science issues, public opinion, position openings, AISES events, and various chapter newsletters.

AISESnet membership is open to all, including non-AISES members. The list owner is Dr. Borries Demeler (demeler@selway.umt.edu) at the University of Montana at Missoula. Open membership is a characteristic of most of the Native listservs on the INTERNET, that is, anyone may subscribe and join the list if they wish. AISESnet and NativeProf-L members are now exploring the idea that open membership may not be desirable. Closing ranks, that is, restricting membership to those who belong to AISES and pay membership dues is being debated.

Because AISESnet was originated to improve communication between all of the different campus chapters of AISES, subscribers to the net generally share common characteristics of being involved in science and engineering and are generally of Indian descent. Of all the listservs with Indian information, AISESnet has the highest percentage population of Indian subscribers. Whereas Nativenet and the BBS systems members may disguise themselves as Indian (online ethnic fraud), the majority of AISES members are Indian. Unlike Nativenet, AISESnet listservs are open, and members may retrieve the e-mail addresses of all subscribers. Each subscriber also fills out a simple, one-screen form, which serves to introduce the new member to the group.

INDIANnet-L

INDIANnet-L is the listserv that is used by the INDIANnet Census Information and Computer Network. INDIANnet-L works in conjunction with the INDIANnet BBS system and ftp/Gopher sites listed in Table 8.1. It is the first national computer network to provide civic information useful to American Indian and Alaskan Natives. This information is provided as a service to anyone with a computer, modem, and telephone. INDIANnet is a computer communication network similar to an Indian radio station, television station, or Indian newspaper. In fact, the National Indian Public Broadcasting Corporation (television), the

Native Communications Group (Indian public radio stations), and the Native American Journalist Association all have representatives on this network. INDIANnet has created many firsts.

For the first time Indians are creating and sharing electronic information about themselves, rather than having others (non-Indians) create that information. For the first time a computer network of information about Native Americans is owned and operated by Native Americans. INDIANnet is multipurpose, acting as a clearinghouse for federal information and opportunities that pertain to Indians, as well as creating a setting for tribes to develop profiles on themselves. INDIANnet has three objectives:

1. To help American Indians and Alaskan Natives in cities, rural areas, and reservations throughout the United States and across the continent to establish free, open access to information about themselves and other tribes.
2. To provide this information through community computer systems linked together into a common network similar to National Public Radio or PBS on television.
3. To help supplement what the local systems are able to produce for their communities by providing them with high quality network-wide services and information resources.

These objectives are accomplished by having the information on the INDIANnet computers shared with an affiliate's computer on a periodic basis. INDIANnet services include computer conferences and private electronic mail for Indian tribes, nonprofit organizations, and individuals. Other useful information includes the Federal Registrar, U.S. Census data, and Geographic Information System (TIGER) files. There is also a specialized collection of American Indian and Alaskan Native research reports extracted from the Educational Research Information Clearinghouse (ERIC) database and an amazing collection of electronic Indian artwork and digitized photographs.

INDIANnet is a project of Americans for Indian Opportunity, a national Indian organization dedicated to enhancing the cultural, social-political and economic self-sufficiency of tribes. It is headquartered on the Santa Ana Indian Reservation in New Mexico, and the President of AIO is LaDonna Harris.

NativeNet

NativeNet consists of four lists that have overlapping memberships. It is perhaps the oldest listserv on the Internet to discuss American Indian and

Alaskan Native issues. Subscribers soon learn that if one wishes to discuss "Indian Education," comments should be posted to NAT-EDU, not the listserv NAT-CHAT. Communication from ALT.NATIVE, a Usenet newsgroup, is netweaved to NATIVE-L, as is information from several of the NATIVENET BBS NETWORK machines and semi-commercial networks, such as Peacenet/Econet. Netweaving occurs when connections between these networks are not automatic and messages must be individually moved by a human volunteer who then becomes a "netweaver."

Postings to the Nativenet listservs are reviewed by the list owner(s) and are either accepted or rejected before they are distributed to the subscribers. The majority of the contributors are from the United States and Canada, but there are a significant number of subscribers from Germany, Australia, and the Netherlands.

Similar to Indian newspapers and radio stations that are run by non-Indian managers, Nativenet is occasionally criticized for having a lack of "editorial control" from Indian people. Gary Trujillo, owner or co-owner of all four Nativenet listservs, volunteers a significant amount of his time and energy managing the network software. His editorial control over the discussion comments places him in the analogous role of a radio or newspaper magnate.

Nativenet is being used by college professors nationwide who are teaching courses in American Indian history, culture, or literature. Book reviews, curriculum guides, and classroom activities are commonly posted to the list. Undergraduate and graduate students in Indian study programs on college campuses often "find" each other through Nativenet discussion threads. Such conversations support the contention that the network provides a "virtual support group" for Indian students on numerous campuses nationwide, and this has led some of the Indian student counselors to speculate that CMC has the capability to improve the retention of Indian students.

In recent months subscribers have been migrating to other listservs, such as NativeProfs-L and NativeLit-L, which are more heavily monitored by the list owner. Common complaints are that there are simply too many postings to the network to follow, or that the quality of the postings is so low that subscribers dislike working through all of them. Many subscribe to the network hoping to communicate with Indian people and become discouraged to find more conversations about Indians taking place among non-Indians than with Native people. Native people are heard to complain that they hate being identified as "Indian" because of the mass of private mail they begin to receive, generally asking them their opinion on an Indian issue. Ethnic fraud, that is, individuals portraying themselves as Natives when they are not, is also a common complaint from the native people who subscribe to these listservs.

NIPRI

The National Indian Policy Research Institute (formerly the National Indian Policy Center at The George Washington University) operates an Internet listserv called NIPRI-L. Policy research papers that have been commissioned by the National Indian Policy Center (NIPC) will be stored in the listserver so that they can be retrieved by sending an e-mail message to the listserv software. This unique service will allow anyone with an e-mail address to retrieve full-text reports or books. At the time of this writing only a bibliography of papers was available through NIPRI.

It is NIPC's intent to eventually mount a more powerful information utility on the Internet that will act as an electronic clearinghouse for federal information for and about American Indians. This network information system will be built contingent on continued funding of NIPC and the eventual configuration of the National Research and Education Network (NREN). NIPC is also exploring collaborative arrangements with institutions such as the National American Indian Resource Information Clearinghouse (NARIS) at Oklahoma University. NARIS, which is an electronic bibliographic retrieval system, is not online and will need to be upgraded to a different system in order to be useable via the Internet or telephone dial-up.

BULLETIN BOARD SYSTEMS

Whereas the Internet primarily serves the academic and scientific community, bulletin board systems are more likely to be accessible to rural and urban Indian populations—if they have a home computer, a modem, and a phone line. For educators in secondary schools, the local bulletin board is only a local phone call away, and if the phone call is a 1-800 toll-free number (as ENAN and the INDIANnet BBS have shown), the BBS system becomes exceptionally accessible to educators.

The BBSs discussed here are only accessible through a phone line. They have no interconnectivity to the Internet or any other e-mail systems. As such, members of the larger community of "tribal networkers" sometimes refer to them as "online Indian reservations" an analogy that compares the electronic isolation of the BBS to the physical isolation of Indian reservations.

ENAN: The Educational Native American Network

ENAN was established in 1988 as the Eastern Navajo Agency Network. It was established and supported by the University of New Mexico, the

Bureau of Indian Affairs (BIA), and Tandy Corporation. ENAN was initially designed to explore how computer-mediated communications might be used to improve the educational environment in the 187 BIA schools by:

- Supporting, expanding, and improving the delivery of innovative technological programs in the rural, geographically dispersed schools;
- Supporting the delivery of inservice education programs for teachers and aides;
- Promoting the basic "computer literacy" of administrators, teachers, and students of the BIA, especially the use of computers as telecommunication tools; and
- Increasing communication among educators. (Gittinger & Schilling, 1989, p. 19)

ENAN began as a TANDY desk-top computer with four 1-800 telephone lines attached to modems. It supports a popular PC bulletin board system called TBBS. System operators plan to connect ENAN to the INTERNET. At the time that this chapter was written, projections suggested that it might be accessible during late 1993. However, at this time, ENAN users may not be reached from any of the other Native networks, nor may ENAN users subscribe to services, such as the listservs on the INTERNET.

During its four years of operation, the managers of ENAN have witnessed a growing user base of teachers, administrators, BIA officials, and students. Although most of the activity on the system represents individuals sharing information, there has been some limited success in allowing advanced learners to take college-level courses.

There are reportedly about 1,000 registered users who make about 2,100 calls per month from locations in 23 states. ENAN administrators report that 30% of the users are teachers, 30% students, and 40% administrators. The most frequently used service is electronic mail. During peak periods of use, an average of 135 calls per day have been recorded by ENAN administrators (Pilz, 1992).

One of the more interesting aspects of ENAN is the fact that Indian children in boarding schools across the nation sometimes have an opportunity to chat with each other, as well as Indian educators and scientists. A special section of the BBS has been set aside for this purpose. Several researchers, including this writer, are now studying the multitribal, interracial nature of the children's conversations.

Iowa Indian Defense Network (IIDN)

The Iowa Chapter of the Native American Law Student Association and the University of Iowa College of Law initiated the Iowa Indian Defense Network in February 1992. IIDN is a free computer network bulletin board service dedicated to the exchange of information, views, data, and material on American Indian Law and Indian affairs.

Robert Clinton, the systop, sees this network as having a number of uses. For example, a tribal attorney involved in a complex Indian water rights case could seek out the views of others using the service as to strategies they might pursue in litigation, or they could transfer computer file copies of their briefs in the case to IIDN for the benefit of others who might be litigating similar cases.

The primary users of this network are the Indian law students at the University of Iowa. There is only one phone line and no direct connectivity to the Internet, nor are any of the conferences on IIDN carried on the FidoNet. Clinton is an Internet user who subscribes to Nativenet and occasionally netweaves (moves the data by hand) from the IIDN bulletin board to the INTERNET listservs of Nativenet and vice versa.

The NATIVENET BBS Network

An exciting development in Indian CMC has been the creation of a FidoNet of numerous Indian owned and operated BBS systems. The typical BBS offers private and public mail as well as computer files that a subscriber can download and use on their computer. FidoNet has three additional services: Netmail, which allows a person to send mail to anyone on any FidoNet BBS (and there are thousands of such BBSs), Echomail, which consists of public conferences on a variety of topics; and binary file transfers, which allow a user to send computer programs and digital files to others.

The NATIVENET BBS network (not to be confused with the Internet listservs "Nativenet") began as an Echomail public conference called "Indian Affairs." Through the Indian Affairs conference, Indian BBS systops met and organized the NATIVENET BBS NETWORK. Several of the systems are hubs that communicate with the other hubs as well as BBS systems in their local telephone-calling region. This minimizes the expense of long-distance telephone calls.

Unlike the "educationally elite" culture of the Internet, FidoNet BBSs are generally owned and operated by individuals employed in the private sector serving the electronic data needs of the computing members of their communities. As such, the NATIVENET BBS systems and their members represent the Indian grassroots computing movement.

Rittner (1992) refers to the FidoNet as "truly the people's network—the heartbeat of world discussion of issues facing us today" (p. 32). FidoNet volunteers are thus the "unsung heroes" of this social movement and contribute considerable personal time and investment to support it.

There are many resources on the NATIVENET BBS NETWORK: Each system has its own specialized collection of information. Because the INDIANnet BBS System exemplifies what is being done on these interconnected systems, it is discussed in greater detail.

The INDIANnet BBS System

The INDIANnet BBS system (formerly the Dakota BBS) is physically located in Rapid City, SD. It supports the communication of a growing number of Indian nonprofit organizations and individuals. Although its stated purpose does not readily identify it as an educational network, it certainly serves that purpose for a number of Indian educators.

For example, one project funded through the Rural America Initiative provided drug and substance abuse training for teachers on the Pine Ridge Reservation during 1993. As part of Project Titakuye, teachers used the INDIANnet system to communicate with each other, program trainers, and to retrieve related information. A 1-800 number, proven successful in the ENAN project, was used in this project to promote connectivity. Unlike ENAN, however, the INDIANnet has Internet connectivity for e-mail and listserv subscriptions.

For reservation educators this means that they have access to the faculty members at major universities everywhere in the world. As more inservice training and college accredited coursework is offered via CMC, the INDIANnet system should be able to provide these to Indian educators.

INDIANnet users may also subscribe to a number of commercial news services and electronic editions of national newspapers, including *U.S.A. TODAY* and *Boardwatch Magazine*. Most remarkable is the use of graphics. Subscribers to INDIANnet may view, download, and purchase Indian Share-Art stored in an "online Indian art gallery." In fact, by using public domain telecommunication software on one's home computer, one can have graphic interface capabilities, similar to the manner of PRODIGY (the Sears network). A graphics library of Indian art is available in several formats for subscribers to download. A number of the graphic files are "slide shows" of traditional Indian stories and legends told in pictures and written tribal languages. These educational "slide shows" were created by Indian teachers and their students as exercises in language, and they can be accessed on both MacIntosh or IBM compatibles. Remarkably, the INDIANnet BBS has the first graphic-based CMC system that is capable of operating in a Native tongue. More remarkably, it works via that common denominator of community telecommunications, the telephone line. INDIANnet has recently received an equipment grant from Apple Computer and has installed two new Quadra 840 A/V machines that will use the ResNova graphics-based telecommunications software.

With support from Americans for Indian Opportunity, INDIANnet is now in the process of posting both U.S. Census Data on Indian people and TIGER geographic information system data on its network. Civic information from a number of government agencies, including the Environmental Protection Agency, Bureau of Indian Affairs, and Department of Agriculture, has also been posted in public areas on the INDIANnet machine.

SciLink: The Kids From Kanata Project

Kids from Kanata is a Canadian national project that involves students in classrooms throughout Canada using a computer network to discuss critical issues facing all Canadians today. During the initial pilot phase, the primary dialogue on the network was the theme of "A First Nations Perspective." The discussions were hosted by youth from native schools across Canada and focused on current issues such as aboriginal rights and native self-government.

According to the Kanata project organizer, Jon Ord, the project is all about discovering how computer networking technology can empower young Canadians to become more involved in their own development and in the future of Canada. Sponsors of the project believe that participants will develop a shared and enhanced view of the many ways of being Canadian through a direct exchange of diverse personal experiences: KANATA Discovery Boxes. The boxes contain pictures, gifts, videotapes, and various community and personal items. In addition to the student exchanges, KANATA provides a forum for participating teachers to engage in their own discussions on a variety of topics.

Thirty-five sites were selected from across Canada for the pilot phase, with about one-third of these native schools. The sites were organized into groups of three, and they were asked to:

- conduct research on project issues
- consult with participating "elders"
- hold online discussions and use various media to communicate with other sites.
- prepare and exchange KANATA Discovery Boxes with other triad members.

- interact with local and national media and organizations
- produce a KANATA newsletter to share with other sites and the media.

Kids from Kanata is based on KIDLINK, a highly successful global telecommunications project that now involves thousands of youth from more than 40 countries. Through KIDLINK, young people around the world form "keypal" relationships, responding to questions about what they can do to make the world a better place. Students participating in Kanata were able to develop keypal relationships with other youth around the world in the KIDLINK forums.

Project coordinators recognized that classroom teachers participating in the project would need support in order for the project to work effectively. Organizers worked with native advisors, teachers, curriculum specialists, and the Canadian Education Association in developing classroom materials. A manual and a quick guide was provided for the computer network, as well as a Canada-wide 800-number hotline for direct project support.

Each site prepared a KANATA Discovery Box for each of the two other sites in their "triad." Triads of schools were organized as Native, English, and French. The boxes could contain pictures, letters, videotapes, information about the local community and a Kids from Kanata newsletter produced by the class.

The SciLink system is a desktop computer running under the UNIX operating system that supports a computer messaging system called CAUCUS. CAUCUS, a true computer conferencing system, supports e-mail to the Internet because it is linked to the Canadian national telecommunication network. CAUCUS is especially well suited for multilingual communication because it allows a user to chose either an English or French language interface.

Unfortunately, there are no Native dictionaries available for Caucus. Thus, it should not come as a surprise to find that all of the recorded conversations have been in English or French.

DISCUSSION

The language problem faced by Native communicators in the CMC environment will likely remain a problem until multimedia networks become more common. The nature of CMC is currently grounded in its emphasis on English writing skills. Educators of Indian students may, for conversational purposes, wish to consider allowing poor grammar, as long as the message inherent in the writing is understandable. This appears to be the informal norm on most CMC networks today. As a method for teaching writing, techniques like this have been called *Communicative Language Teaching* (Brown, 1990). The communicative language approach states that the child's second language literacy is defined by how well he or she communicates his or her ideas within a wide range of social situations. Communicative abilities depend not so much on the time spent in rehearsing grammatical patterns, but rather on the opportunities given to interpret, express, and negotiate meaning in real-life situations. On the Pine Ridge Reservation, the Zuni Reservation, as well as at other sites around the country we find Indian educators experimenting with newer multimedia machines, especially the Apple Macintosh platform, text, sound, and motion video offer remarkable learning opportunities for Native students. These educational experiments are on the verge of going online as Indian networks extend themselves across the boundaries of "ascii cage" to include Quicktime video and digital stereo sound.

For Indian students and teachers alike, CMC quickly becomes a real-life activity when they are in communication with strangers who are of different cultural backgrounds. As secondary schools around the country begin to experiment with CMC as a learning tool, there is a growing interest in providing electronic pen-pal encounters between non-native and native students. Children who learn via this medium will learn an array of skills related to the communicative success required in today's information society. On the Native CMC networks we witnesses the emergence of powerful online personalities similar to those we have seen on television and film. These Native people are the role models for the next generation of computer and teleliterate Indian children. The communicative behaviors expressed by them reflect the attitudes, values, and opinions of Native people to an audience of hundreds, perhaps thousands. The survival of those voices and the cultural beliefs of which they speak are dependent on the continued development and control of this new medium by Native people.

Several projects are currently underway that will determine the future of Indian controlled telecommunications. The desire by Indian leaders is to see this technology used to strengthen tribal communities (Odasz, 1990). One project is the American Indian Higher Education Consortium's satellite video network. This group of 26 Indian-controlled colleges has a computer subcommittee examining the possibility of carrying the Internet on the C-band-based video network they are building with funding from the Department of Commerce. Another project is being sponsored by the American Indian public radio stations. They have proposed linking together to share programming, forming the American Indian Radio On Satellite (AIROS) network. It is not clear how

AIROS will broadcast and distribute their signal, but both V-SAT and C-band satellite technologies have been proposed.

These two groups and the INDIANnet civic computer network are closer than ever to merging into one "virtual Indian communication network." The Corporation for Public Broadcasting recently requested proposals to fund Community-Wide Education and Information Services, essentially Freenets managed by public radio stations. These networks will link community schools to local public radio stations that manage the CMC network. A joint proposal is forthcoming from AIROS, INDIANnet, and the National Indian Public Broadcasting Corporation to create a network link between Indian public schools and the Indian-controlled colleges via the Indian public radio stations.

Indian leaders believe strongly that the path to cultural survival is the adaptation of these communication technologies to the needs and values of Native people. Our future will be determined by Indian ownership of the telecommunication infrastructure, the creation of Indian source material and programming, and by finding a balance between the cultural values and beliefs that are influenced by these technologies. The changes to society wrought by communication technologies are profound (Baldwin, 1994). It is imperative that Indian educators begin to develop a critical perspective for understanding network information systems so that they may be harnessed to serve the needs of tribal communities.

REFERENCES

American Indian Higher Education Consortium. (1992, November 30). *Campus telecommunications facilities and profiles: The current capability of AIHEC Colleges.* (Interim Report #3, AIHEC Tele-communications Project). Washington, DC.

Americans for Indian Opportunity. (1994, January). *Native American telecommunications forum: Final report to the National Science Foundation.* Bernalillo, NM.

Aronowitz, S., & Giroux, H. (1988). *Ideology and practice in schooling.* Philadelphia, PA: Temple University Press.

Bakhtin, M. (1986). *Speech genres and late essay.* Austin TX: University of Texas Press.

Baldwin, G.D. (1994). Public access to the Internet: American Indian and Alaskan Native issues. In B. Kahin (Ed.), *Public policy and public access to the Internet.* New York: McGraw-Hill.

Barnhart, C. (1984). *Let your fingers do the talking. Computer communication in an Alaskan rural school.* Washington, DC: National Institute of Education.

Bartelt, H.G. (1986). Language contact in Arizona: The case of Apachean English. *Anthropos, 81*(4/6), 22.

Basso, K.H. (1990). To give up on words, in language and social contest. P.P. Giglioli (Ed.), New York: Penguin Books.

Brown, D.B. (1990). Learning styles and Native Americans. *Canadian Journal of Native Education, 17*(1), 23-35.

Cattey, M. (1980). Cultural differences in processing information. *Indian Education*, pp. 2-5.

Charleston, G.M. (1990). Indian nations at risk: Solutions for the 1990s. Department of Indian Education, Washington, DC.

Cook-Gumperz, J. (1986). *The social construction of literacy.* London: Cambridge University Press.

Diessner, R., et al. (1985). English fluency via computers at Yakima Tribal School. *Journal of American Indian Education, 25*(1), 17-24.

Donahue, B. (1990, Spring). Computer program helps revive ancient language. *Winds of Change*, pp. 20-25.

Freire, P., & Macedo, D. (1987). *Literacy: Reading the word and the world.* South Hadley, MA: Bergin and Garvey.

Gittinger, J., Jr., & Schilling, N. (1989). The Eastern Navajo agency network: Computer networking for native American schools. *Winds-of-Change, 4*(2), 47, 49-50.

Harasim, L. (1986). Computer learning networks: Educational applications of computer conferencing. *Journal of Distance Education, 1*, 59-70.

Harasim, L. (1987, Spring). Teaching and learning on-line: Issues in computer mediated graduate courses. *Canadian Journal of Educational Computing, 16*(2), 117-135.

Heffron, K. (1984). Native children interface with computers. *Canadian Journal of Native Education, 11*(3), 15-26.

Hiltz, S.R. (1986). The virtual classroom: Using computer-mediated communication for university teaching. *Journal of Communication, 36*(2), 95-104.

Hiltz, S.R. (1988). Learning in a virtual classroom (Vol. 1, Virtual Classroom On EIES: Final Evaluation Report, Research Report 25). Newark, NJ: Computerized Conferencing and Communication Center, New Jersey Institute of Technology.

Higgons, H.S. (Ed.). (1992). *Ethnic minority media.* Beverly Hills, CA: Sage.

Hymer, R. (1988). Computers and writing. *Journal of American Indian Education, 27*(3), 35-41.

Hualapai Bilingual Academic Excellence Program. (1988). *Tradition and Technology Project TNT.* Peach Springs, AZ: Peach Springs School District #8.

Jacobi, C. (1985, April). Project developing Indian software curriculum. *The Computing Teacher*, pp. 12-16.

Kinder, M. (1991). *Playing with power in movies, television, and video games: From Muppet Babies to Teenage Mutant Ninja Turtles*. Berkeley: University of California Press.

Kozol, J. (1985). *Illiterate America*. New York: Doubleday.

Leap, W. (1977). *Studies in Southwestern Indian English*. San Antonio, TX: Trinity University Press.

Leecham, D., & Hall, R. (1955). American Indian Pidgin English: Attestations and grammatical peculiarities. *American Speech*, p. 30.

McLaren, P. (1988). Culture or canon? Critical pedagogy and the politics of literacy. *Harvard Educational Review, 58*(2), 33.

McLaughlin, D. (1991). Curriculum for cultural politics: Literacy program development in a Navajo school setting. In C. Biomeyer, Jr., & D. Martin (Eds.), *Case studies in computer aided learning* (p. 83). London: The Falmer Press.

Means, R. (n.d.). The same old song. In W. Churchill (Ed.), *Marxism and Native Americans* (pp. 19-34) Boston: South End Press.

Novelli, J. (1990, April). Culture meets curriculum. *Instructor*, pp.31-34.

O'Brien, E.M. (1990, March). The demise of Native American education, Part 1. *Black Issues in Higher Education, 7*(1).

Odasz, F. (1990). Strengthening Native communities through networking. *Online Journal of Distance Education and Communication*.

Office of Technology Assessment. (1989). Linking for learning: A new course for education. (OTA-SET-430). Washington, DC: OTA, Congress of the United States.

Pilz, A. (1992). Seeking digital connections: Reaching out beyond the traditional classroom. *Journal of Navaho Education, IX*(2), 30-36.

Pilz, A., & Resta, P. (1991, March). *Bureau of Indian Affairs School Technology Survey Results Report*. Albuquerque, NM: ENAN Office, University of New Mexico.

Rittner, D. (1992). Echolinking: Everyone's guide to online environmental information. Atlanta: Peachtree Press.

Ross, C.A. (1982). Brain hemispheric functions and the Native American. *Journal of American Indian Education*, pp. 2-5.

Schaefer, R. (1990). *Racial and ethnic groups*. Glenview, IL: Scott, Foresman, Little and Brown.

Seaton, B.A., & Valaskakis, G. (1984). *New technologies and Native people in Northern Canada: An annotated bibliography of communications projects and research*. Prepared for the Canadian Commission for UNESCO and the Department of Secretary of State. Montreal, Quebec: Concordia University.

Souder, M. (1990, Autumn). Zuni school district fosters cultural preservation. *Winds of Change.*

Turnbull, G., & Hoebel, H. (1990, October). *Projects and activities: The educational technology Centre of British Columbia.* Vancouver: The Educational Technology Centre of British Columbia, University of British Columbia.

Chapter Nine

The Fractal Factory:
A CMC Virtual Laboratory
for Instruction & Research*

John J. Sarraille

Thomas A. Gentry

California State University, Stanislaus

The "Fractal Factory" is a figment of the collective imagination made possible by computer networks. It is a whimsical shorthand name for an ever-changing mixture of people who form a cooperative computer-mediated communication (CMC) environment concerned with the issues frequently described as "chaos science." Central concepts in this area are "fractals" and "fractal dimensions." Because of the general need for improved methods to describe natural phenomena, the advent of fractal geometry is producing a rapidly expanding range of applications. Although the roots of this revolution in analysis predate electronic computing machines, it has

*The authors gratefully acknowledge the numerous and diverse contributions of Frederick Abraham, Annhenrie Campbell, Thomas Carter, Allan Combs, Timothy Elliot, Dorothy Gampel, Sally Goerner, James Goodwin, Julie Gorman, Shelle Hay, Frances Jeffries, Krista Kern, Kelly Lautt, Debbie Lillie, David Lindsay, Phillip Moose, Gary Morris, Lin Myers, Richard Savini, Mary Silveira, Lucinda Smith, Teri Stueland, Larry Vandervert, Gary Vankirk, James Wakefield, Jr., Kim Winters, and Jennifer Young.

been the rapid calculation and graphical display features of modern computers that makes these methods both practical and popular.

Our notion of creating a virtual laboratory concerned with the study of fractals evolved from interdisciplinary collaboration while developing a new degree program in Cognitive Studies that included instruction on chaos science (some of the major contributions to defining this field include: Barnsley, 1988; Briggs & Peat, 1989; Gleick, 1987; Kaye, 1989; Mandelbrot, 1977, 1982; Moon, 1987; Prigogine & Stengers, 1984; Schroeder, 1991). Expanded cooperation with colleagues at other institutions grew out of a 1991 meeting to inaugurate the Society for Chaos Theory in Psychology and the Life Sciences. In the interval between the first and final draft of this chapter, significant new online resources have become available that provide dimensions to this virtual laboratory beyond our original concept. The establishment of the Usenet newsgroup "sci.fractals" with an associated frequently asked questions (FAQ) (Shirriff, 1992), a Chaos-related ftp archive at "lyapunov.ucsd.edu," and a listserver for the Society at "CHAOPSYC@moose.uvm.edu" have greatly expanded what can be utilized for research and instructional activities. (Instruction on how to access listserv groups and ftp archives can be found in Sudweeks, this volume.) There has been a corresponding growth in the published software (Sprott & Rowlands, 1992), and a multivolume textbook, *Fractals for the Classroom* (Peitgen, Jurgens, & Saupe, 1992a, 1992b, 1992c, 1992d) being particularly suitable for CMC-based instruction as each chapter ends with a program in Basic that can be implemented on most microcomputers.

WHAT IS A FRACTAL? DOES ANYBODY KNOW EXACTLY?

It is perhaps ironic, and possibly inevitable, that the layman's definition of the word is "fuzzy." We will not attempt to give a rigorous definition here, but it should be noted that there are formal mathematical definitions that have been used in order to allow for the precise statement of theorems relating to fractals. There is, however, no single definition of a fractal to which all of mathematics has agreed. The following is what we think fractals are.

In popular terms, fractals are objects that appear to have complex structure no matter what scale is used to examine them. For example, a spiral is a type of fractal. You can zoom in on it forever, and it still looks the same. Another example might be a fern-like object. From a distance, a frond has a certain look. As you zoom in, small parts of the frond are seen to be almost exactly the same shape as the frond itself, except much smaller. Imagine, too, an "idealized" coastline. As you zoom in, parts of the coast that appeared to be straight or smoothly curving now are seen to have "jagged" features such as inlets and peninsulas. The more you zoom in, the more of these features you can see. No matter how close you get, the outline never looks completely flat or smooth.

Mathematicians think of "true fractals" as sets of points in some Euclidean space. In order to have complex structure at any scale, such a set of points is necessarily infinite. Often, but not always, fractals have the same granularity across scales, or are even "self-similar" across scales, so that one tends to see the same quality of structure in a fractal as one zooms in on it. The examples just described are all this sort of "well-behaved" fractal. They have a well-defined fractal dimension. Mandelbrot's "ball of yarn" is an example of a fractal that does not have the same granularity across scales. Viewed from a distance, a ball of yarn appears to be a point, which is zero-dimensional. As one approaches more closely, it looks like a solid sphere—three-dimensional. When one gets even closer, it has the look of a complicated, tightly wound curve—one-dimensional. If one zooms in further, the yarn looks like columns—three-dimensional again.

Fractal curves can "fill space," much like the yarn in the example above seems to fill up a sphere. The highly convoluted surfaces of the human brain and the endoplasmic reticulum of living cells are examples of fractal-like surfaces that seem to fill up a volume of three-dimensional space. The Peano curve has been a well-known mathematical example since 1890. It lies in a square in the Euclidean plane. It is extremely convoluted, and (as hard as this may be to believe) it "fills up" the entire square. In other words, every point in the square is on the curve.

HOW DO FRACTALS RELATE TO CHAOTIC SYSTEMS?

The phase-plane and Poincare maps of chaotic systems have a fractal structure. We can hope to recognize, classify and understand such "maps of chaos" by measuring their "fractal properties." This in turn shows promise for increasing our understanding of the complex forces, processes, and phenomena that affect ourselves, our world, and even the universe. The fractal dimension is such a "fractal property." Its use as a classification tool holds promise. It is relatively easy to estimate the fractal dimension of a plot of a phase space. If the dimension is not a whole integer, then the system that the plot was derived from is chaotic, and the actual value of the dimension gives some indication of what the system might be.

Fractal dimension is a generalization of the common idea of the dimension of an object. Points have fractal dimension 0, lines 1, planes 2, and so on. A highly convoluted idealized coastline curve might have a fractal dimension of 1.3. Its fractional dimension is a measure of how much of the surrounding space it "comes near." The Peano curve has a fractal dimension of 2 because it fills a square area. The Cantor "middle thirds" set is constructed from a line segment by removing the middle third, then removing the middle thirds from the remaining two segments, then the middle thirds from the remaining four segments, and continuing in this manner ad infinitum. It can be shown that the Cantor set is (uncountably) infinite. In some sense it has the same amount of points as a line segment. Yet, it contains no line segment, no matter how short, and its fractal dimension is approximately 0.63.

OBJECTIVES THAT THE FRACTAL FACTORY ADDRESSES

A common challenge when developing curricula for the online environment are the facilities traditionally associated with laboratory classes. CMC-based courses are easier to plan and provide if the students do not need the specialized paraphernalia often associated with a laboratory. Fortunately, in our Cognitive Studies program the "laboratory" often is the network in which Santoro's (this volume) triad of conferencing, informatics, and computer-assisted instruction (CAI) are the subjects of study. Our particular emphasis on fractal geometry grew out of a combination of courses concerned with teaching nonlinear analysis methods, existing traditional courses that wanted to incorporate the emerging methods of chaos science, and the research interests of the participating faculty.

The spatial properties of natural forms and fluctuations in time-series data have historically represented formidable challenges to quantitative analysis. The great diversity in shapes and behaviors of the animate and inanimate worlds provide a seemingly inexhaustible supply of unique patterns. However, the human brain has evolved to make some categorical sense out of the complex, dynamic flood of sensory experience. Indeed, the ever-changing energy patterns playing on our numerous sensory channels are necessary for perception. In the absence of sensory changes the brain will assume that nothing is "out there" as in the case of stabilized retinal images, in which the experience is one of blindness to the invariant aspects of the visual field (Prichard, 1961; Yarbus, 1967).

Making generalizations about the world in order to create cognitive categories represents a major occupation of the human brain (Edelman, 1987, 1989, 1992), especially in its continuous need to make subtle discriminations between the generally fuzzy categories attributed to the ever-changing patterns. The "just noticeable difference" experiments of Fechner (1860) gave us the initial analysis issues that continue as central threads in experimental psychology and now in machine intelligence research. For example, if you want an artificial visual system to match or exceed a good observer's ability to detect a change in the appearance of a fracture line, you can use human data for the benchmark measures. A human observer can detect the change in a fracture line with an estimated fractal dimension of 1.15 at an average shift of 0.0085 in the dimension (Westheimer, 1991). In other words, the human is very sensitive to properties of natural forms that can now be given quantitative values of great precision.

FRACTAL GEOMETRY APPLICATIONS

Table 9.1 identifies five general areas in which fractal geometry is being applied.

The discovery that small equations iterated in a self-reflective fashion can yield computer graphics with elaborate complexity and the concept of fractal geometry were concurrent creations of Mandelbrot (1977, 1982). Using computers to generate these images of complexity is a common first encounter with fractal geometry. The Mandelbrot set (see Figure 9.1) is appropriately one of the most recognizable icons of Chaos science, and this equation derived pattern is an example that includes the property of having an unusually exotic border which is fractal.

Numerous freeware programs for creating the Mandelbrot set, "strange attractors" and other interesting fractals are available via anonymous ftp at the sites listed in the FAQ of the Usenet newsgroup sci.fractals, which should be consulted for the current status of these online archives (see Sudweeks, Chapter 12, for information on accessing newsgroups).

The public domain programs for creating images using the methods of fractal geometry are especially helpful as introductory materials in teaching this subject. The ability for students to see the complexity of an image being generated out of the iterations of small equations generally has considerable appeal for all age groups. Some programs provide access to the equation variables, allowing students to explore these image-generating procedures, and it is not uncommon for this aspect to provide the motivation for learning more about the mathematics behind the often elaborate and beautiful patterns.

Table 9.1. Fractal Geometry Applications

Image construction
Image compression
Image analysis
Time-series data analysis
Strange attractor analysis

The second major application area for fractal geometry was derived by running the problem in reverse. Given complex patterns, can equations be discovered that will encode this information in a highly compressed form? Using fractal geometry methods for image compression is described in Barnsley and Sloan (1988), Jacquin (1990), and Barnsley and Hurd (1993), and Brammer (1989). This area has considerable promise for new solutions in the unending quest for getting more information over less bandwidth.

The analytical uses of the fractal dimension identified in Table 9.1 were the initial interests that gave birth to the Fractal Factory concept, and the remainder of this chapter will be concerned with those applications.

Figure 9.1. The Mandelbrot set (M-set) has a single basin of attraction which is represented by the solid black "snowman"-shaped area in the center of this figure. The banded regions around the M-set represent different zones indicating the number of iterations needed before the computation assigns a point to infinity. It is the boundary of the M-set that exhibits a complex fractal structure.

Table 9.2 shows the distribution of 1,461 recent publications with the keyword "fractal(s)" from 415 different journals indexed by the Current Contents and Medline databases. The third column in Table 9.2 is the distribution of "fractal geometry" articles provided by the National Science Foundation Japanese Database "Custom Hot Topics" search service (e-mail requests for searches can be sent to nacsis@nsf.gov, and a press release describing this service can be obtained by anonymous ftp at stis@nsf.gov in file pr9258). Assigning an article to a subject area is often problematic with these papers, which are frequently interdisciplinary in nature; hence, the values are approximations.

The use of fractal geometry to characterize properties of natural phenomena is occurring over a wide assortment of disciplines, but as Table 9.2 indicates, these applications are currently concentrated in a few areas. Some of this variance is attributable to the human and material resources associated with these fields. Educational and equipment deficits are frequent obstacles to many researchers who could use these new quantitative methods for some of our more pressing social and economic problems. For example, the productivity of manufacturing processes may exhibit fractal characteristics (Bendler & Shlesinger, 1991), and new fractal models of economic systems are being hypothesized (Brock & Sayers, 1988; Peters, 1989). One particularly generic application with the potential for broad use is described by Milne (1992), who has developed fractal geometry models used in estimating the consequences of environmental changes on species populations.

Table 9.2. Distribution of Recent Publications with "Fractal(s)" as a Keyword

Subject Areas	Medline and Current Contents (%)	NSF "GAKKAI2" Database (%)
Physics & Materials Sciences	46.5	30.2
Physiology / Medicine	10.1	17.0
Geophysics / Geology / Geography	8.7	1.9
Chemistry	8.0	13.2
Biophysics / Biology	7.7	5.7
Mathematics	6.5	5.7
Computer Science & Information Technology	4.5	24.5
Agriculture / Botany	1.3	0.0
Astronomy	1.2	0.0
Psychology	0.9	1.9
Arts	0.7	0.0
Other	3.5	0.0

PROVIDING ACCESS TO A GENERAL PURPOSE
FRACTAL COMPUTING ENVIRONMENT

Our initial experiences in computing fractal dimensions using manual methods proved to be a laborious chore and yielded only a single estimate known as the "capacity dimension" (Gentry & Wakefield, 1991; Kern, 1992). DiFalco (1991) and Sarraille (1991) have produced an algorithm for the rapid computation of the capacity dimension, which was subsequently expanded by Sarraille to include estimates of the "information" and "correlation" dimensions. The program is called "fd3," and it provides the central engine in the "factory" for computing these estimates of the fractal dimensions for course projects and research. (Copies of this program are available for anonymous ftp at lyapunov.ucsd.edu and csustan.csustan.edu.)

A remaining initial obstacle to automation of the process was the technology needed for porting real-world patterns to the fd3 program, which requires data sets of organized columns similar to a spreadsheet. Scanners and video "framegrabbers" for converting analog television signals into digital image formats provide general purpose solutions. For example, one project involves measuring areas and shapes in magnetic resonance image (MRI) scans of brains (Lillie, 1992). A camcorder records the MRI scans illuminated with a light box, and the video image is digitized with a framegrabber. Both proprietary and public domain software are available for tracing the outlines of digital image structures and converting them into lists of (x,y) coordinates. Each ordered (x,y) pair corresponds to one position on the outline. At this stage we had achieved the basic components of the Fractal Factory process in which microcomputers, equipped with framegrabbers and image analysis programs, provide the "retinas" for this approach to image analysis and the fd3 algorithm, the "neocortex" extracts the desired information from the images.

The next technical additions originated from an interest in estimating the fractal dimensions of drawn patterns produced during psychological examinations. We selected examples of drawings from the Bender-Gestalt and Draw-A-Person tests that had been collected during psychometric evaluations.

The psychologist who directed this research requested that we use fd3 to compute estimates of the fractal dimensions of the complete drawing. This presented a problem because we had to record an entire two-dimensional image area in a form that fd3 could use for input. Unfortunately, we could not find a practical way to use the camcorder and framegrabber combination described earlier to create a plain text list of all the pixel points in a two-dimensional image. Try as we might to illuminate the drawings evenly, we found that they did not transfer very well. There were always brightness variations on the blank parts of the paper that showed up in shades of grey on the digitized frames. This "noise" would have to be filtered out if we were to measure only the drawings themselves.

We eventually decided that it would be better to search for a simpler method. We located a small scanner attached to a Macintosh computer and did some tests. We found that we could set the scanner and the software on the computer so that scans would be made in black and white (as opposed to greyscale). The resulting TIFF graphic image files looked very good. When displayed on the computer screen, they were true to the pages we had scanned, except for a few very small areas in which blank paper came out black, but most image software provides utilities to remove these blemishes, and we did so.

Scanners can be set to various resolutions. We found that using a very high resolution creates more artifacts in the images. The small pixel size would give rise to very small-scale features in the drawings that were "not really there," but which fd3 could pick up, thus biasing its estimate of the fractal dimension. For this reason, we used resolutions in the neighborhood of 70-80 pixels per linear inch.

We still had the problem of translating the images, recorded as TIFF files, into plain text lists of the coordinates of the points in the image. We made some inquiries to see if anyone knew of a program that could read a TIFF file and output the type of listing we needed. No complete solution turned up, but we did learn of several software packages for transforming image files of one type to another. We settled on one package called "pbmplus" (this is shareware available from uunet). We were able to use it to transform the TIFF files into another format called "Usenet face format." Usenet face format is especially simple. It represents the image using ASCII characters for the binary pixel values.

One of us wrote a small C program that translates Usenet face files into lists of points. Once we had pieced together a procedure for transforming a TIFF file from the scan phase into a list of points, we made a script file and used it to process large batches of TIFF files on a workstation. The script produced the point lists, ran them through fd3, and left the results of the dimension estimation in an appropriate report file.

Incidentally, we needed a way to check on the correctness of the lists of points we were getting from our translation procedures. We did this check by using a plotting program called "gnuplot" (also shareware available from uunet) to plot the lists of points and generate PostScript files containing the resulting images. We knew that our translation operations were working correctly when we saw that the PostScript files were faithful images of the original drawings.

This completes the description of how we were able to get estimates of the fractal dimensions of two-dimensional images drawn on paper. This project probably could not have been done if it had not been a collaborative effort by faculty with a wide range of skills, notably in psychology, art, and computer science. If funding had been available, we undoubtedly would have attempted to purchase some software tools to make the manipulations of the data more straightforward. We have not looked, but we trust that there must be image-processing software "out there" that makes it easy to derive a list of points from an image.

THE FRACTAL FACTORY IS A "MAGNET" RESOURCE THAT FACILITATES LEARNING FOR FIRST TIME USERS OF COMPUTER NETWORKS

Motivating both students and colleagues to learn the advantages of CMC can be enhanced when the basis for these communications involves a significant savings in costs and time on projects of interest to the new user. Like many other types of mathematics, once the learner has manually calculated a fractal dimension (Barnsley, 1988, p. 190), the idea of having a computer do it takes on a greater appeal. Following the completion of the initial technical assembly of the Fractal Factory, it rapidly became an effective attraction for people to use e-mail, Telnet, anonymous ftp, and other network programs in order to utilize these online resources. It is now standard procedure to get the potential new user interested in the benefits of using fractals in their work, after which they are informed, "Oh, by the way, you will need to know how to use computer networks to get access to these resources." We are finding that this "bait and connect" strategy is an effective way of introducing people to the advantages of the CMC environments.

FACILITATING COOPERATIVE PROJECTS BETWEEN FACULTY AND STUDENTS FROM DIFFERENT DISCIPLINES AND INSTITUTIONS

The Internet has enabled us to provide an expanding CMC-based utilization of the instruction and research associated with the Fractal Factory. A network of cooperative computing projects on our campus and with other universities has emerged and was the subject of a recent conference workshop (Abraham, Combs, Gentry, & Goerner, 1992). We are using this CMC project to create a seamless transition from secondary education through college to commercial enterprises.

One of our current projects involves what we are calling the "Fractal Garden," and it provides an example of using CMC to promote vertical integration in our educational efforts. A teacher in a nearby middle school has developed an innovative strategy for teaching English as a second language (ESL) using raised bed gardens and "appropriate technology." She is working on a thesis project that will take students from learning English words for the plants to the fractal analysis of their structures and the composts on which they are grown.

Root systems, aquifers, and soils are particularly good candidates for using estimates of the fractal dimensions to do research on variables that alter their structure (Ahl & Niemeyer, 1989; Hoyez, 1992; Klinkenberg & Goodchild, 1992; Streitenberger & Forster, 1992; Wheatcraft & Tyler, 1988). In fact, we expect to do some serious science while young children learn English, grow some food they can use, and port video pictures of their garden to the Fractal Factory for agronomy research projects. The Fractal Garden project represents an implementation of this seamless world of cyberspace in which school, work, and play can have very fractal boundaries.

THE FRACTAL FACTORY IN TEACHING AND RESEARCH

A class on Comparative Animal Behavior is yielding a diverse range of problems for using estimates of the fractal dimension. The fractal dimensions of fish swimming, snail and slug foraging trails, barking patterns in groups of dogs, spider web spinning behaviors, and ants challenged by obstacles on their foraging trails have provided a good mix of humor and high tech for laboratory projects. The video camcorder is an adaptive general-purpose data collection technology for fractal analysis methods. One low-cost way to extract fractal dimension data from videotape uses a standard playback monitor and VCR, plus a stock of acetate sheets and pens that mark on plastic. With a clear plastic sheet on the monitor face, a selected point on the images of interest can be tracked from frame to frame and marked on the acetate overlay to create a "cloud of points" that can then be used to manually calculate a capacity dimension as outlined by Barnsley (1988, p. 190).

A more sophisticated technology uses a large rear-projection digitizing tablet to compute XY coordinates of the target object in successive frames from a videotape run in a frame-by-frame mode. A computer mouse equipped with a gunsight cross-hair locates the target on the rear-projection tablet, and Jandel Scientific's *SigmaScan* system records the coordinates in a spreadsheet. One of the continuing applications of our fractal analysis technology was provided in the original problem concerning human spatial cognition (Gentry & Wakefield, 1991). In this work we are attempting to describe the geometry of human imagination and have adapted the use of videotape analysis to this research program.

Barnsley (1988) had claimed that the fractal dimension would prove to be both a robust and sensitive measure, and our study of human behavior and cognition has supported his claim. We now find ourselves working with significant effects in the data values to the right of the decimal point. For example, Moose (1991) found significant differences in the fractal dimension of sketch maps drawn by subjects under different conditions that reflected changes as small as a hundredth of a fractal dimension. Kern (1992) demonstrated that the fractal dimension analysis of videotape records of humans pointing to the locations of imagined targets was consistent with the classical brain asymmetry literature. She found significant differences between pointing with the left versus the right arm at the thousandth place in the estimate of the fractal dimension. For behavioral and social scientists, this type of precision represents a considerable advance over our usual effect sizes, which we have previously expected to be to the left of the decimal point.

CONCLUSION

Overall, we are finding that the CMC virtual laboratory is a very general-purpose environment in which to develop cooperation between vertical levels in educational institutions and horizontally with colleagues at other universities. We conclude with our opening invitation to any and all with an interest in "working" at the Fractal Factory to contact us. Needless to say, CMC methods will provide the most effective way to do so.

REFERENCES

Abraham, F., Combs, A., Gentry, T. & Goerner, S. (1992, August 13-15). *Cooperative computing on chaos science projects: a dialogue and workshop.* Paper presented at the Conference of the Society the for Chaos Theory in Psychology, Washington, DC.

Ahl, C., & Niemeyer, J. (1989). The fractal dimension of the pore-volume inside soils. *Zeitschrift fur Pflanzenernahrung und Bodenkunde, 152*(6), 457-458.

Barnsley, M.F. (1988). *Fractals everywhere.* Boston: Academic Press.

Barnsley, M. F. & Sloan,A.D. (1988, January). A better way to compress images. *BYTE,* pp. 215-223.

Barnsley, M. F. & Hurd, L. (1993). *Fractal image compression.* Wellesley, MA: A.K. Peters.

Bendler, J.T., & Shlesinger, M.F. (1991). Fractal clusters in the learning curve. *Physica A, 177,* 585-588.

Brammer, R.F. (1989). Unified image computing based on fractals and chaos model techniques. Optical Engineering, 28, 726-734.

Briggs, J., & Peat, F.D. (1989). Turbulent mirror: An illustrated guide to chaos theory and the science of wholeness. New York: Harper & Row.

Brock, W.A., & Sayers, C.L. (1988). Is the business cycle characterized by deterministic chaos? Journal of Monetary Economics, 22, 71-90.

DiFalco, P., (1991, August 15-16). A new program for computing the fractal dimension of a 'cloud of points.' Paper presented to the Inaugural Conference for a Society for Chaos Theory in Psychology, San Francisco.

Edelman, G.M. (1987). Neural Darwinism. New York: Basic Books.

Edelman, G.M. (1989). The remembered present. New York: Basic Books.

Edelman, G. M. (1992). Bright air, brilliant fire: On the matter of mind. New York: Basic Books.

Fechner, G.T. (1860). Elemente der psychophysik. Leipzig: Breitkopf & Harterl. (English trans. by H. E. Adler, D. H. Howes & E. G. Boring, Eds. New York: Holt, Rinehart & Winston.)

Gentry, T.A., & Wakefield, J.A., Jr. (1991). Methods for measuring spatial cognition. In D.M. Mark & A.U. Frank (Eds.), Proceedings: NATO Advanced Study Institute on the cognitive & linguistic aspects of geographic space (pp. 185-217). Dordrecht: Kluwer Academic Publishers.

Gleick, J. (1987). Chaos: Making a new science. New York: Viking.

Hoyez, B. (1992). Fractal analysis of sand grain shape. Comptes Rendus de L Academie des Sciences Serie II-Mecanique, 314(9), 954-951.

Jacquin, A.E. (1990). A novel fractal block-coding technique for digital images. In Proceedings of the International Conference on Acoustics, Speech and Signal Processing, 4, 2225-2228. New York: Institute of Electrical & Electronics Engineers.

Kaye, B.H. (1989). A random walk through fractal dimensions. New York: VCH Publishers.

Kern, K. (1992). The geometry of imagination: Using the fractal dimension to search for relationships between a new measure of spatial cognition and individual differences in personality and intelligence. Unpublished master's thesis, California State University, Stanislaus, Turlock, CA.

Klinkenberg, B., & Goodchild, M.F. (1992). The fractal properties of topography—a comparison of methods. Earth Surface Processes and Landforms, 17, 217-234.

Lillie, D. (1992). A study of corpus callosum: Reliability of measurements. Unpublished master's thesis, California State University, Stanislaus, Turlock, CA.

Mandelbrot, B.B. (1977). Fractals: Form, chance, & dimension. San Francisco: W.H. Freeman & Co.

Mandelbrot, B.B. (1982). *The fractal geometry of nature.* New York: W.H. Freeman and Company.

Milne, B.T. (1992). Spatial aggregation and neutral models in fractal landscapes. *The American Naturalist, 139,* 31-55.

Moon, F.C. (1987). *Chaotic vibrations.* New York: Wiley.

Moose, P. (1991, August 15-16). *How long is the coastline of a cognitive map?* Paper presented to the Inaugural Conference for a Society for Chaos Theory in Psychology, San Francisco.

Peitgen, H.O., Jurgens, H., & Saupe, D. (1992a). *Fractals for the classroom, part one: Introduction to fractals and chaos.* New York: Springer-Verlag.

Peitgen, H.O., Jurgens, H., & Saupe, D. (1992b). *Fractals for the classroom, strategic activities: Volume one.* New York: Springer-Verlag.

Peitgen, H.O., Jurgens, H., & Saupe, D. (1992c). *Fractals for the classroom, part two: Complex systems and Mandelbrot set.* New York: Springer-Verlag.

Peitgen, H.O., Jurgens, H., & Saupe, D. (1992d). *Fractals for the classroom, strategic activities: Volume two.* New York: Springer-Verlag.

Peters, E.E. (1989). Fractal structure in the capital markets. *Financial Analysts Journal,* pp. 32-37.

Prichard, R.M. (1961). Stabilized images on the retina. *Scientific American, 204,* 72-78.

Prigogine, I., & Stengers, E. (1984). *Order out of chaos.* New York: Bantam Books.

Sarraille, J. (1991, August 15-16). *Developing algorithms for calculating fractal dimensions.* Paper presented to the Inaugural Conference for a Society for Chaos Theory in Psychology, San Francisco.

Schroeder, M.R. (1991). *Fractals, chaos, power laws.* New York: W.H. Freeman and Co.

Shirriff, K. (1992). Fractal FAQ (Frequently Asked Questions) from the Usenet newsgroup sic.fractals.

Sprott, J.C., & Rowlands, G. (1992). *Physics academic software: Chaos data analyzer, IBM PC version 1.0.* New York: American Institute of Physics.

Streitenberger, P., & Forster, D. (1992). The effect of fractal dimensionality on self-similar grain growth. *Physica Status Solidi B-Basic Research, 171*(1), 21-28.

Westheimer, G. (1991). Visual discrimination of fractal borders. *Proceedings of the Royal Society of London B, 243,* 215-219.

Wheatcraft, S.W., & Tyler, S.W. (1988). An explanation of scale-dependent diversity in heterogeneous aquifers using concepts of fractal geometry. *Water Resources Research, 24,* 566-578.

Yarbus, A.L. (1967). *Eye movements and vision.* New York: Plenum Press.

Chapter Ten

Online Scholarly Discussion Groups

Raleigh C. Muns
University of Missouri, Saint Louis

In this chapter I discuss the context, the means of analyzing, and specific mechanisms relating to online scholarly discussion groups. In addition, synoptic descriptions of a number of specific discussion groups serve to give concrete examples to neophytes about this burgeoning area of telecommunications in academia. Technical obfuscation has been avoided when possible; nonetheless, new terms and concepts must inevitably be introduced. For some, the descriptions of two of the actual mechanisms used by scholars to communicate online (Usenet and listservs) may be particularly onerous.

The network revolution is raging on college and university campuses across our fair orb. Remaining civilians must either step aside or enlist in the ranks of the network literati. The information that follows is an invitation to the latter group to "come on down!" and is intended to give them a working knowledge of the existing systems and the intriguing possibilities of online scholarly discussion groups.

The history of prenetwork scholarship has been dominated by tongue and paper. Those still communicating exclusively by voice and ink, save the ever-present and hardy population of Luddites (erstwhile destroyers of machinery in early 19th century England), need to understand what some of the typical network mechanisms used for carrying on scholarly discussions are and how to access them. Similarly, as talking about a subject is functionally different from writing about a subject, there are functional variations between the operating mechanisms of network communications that need to be understood.

Understanding how to use the network is a technical exercise requiring time and the intellectual ability to follow directions only slightly more difficult than a good set of origami instructions (of course, you may need a translator because the instructions will not be in standard English!). Surmounting that problem, the obstacle of identifying which among the growing thousands of electronic conversations is of appropriate interest is a more difficult matter. As inventor, editor, writer, and publisher of the *List Review Service*, a modest newsletter designed to assist network denizens to locate relevant online discussions, my self-anointed expertise is at your disposal.

SOCRATES TO SHMOOZING

Socrates's tragic failure to attain tenure from the Athenian elite attests to the importance of fully understanding the mechanisms used for scholarly communication. Contemporary scholars who fail to respect their profession's rules of communication rarely commit suicide. Nonetheless, negative consequences may still accrue to those modern thinkers who choose not to respect the unspoken professional rules of their disciplines. Famed cold-fusion physicists Stanley Pons and Martin Fleischman have been looked on with disdain as much for circumventing the traditional peer review process as for questionable research results (Cowen, 1991).

The advent of computer-mediated communication (CMC), specifically the ready availability of international electronic mail (e-mail) networks, has not yet sounded the death knell to existing scholarly communication structures and mechanisms. Neither has CMC yet created radically new conceptual means of communicating. What has happened is that the distinct characteristics of informal dialogues, invisible colleges, oral presentations, and scholarly publication have begun to merge. To varying degrees, online scholarly discussions can easily encompass the informality of a casual dialogue, the pseudo-formality of conference presentations, the social mechanisms of the invisible college, and, increasingly, the rigor of scholarly publication. The following should demonstrate, by describing these mechanisms, how this is taking place.

The oral tradition of transmitting scholarly knowledge can be dated usefully as beginning with Socrates's Athenian school. The written tradition was espoused by his student, Plato, who passed to his students the early written versions of Socratic thought. Within this body of classical knowledge is a recurring theme of reactivity: Knowledge is exchanged among individuals who, over time, react to and refine this transmitted information. This is exemplified by the classic dialogue.

I wrote this while attending what one of my non-librarian colleagues calls the "library techno-geek conference" (Third Annual Library and Information Technology Association Conference). In this exemplary setting, the Socratic dialogue has been only slightly modified into modern shmoozing; information is, to this day, being transmitted between scholars via informal and relaxed dialogues.

Scholarly presentations at conferences serve to alert attendees to the extending horizons in their area of interest. Though tending to the informal, such presentations acquire at least a patina of organization. Oral scholarly presentations often precede the official debut of an idea in a scholarly journal.

Articles published in these refereed journals seldom surprise their readership. After all, their purpose is to officially stake out intellectual territory by stating, "I was here first." Similarly, they serve to point out to tenure review committees how often "I was there," as well as "Who cares that I was there" (i.e., frequency of citation by other scholars). Publication of scholarly information in peer-reviewed journals is marked by formality and rigor and is often a direct result of the informal dialogues and oral presentations previously mentioned.

Another familiar mechanism of scholarly communication involves the term *invisible college,* originally used by the Royal Society of London in the 17th century, to refer primarily to the Society's lack of a campus (Paisley, 1972). Crane's seminal volume, *Invisible Colleges* (1972), looked at the sociology of modern communities of scholars and indicated that informal communication of scholarly information affects publication patterns in the formal literature. The phrase *modern communities* must now be updated to include the new telecommunications technologies that have created online communities of scholars. Usenet and list servers are two of the dominant mechanisms used to form virtual communities of telecommunicators.

USENET AND LIST SERVERS

Usenet newsgroups and BITnet (Because It's Time Network) and Internet listserv groups are types of electronic discussion groups. Both models are characterized by being, first, an alphabet-based means of communication (i.e., information transmitted as strings of words either read on a screen or printed out on paper), and second, reactive. These electronic dialogues do not possess the immediacy of real-time verbal exchanges. Conversely, they do not have the glacial characteristics of print dialogues in the professional literature.

"Usenet is the set of people who exchange articles tagged with one or more universally-recognized labels, called newsgroups" (Spafford, 1993, p. 1). From a Usenet reader's point of view, one must actively seek out a Usenet newsgroup, then explicitly choose to read, or not read, individual postings. Active control over the amount of messages one wishes to receive is the functional component that distinguishes Usenet from list servers, which are described later.

List servers, commonly called *listservs*, are (usually) computer programs operating on mainframe computers, utilizing Eric Thomas's Revised Listserv software. This software maintains lists of the electronic mail addresses of subscribers. Electronic mail received by a list server is re-distributed to all subscribers. List subscribers are thus passively supplied with the list's common message traffic. Such mandatory serendipity can be costly in time. The Women's Studies List (WMST-L), for example, distributes up to 100 messages in a given week (Muns, 1992a). Individuals with eclectic interests can easily suffer information overload just by subscribing to two or three active lists. This functional component of listservs, that of receiving all messages, has been referred to as "drinking from a firehose." This is in contrast to the Usenet news reader who "sips from a tap."

In their functional differences, listservs and Usenet serve as paradigms for the two main mechanisms of information distribution: passive (listserv) and active (Usenet). In actual practice, listserv messages may be simultaneously posted to Usenet newsgroups; Usenet messages may be distributed transparently to listserv subscribers; private or commercial computer bulletin board messages may find their way into both listservs and Usenet. For example, the listserv LHCAP, an online discussion of issues relating to the other-abled, regularly distributes an electronic dialogue as a single *Handicap Digest*, compiled from such diverse sources as private computer bulletin boards (e.g., FIDONET), the CompuServe commercial service, Usenet, and the listservs. An extremely important implication is that identical pieces of information (i.e., electronically posted e-mail) are distinguished by the mode in which they are received, that is, passive (listserv) or active (Usenet). In the very recent past there were apparent differences between the intellectual component of the information streams on Usenet and distributed by listservs. Typically, Usenet was thought of as the place where all the pornography was posted, and listservs were stereotyped as used by academics to discuss weightier matters. With the increasing overlap between the information posted on all internet systems, it is these functional differences of the distribution mechanisms that are distinguishing, rather than any previously perceived differences in intellectual content.

Posted messages in electronic forums are dangerously less ephemeral than spoken conversations. In my review of a general anthropology listserv, ANTHRO-L, I used the metaphor of anchovies on pizza to describe the spicy nature of what I found to be a fascinating range of messages. The subject of cliterectomy appeared in a subsequent paragraph along with other examples of ANTHRO-L's discussions (Muns, 1992b). An irate reader wrote to me, privately, wondering how I could so callously insult women, circling on a printed version of my review the two elements just mentioned. Whether the metaphor was appropriate, callous, or inadvertent is not the point. Utterances in electronic scholarly discussion lists become part of a printed and referencable record. Unlike spoken words which dissipate into the air (unless recorded somehow), electronically transmitted information glows on computer video screens for all to ponder, can be downloaded to diskette, and may be part of a listserv or Usenet archive of messages stored on more than one mainframe computer. In addition, when participants can number in the thousands, the probability of extreme reaction is near certain. Protests over one's intellectual prowess, viewpoint, political correctness, and spelling are regularly paraded before the list's readership within hours of the original posting, unless screened out by a list moderator.

ACCESSING FORUMS: USENET AND LISTS

The Usenet universe is organized hierarchically into seven major groups at its top level: "comp," "sci," "soc," "talk," "news," "rec," and "misc." Within each group chains of e-mail postings on specific subjects are organized into "newsgroups." "Comp" encompasses newsgroups discussing computer hardware and software. "Sci" covers research and practice in the recognized sciences. "Soc" newsgroups consider social issues and relationships. "Talk" is the umbrella for endless debate on anything (focus on debate). "News" delves into Usenet issues, such as standards, hardware, software, and Usenet sociology. "Rec" collects messages about recreation and hobbies. "Misc" deals with anything that doesn't fit within the other groups.

Beyond this standard Usenet hierarchy lies an amorphous universe of other newsgroups. For example, there are an indeterminate and varying number of discussions taking place in what are designated as the "alt" hierarchy of newsgroups. The "alt" newsgroups pledge fealty to no creature and range from the infamous sex newsgroups (e.g., alt.sex.stories which lists pornographic short stories), to the mysterious (e.g., alt.butt-keg.marmalade), to the mundane (e.g., alt.backrubs).

Many think that Usenet embodies the antithesis of the scholarly online discussion group. However, my local University of Missouri Usenet news feed contains a number of bit.listserv.name newsgroups mirroring network listservs. For example, the list PACS-L (discussed later) is mirrored by the "bit" newsgroup bit.listserv.pacs-l. The same scholarly discussions in PACS-L are simultaneously available as a Usenet newsgroup.

Because not all Usenet locations carry all Usenet newsgroups, the perception of what Usenet is may be biased by the local Usenet configuration, as it is the site, not the individual, that subscribes to Usenet. Users only have access to those newsgroups to which their site subscribes. The idea of a "site" becomes ambiguous, however, when one learns to connect to another computer (which may have an entirely different set of Usenet newsgroups) via the offending, censoring, or deficient home site.

Usenet, with modes of access varying from site to site, is not a subscription service. It is available to anyone with a connection to any Internet site maintaining a Usenet feed and appropriate software. Lists, on the other hand, are characterized by the fact that an individual does indeed subscribe to them. To subscribe to a list, follow these three steps: first, identify the existence of a list to which you want to subscribe; second, find the e-mail address of the list server maintaining the list; and third, send an e-mail message telling the server that you want to subscribe to the list it controls.

The annotated *Directory of Electronic Journals, Newsletters and Academic Discussion Lists* lists 1,152 e-mail addresses of lists and their servers (Kovacs & Strangelove, 1993). More extensive and up-to-date directories of online discussions are available on the networks themselves. *The Directory of Electronic Journals* is, in fact, a product of network sources. These online sources are of limited utility because the people who need them the most are those who do not have access to, or experience with, computer networks. The printed *Directory of Electronic Journals* (or any similar publication) is absolutely essential to the neophyte network participant.

Subscription requests to servers are usually sent as e-mail messages in the form:

To: LISTSERV@NODENAME
SUBSCRIBE listname yourfirstname yourlastname

For example, if John Doe wishes to subscribe to the aforementioned L-HCAP list, he would look up L-HCAP in the Directory of Electronic Journals and would find the BITnet address to be LISTSERV@NDSU-VM1. Next, Mr. Doe could send an e-mail message to LISTSERV@NDSU-VM1 telling the listserv program to register him on the subscription list for L-HCAP. An example of his request would look like this:

To: LISTSERV@NDSUVM1
SUBSCRIBE L-HCAP John Doe

The sender's e-mail address is automatically included in any outgoing message, thus, LISTSERV@NDSUVM1 automatically "knows" where to send L-HCAP traffic. "John Doe" is how the program will address this subscriber in messages sent to and from the list.

One does not subscribe to the server, rather, the server is a gate-keeper that processes requests for addition to, or deletion from, the list. A common error is when requests to unsubscribe are sent to the list address, instead of to the server address. If a list is unmoderated, such messages of one's inadvertent ignorance are then forwarded to all list subscribers.

E-mail is the primary method used to read and contribute to online discussions, thus, there is a premium on knowing a discussion group's electronic location. E-mail address conventions, however, are light years beyond the scope of this essay. In-depth analyses of network mail pathways give new meaning to the word *byzantine*. The brave, or masochistic, are directed to Frey's *!%@:, A Directory of Electronic Mail Addressing and Networks* (1991) and LaQuey's *The User's Directory of Computer Networks* (1990) for some painfully thorough explanations and listings of network pathways and their corresponding e-mail address conventions. Even though LaQuey's and Frey's books are both extreme-ly well written, the technically faint of heart are warned to stay away. Personal experience tells me that the most efficient way to solve most e-mail address problems is to contact local network support staff. And the most sure way of finding out someone's email address is to ask them.

Many list owners set up their lists to automatically send intro-ductory messages to new subscribers explaining in detail their editorial policy, how to communicate with their lists, general network e-mail eti-quette (called netiquette), and how to obtain further documentation. Subscribers unafraid to actually try some of the directions in these intro-ductory messages will experience a cascade effect. For example, the introductory material to list PACS-L explained to me, in plain English, how to obtain the text file LISTDB MEMO. LISTDB MEMO explained how to search the message archive files of a list. Searching the archives of list PACS-L taught me how to do an "anonymous FTP." Using anonymous FTP (File Transfer Protocol) obtained the online version of *Zen and the Art of the Internet* (Kehoe, 1992), which directed me to further sources of information obtainable through networked computers.

DATABASES OF MAIL

Most scholarly discussion lists maintain archives of their e-mail messages. These databases of mail represent unique information resources. In practice, I have searched library-oriented discussion lists for comments on software and hardware that the library may be planning to purchase. A mathematician colleague recalled a mention of an obscure proof months ago on the mathematics list, NMBRTHRY, and a search of the list's archive of messages easily turned up the relevant citation. I regularly search list archives to determine a list's overall personality by inspecting retrieved index files. Index files contain single subject lines written by each message's author when the message was posted.

The scholarly value of these archives is still unproven as their prevalence and existence are relatively new. Further, wide variation exists in the availability of archives, as well as the means by which they may be searched. The subtle, yet critical issues of bibliographic control, future availability, and copyright are also unresolved. Nonetheless, these archives exist, giving subscribers access to more than just the passing current of messages. Online scholarly discussions are a matter of record.

ANALYSIS OF FORUMS

Librarians constantly evaluate information sources in order to filter out the noise of undifferentiated information. The basic question about any information source is "what good is it?" A variety of procedures and tools have evolved over time and have been used by information professionals, such as librarians, to deal with the glut of all possible information that could be made available to one's clients. I, and other individuals responsible for developing accessible information resources, spend a good deal of time reading reviews in order to identify possible useful sources. Certain evaluative tools are published solely to satisfy that need. No individual can examine all items, so such information leverage tools are necessary (e.g., *Choice*, Chicago: American Library Association, which annually reviews approximately 6,000 reference books). Books and journals are no longer the only types of items being evaluated by such tools. Increasingly, reviews of nonprint items, such as compact disc (CD-ROM) and online databases, have become more prevalent.

When it is practical, prospective additions to any information resource pool are examined firsthand. The reference department in which I work tested 21 CDROM products last year alone. Properties considered in examining possible additions to a collection include an item's format, structure, language, style, useability, source, intended audience, applicability to institutional mission, and cost.

It was a simple conceptual leap for me to apply my librarian training, as an evaluator of information resources, to electronic discussion lists. Thus was born the *List Review Service*, an irregular periodical, fee-free, online only publication, combining the elements of book and restaurant reviews. As a restaurant reviewer, I enter a list through the open network door, look at its offerings, sample its wares, make notes, then broadcast to my subscribers my impressions of the experience. As a book reviewer, I apply the rigor of professional librarianship to analyze the list's possible information utility. My intent is to give potential subscribers enough information to determine whether or not to subscribe to the list, without having to use their own time to discover that for themselves.

The basic information within each review is divided into two broad components: qualitative and quantitative. The qualitative components consist of a prose description of the list as well as suggested uses for it. The quantitative elements describe the level of message traffic over time and give the ratio of queries to nonqueries. This latter statistic was implemented as an attempt to objectively describe a list's usefulness. Ideally, each posted question would receive an answer. A superior scenario would have multiple answers for each question. A list bogged down with many queries and few responses may not be of much use. The relevance of this statistic is determined by the reader of the review.

The methodology used for a list review has evolved with each published issue. There are no other established processes to specifically evaluate these new sources of information. In a sense, more than mere text needs to be evaluated. Lists are not just packets of messages;they are also communities of individuals dynamically producing those packets. Because of this dynamic nature, the problem of creating classification schemes for discussion groups is intriguing. In most cases, a listserv or newsgroup self-classifies itself by simply stating its intended subject area and audience. Alternatively, classification by an external analyst is usually something like the methodology of simple human judgment as employed in the *Directory of Electronic Journals* (Kovacs & Strangelove, 1993, p. 85). This should not be seen as a failing of that work, but as a signal judgment on the ambiguity inherent in classifying discussion groups. The entire idea of an "online scholarly discussion group" begs for a discussion on the definition of the problematic term scholarly.

Discussion groups can be more easily classified by how they function. For example, a list may be moderated or unmoderated. The degree of moderation varies among individual moderators, but the idea of moderation at least implies human control over message traffic with some sort of message filtering taking place. The level of message traffic can also be used to functionally classify discussion groups. Rather than use terms such as heavy or light message traffic, in the *List Review Service* I simply post the number and length of all messages for a given time period, and once again rely on the reader's judgment to determine its importance.

There are other existing analytical methods that can be applied to the list evaluation process. Forum analysis, for example, appears to be a useful concept for analyzing and describing online scholarly discussion groups. "I believe we need to develop audience heuristics that begin by placing the writer and audience on a different relational footing altogether: that begin by guiding the writer toward interaction with (not control over) audience" (Porter, 1992, p. 142). Electronic forums epitomize the interaction between writer and audience because they are, in essence, interchangeable. Forum analysis incorporates the description of an audience, the background of the forum, and the conventions by which communication takes place into a single evaluative statement.

Some lists require biographical sketches as a precondition for subscribing, such as the Library Research List (LIBRES-L). Such databases of biographical information could be used as an element of forum analysis in classifying the list by describing the subscribers. Orwellian "Big Brother" considerations aside, the assumptions are, first, that no one is lying (a risky assumption when the only clues one has is ASCII text), and, second, that knowing who the contributors are validates the information in a scholarly discussion. One of the inherent charms of most online scholarly discussion groups is that one need not be a card-carrying academician to contribute. Conversely, erudite academics judged solely by their posted e-mail messages can appear to be idiots. Heavens! Is it who we are? What we say? Or how we say it?

WHAT'S OUT THERE?

As of February 10, 1994, 4,615 Listservs were known to the network backbone server LISTSERV@UBVM. The *Directory of Electronic Journals* publishes a list of 1,152 discussion groups "of interest to scholars" (Kovacs & Strangelove, 1993). To date, I have disseminated 25 list reviews. Even though user-friendly network software, with intriguing names like "Gopher," "Archie," and "Veronica," is evolving to lead prospective users to online scholarly discussion groups (among other network resources), most participants find their way to relevant lists by word of mouth. In most cases, that mouth is online! The next section describes some of the sources that I have found particularly valuable for uncovering other, more discipline-specific online discussions.

The most useful online discussion groups for this purpose tend to be either in the field of information science/librarianship or communication studies. The librarian lists generally emphasize finding, evaluating, organizing, and disseminating what is out there. The communication studies groups tend to be best at exploring the processes of online communication, both philosophical and technical. Such generalizations have led to simplification of the coverage described in the following lists, indicating a narrower coverage of subject matter than actually occurs.

Public-Access Computer Systems (PACS-L)

The subject material covered by all of the other sources enumerated has been, or will be, covered by PACS-L. PACS-L, with more than 7,800 subscribers in 66 countries, is a forum for discussing the practical and theoretical issues surrounding the supplying of public access to electronic information resources. If any discussion group could be called "The Librarians List," it would be PACS-L. Although it is moderated (i.e., messages are filtered by one or more list editors based on explicit submission guidelines), after two years of subscribing I still find myself frustrated by the amount of noise (postings irrelevant to the stated list topic) on this list. Its true value lies in that. Because everyone "knows" that PACS-L is such a monolithic list, it inadvertently serves as a virtual clearinghouse for information on the rest of the network. Most of what I have learned about cyberspace can be traced, at least indirectly, to PACS-L.

PACS-L consistently draws one's attention to new lists, online directories, library catalogs, archives, software, information and library-related legislation, awards, conferences, books, problems, and philosophies. It is this wide range of material that makes PACS-L most valuable for the neophyte. Equally worthwhile are the conversations themselves, among mostly information professionals, about the theory, problems, and resources relating to public access. PACS-L also disseminates several online publications; one of which, *PACS Review,* is a peer-reviewed journal covering library science research results and issues.

The Communication Institute for On-line Study (CIOS)

CIOS maintains the online mother lode of network communications studies information via its Comserve server. Online documentation cites annual statistics of upwards of 300,000 Comserve commands from more than 25,000 users in over 47 countries.

Instead of lists, Comserve maintains 27 "Hotlines" covering distinct subject areas, such as mass communication (MassComm), communications in the health fields (HealthCo), computer-mediated communication (CMC), communications research methods (Methods), and so on. Like PACS-L, this breadth of subject matter makes Comserve another appropriate first stop for a beginner. Unlike PACS-L, the amount of information one receives can be ameliorated by selecting only a few Hotlines. A specific Hotline, Intercom, serves as a means of communicating common information to all Hotline subscribers.

New subscribers to Comserve Hotlines automatically receive a text file called STARTER KIT, which is the best introductory "how to" information I have ever received online. The STARTER KIT file explains how subscribers with e-mail accounts on VAX or CMS machines can obtain and use the EASYCOM software for those platforms. EASYCOM, a menu-driven interface for interacting with Comserve, makes searching for archived messages, retrieving files, and getting help a matter of choosing the appropriate menu item, requiring only that one respond to plain language prompts. The term *plain language* is used because EASYCOM can be configured to speak English or Spanish.

Interpersonal Computing and Technology List (IPCT-L)

IPCT-L's primary focus is on ideas. The questions—"What good is it?" "How good is it?" and "Why is it good?"—are rigorously explored by this list. As this list concentrates on the interaction between humans and technology, it serves to present, and in most cases clarify, network communication issues. In so doing it regularly points to, and extracts from, other lists that explore narrower viewpoints (e.g., copyright issues in the electronic environment).

This list's moderated dialogues are some of the most cogent and lively that I have encountered. The personality of the list is extremely civilized, which is not to say there are no sparks. Advanced communication theorists regularly exchange ideas with nuts-and-bolts educators, with the reader left to determine the value of the exchange.

Almost all lists explore these same issues of humans interacting with technology, but usually diffusely and only in passing. I have dubbed this the "look at what we are doing and isn't it neat" phenome-non. IPCT-L's explicit focus on such concerns makes it an excellent tool to help new networkers learn in a more coherent manner about the over-all issues of the academic network environment.

Electronic Journals List (VPIEJ-L)

This technically oriented list provides a gateway to a discussion of the problems, and requisite resources, concerning online electronic journals (e-journals). VPIEJ-L points to e-journal locations and explains how they can be obtained. VPIEJ-L expounds on subjects such as e-journal format, the implications and appropriateness of using specific formats (e.g., ASCII, Postscript, TEX, SGML), and the issues of maintenance and dis-semination of e-journal collections.

Reference Librarians List (LIBREF-L)

The policy of LIBREF-L is not to be an online reference assistant. Rather, LIBREF-L is the place to go to eavesdrop on the shared experiences and discoveries of reference professionals. Reference librarians are very good at uncovering things. This is the list that points to such discoveries.

As the list attuned to my specific profession, this is the one in which the *List Review Service* is regularly posted. I hesitate to recommend that nonlibrarians subscribe, due to heavy levels of message traffic (caveat emptor!), but LIBREF-L regularly receives announcements cross-posted from other sources of "things" that are available on the network. Notification of the availability of full-text, public domain works, new e-journals, data depositories, and network aids regularly debut on LIBREF-L.

SUMMARY

I have found the five discussion groups listed to be of great and immedi-ate practical value for the task of harnessing the torrent of information generated by the huge numbers of discussion lists. PACS-L and Comserve are used as broad, interdisciplinary, general awareness tools. IPCT-L serves to keep one aware of people-oriented network issues. VPIEJ-L works as a resource for discussing technical issues. LIBREF-L seems to be best at pointing to a wide range of useable network items. By subscribing to four of the five, Comserve being the exception, I regu-larly receive 50-100 messages per day.

CONCLUSION

I have covered the basic context of scholarly communication, discussed some of the means by which online discussions take place, described an existing mechanism's evaluative methodology for online discussions, and supplied a number of specific examples of existing discussion groups. What has been covered is introductory and incomplete, but should serve as a departure point to those wishing to place the words printed here in a practical context (i.e., wishing to put fingers to keyboard).

As a reference librarian, my job requires me to continually seek out and evaluate new information resources. Individuals with specific information needs seldom have the time or inclination to adopt such a systematic exploratory approach. By doing this for them, I have become both more facile with the mechanisms for accessing online scholarly discussion groups and more familiar with the growing array of specific groups themselves. I have also become more frustrated at the paucity of activity I see in my profession in analyzing these dynamic network resources. I sense that librarians as a group are missing an opportunity to fulfill one of the profession's traditional roles as intermediaries between patrons and information. So, in addition to being (hopefully) at least a minor education for some, this discussion ends with a traditional call for action by my well-heeled researcher colleagues.

REFERENCES

Cowen, R.C. (1991, July 10). Epitaph written to cold-fusion follies. *The Christian Science Monitor*, p. 13.

Crane, D. (1972). *Invisible colleges: Diffusion of knowledge in scientific communities*. Chicago: University of Chicago Press.

Frey, D. (1991). *!%@: a directory of electronic mail addressing and networks*. Sebastopol, CA: O'Reilly & Associates.

Kehoe, B.P. (1992). *Zen and the art of the internet*. Chester, PA: s.n.

Kovacs, D., & Strangelove, M. (1993). *Directory of electronic journals, newsletters and academic discussion lists*. Washington, DC: Association of Research Libraries.

LaQuey, T.L. (Ed.). (1990). *The user's directory of computer networks*. Bedford, MA: Digital.

Muns, R.C. (1992a) ANTHRO-L: General Anthropology. *List Review Service*, 1(8).

Muns, R.C. (1992b) WMST-L: Women's Studies. *List Review Service*, 1(6).

Paisley, W.J. (1972). The role of invisible colleges in scientific information transfer. *Educational Researcher*, 1(4), 5-19.

Porter, J.E. (1992). *Audience and rhetoric*. Englewood Cliffs, NJ: Prentice-Hall.

Spafford, G. (1993). What is Usenet? In Usenet newsgroup news.announce.newusers posted 11 Jan. 1993 (expires 13 Mar. 1993).

Chapter Eleven

Enhancing the Interactive Classroom Through Computer-Based Instruction: Some Examples From Plato

Michael Szabo
University of Alberta

The purpose of this chapter is twofold. The first is to provide a brief historical overview of one of the most powerful systems for the computer-assisted instruction form of computer-human interaction, namely PLATO. The developers of PLATO pioneered conferencing, messaging, and database management and integrated it into the context of computer-based instruction. The second purpose is to examine several of PLATO's specific features designed to support and promote a wide range of communication for student learning. Examination of these features should stimulate ideas to aid future communications development using evolving network systems.

SOME USEFUL TERMS AND CONCEPTS TO REMEMBER

The author chose to follow the standard usage of masculine pronouns, although keenly aware of the inadequacies of this approach. For consistency the following terms are used throughout this chapter.

Author, authoring: The individual or team that creates instructional lessons or courseware to be delivered by computer; the processes used to create instructional lessons or curricula.

Authoring System: A natural language interface for directing the flow of a computer to carry out the specialized task of tutoring a learner. Such systems do not require special syntax beyond standard conversational terminology.

Computer Based Instruction (CBI) (Learning): The use of computer technology to provide direction, instruction, or management of instruction to the student. Excluded from this definition is the use of the computer as a tool, such as programming, problem solving, running application programs, developing computer architecture, and administrative applications outside the domain of instructional and student management. The three major components of CBI are (a) computer-assisted instruction (CAI), (b) computer-managed instruction (CMI), and (c) electronic messaging (EM) as defined below.

Computer-Assisted Instruction (CAI): In CAI the computer provides a direct instructional tool for a student or small group of students with the goal of having the student learn a defined body of content, skills, or instructional objectives. CAI employs several different approaches to instruction; the most often used are tutorial, review and practice, simulation, and more recently navigation.

Computer-Managed Instruction (CMI): In this other major category of CBI, the computer assesses each individual student on knowledge of a specific body of content, skills, or instructional objectives and informs the student of his level of knowledge (diagnostic). The computer also communicates to the learner what study assignments are to be undertaken to remove the areas of weakness identified in the diagnosis (prescriptive). CMI is thus referred to as diagnostic and prescriptive testing. (For more information, see Szabo & Montgomerie, 1992.)

Electronic Messaging (EM): EM is the ability to capture, store, and distribute information among humans using public and private telecommunications facilities. Information transmitted may be data, graphic, video, and audio, all in digital format.

Computer-Based Interactive Multimedia (CBIM): CBI is delivered in a combination of computer and media formats. In other words, this is CBI with the integration of audio and video media, such as text, still/animated computer graphics, still/moving video images, and audio, all in digitized format. Today's telecommunications networks are just beginning to be powerful enough to handle the intense requirements to transmit multimedia data.

Courseware: The instructional materials that are delivered to learners via computer technology in order to impart knowledge, skills, and/or attitudes. Courseware can be identified by looking at the computer/video screen.

PLATO: Programmed Logic for Automated Teaching Operations is the name given to a large mainframe hardware/software computer system that was designed expressly to provide CBI.

TWO PIONEERING INTERACTIVE CLASSROOM SYSTEMS

The IBM 1500 Systems

A discussion of PLATO would not be complete without a brief mention of the system it replaced. IBM pioneered CAI when they produced two dozen IBM 1500 systems in the mid-1960s. These systems each drove 32 student learning stations, each capable of computer text/animation plus random access to audio and still imagery. For their time, they employed the most advanced arsenal of communication tools available to educators.

In the mid-1970s these systems were decommissioned. But during their lifetime, they made several significant contributions to the furthering of CAI. These included successful demonstration or applications of:

- multimedia learning stations
- special authoring languages and tools
- key training grounds for future workers in the field, and
- seminal research that validated the effectiveness and efficiency of CAI as a learning tool.

Although a commercial "failure" (IBM never again marketed a dedicated mainframe-based training system), the 1500s helped IBM become one of the largest consumers of internal CAI training in the world.

Another historical first was realized when the potential of the courseware to provide distance learning (inservice) to educators and health care professionals became known. Because public telephone networks were insufficient to deliver the courseware, a contract was let to fabricate 3 mobile van systems that would carry a smaller version of the 1500 system (16 learning stations instead of 32) to locations across North America. Using the "concrete networks," these 8 by 40-foot mobile vans carried two expandable modules that would convert to a 26 by 40-foot stationary classroom. They were developed at the CAI Laboratory at Penn State University and delivered thousands of hours of training in the United States and Canada.

PLATO

In the early 1960s, approximately a dozen years after the first commercial computer became available, a team at the University of Illinois began work on a flat plasma panel for computer terminals and software for a CAI system that was to become known as PLATO. Funded by numerous federal agencies, including the National Science Foundation and the U.S. Office of Education, this effort eventually produced a training system that represents some of the most advanced thinking in the interactive process of communicating learning. Many of the PLATO software tools developed to support learning still serve as models for present-day efforts and are described in a subsequent section.

The primary function of PLATO was to provide a rich environment in which educators and trainers could create and deliver high-quality interactive courseware to students in classrooms, homes, and offices, with or without the presence of an instructor.

PLATO was developed using a commercial mainframe and telecommunications package available from Control Data Corporation (CDC). The student learning stations were designed using flat panel plasma technology. The user had to be connected to the mainframe with a specific type of terminal. It also meant that the courseware and vast amounts of performance data were stored on the mainframe, making it easy to collect and process data, update courseware, and promote communication among users at all levels.

Commercial interest in CAI was rekindled by CDC, which decided to acquire the rights to market PLATO as a training system. CDC at the time was a solid company that was generating significant revenues from its computer business. More importantly, CDC's CEO,

Mr. William Norris, had a vision of using technology to address some of society's more pressing problems. His corporate motto was to address society's unmet needs as a profitable business venture. One of the early applications of PLATO was the development of a complete curriculum for illiterate adults functioning between grades 3 through high school in math, language arts, and reading (Basic Skills and GED Curricula).

During the heyday of CDC-PLATO, a major CMI system was added, an Education Company formed, thousands of hours of courseware developed, and over 100 mainframe systems installed worldwide. Many of these mainframes were linked via high-speed telecommunication hookups.

In the early 1980s, competition began to erode CDC's profits, microcomputers made their appearance, and the era of the mainframe started its now famous slide and decline. The combination of lost revenues and inability to rapidly accommodate the microcomputer market eventually led to the decline of CDC and its mainframe PLATO. It was sold to a Chicago firm which continues today to market a local area network variation of some of the original courseware. CDC itself barely survived as a corporate entity.

The University of Illinois PLATO system continues to operate. In recent years, they developed a system to expand the mainframe's CPU, accommodate standard microcomputers as terminals, and distribute courseware using a sophisticated satellite broadcast system. They are making substantial progress toward their goal of providing instruction to 40,000 simultaneous users across North America at a cost of 50 cents per student per hour.

A local area network subset of PLATO, consisting of the best courseware, was spun off and is now actively marketed under the name PLATO. This version of PLATO retains little of the processing, telecommunication, and database power of the mainframe system and obscures the rich history of the mainframe version described in this chapter.

During the era of PLATO, extensive software utilities were created to enhance the delivery of courseware. Much of this software has never been duplicated, in part due to the orientation of microcomputers and the limitations of local area networks. Now, however, there is extensive development in distance delivery, and the human-computer communication concepts pioneered by PLATO deserve to be examined, for they have much to offer newly developing interactive classrooms.

THE CBI COMMUNICATION PARADIGM

CBI as Communication

Although only a small proportion of the world's population is capable of the sophisticated use of computers, CBI has been used to teach an enormous range of subjects to millions, regardless of their individual level of expertise in communicating with a computer. This requires that the CBI system be so simple and foolproof that lack of experience with a computer can be overcome in a matter of minutes. This term is sometimes called *user-friendly* but I prefer to call it *transparent*. The operation of the computer must be transparent so as not to negatively impact the quality of the learning experience. PLATO provided outstanding examples of transparency. Once the structure of a curriculum was established, a naive computer user could learn to enter and move through it in literally a few minutes time. Even a lack of keyboard skills was no problem due to specially marked keys and the touch-sensitive screen.

Communication with computers made major strides beyond the keyboard by the widespread application of the pointing device (some 20 years after it was invented) and the graphical user interface (GUI). These advances burst on the scene in the early to mid-1980s and are quickly being adopted by many CBI interfaces and electronic message systems, such as QuickMail and Microsoft Mail. Both the pointing device, in the form of a finger-activated touch screen, and the graphics interface were implemented in PLATO in the 1960s.

The Computer as Instructor

CBI is an advanced form of human-computer communication. Early on, it was recognized that computers are superb vehicles for transmitting data and information from one location to another. Fortunately, text-books were once much cheaper, and this discouraged (but did not eliminate) "electronic page turning" and the promotion of "information transmission" as the dominant mode of instruction.

Research conducted by Bloom (1984) suggests that the intelligent one-on-one human tutor results in greater achievement than other forms of instruction. One might hypothesize that this could be due to the individualized and interactive nature of the tutorial situation. One view of CBI attempts to use the computer to "capture" some of the essence of the effective tutorial environment while minimizing unwanted side effects.

Information-Transmission and Information-Processing Models

The cognitive science model of human learning began to gain respectability during the 1960s. In its simplest form, this model suggests we learn best by processing information and constructing our own mental models of our environments, as opposed to passively receiving information. Unlike conventional instruction and most other forms of media, the computer possesses the capacity to engage the learner in a highly individualized form of information processing. This might be said to be the point at which the technological interactive classroom was born.

All forms of instructional media prior to the computer use information transmission models. With the advent of the computer as an instructional tool, interest in the processing of information and analogies with the learning process grew and was translated into many CBI lessons. Interest was renewed in examining learning as a function of the processing performed by the learner (e.g., Anderson et al., 1975; Tenneyson, 1981). The discovery of short-term memory strengthened the resolve to communicate information in ways that would avoid the limitations placed on short-term memory.

At their worst, CBI programs rely on information transmission models of learning in which the emphasis is placed on forming, shaping, and transmitting information to the learner. They may also ignore communication persuasion and motivation theory and practice and in so doing have earned the well-deserved reputation of "electronic pageturners." Adding insult to injury, the ineffectiveness and weakness of electronic pageturner forms of CBI can be masked through another form of communication: excellent or attractive use of graphic design, color, animation, fonts, and other presentation forms.

The information-processing model, loosely applied to instruction, intersperses the presentation of information with activities that cause the learner to think about or process the information. The processing of information allows the learner to compare new information with old and use them both to form new schema or mental models of the world. And so the process continues—presentation and processing in an organized iterative manner. The distinctive feature of CBI is that the interaction occurs frequently, for example, over minutes, rather than the longer periods of time we associate with lecture or other group-paced forms of instruction. The major strength of CBI is its ability to teach using a combination of individualization and information processing (Alessi & Trollip, 1991).

The communication aspects of CBI are numerous. The instructor communicates the information, skills, and concepts deemed important by the choice of learning activities. The author communicates how the instruction will proceed. The student communicates by "depositing'" performance data in data structures from which they can provide valuable feedback to the student, instructor, and lesson author. This information is then used to assist each individual student where he or she is having difficulty and to improve the quality of the instruction. Finally, the tutor communicates information to the learner about his performance on items, groups of items (objectives), time expended, and performance relative to similar students or to preset criteria of quality.

Effectiveness of Learning with CBI

Hundreds of research and four meta-analytic studies comparing CBI with conventional instruction have been conducted. The studies cover elementary, junior high, secondary schools, adult education and training, and mathematics education (e.g., Bangert-Drowns, Kulik, & Kulik, 1985; Kulik, Kulik, & Cohen, 1980; Kulik, Kulik, & Schwalb, 1986; Lee, 1990; Niemiec, Samson, Weinstein, & Walberg, 1987).

Three major conclusions arise from these meta-analyses studies. First, achievement is modestly but significantly better under CBI. Second, learning efficiency or amount learned per unit time is strongly and significantly better under CBI (studies have reported reductions in learning time of 20% to 33%). Finally, student attitude toward learning and content is significantly and positively affected by CBI.

These advantages are viewed positively by commercial trainers because trainees can learn well in less time. Because wages of trainees are being paid by the organization, the bottom line is improved if training can be minimized. Professional educators, on the other hand, place limited or no value on trainee time and thus generally do not perceive these research findings as major advantages.

A THREE-PART COMPUTER-BASED INSTRUCTION MODEL OF COMMUNICATION

A three-part model serves to illustrate the fundamental components of communication in CBI. These models include the basic CBI paradigm (Figure 11.1), the CBI paradigm in which both the instructor and computer are directly involved with the student (Figure 11.2), and a model in which data/information plays a vital role (Figure 11.3).

This process can be thought of as the courseware author "cloning" a part of himself into a computer that tutors the student. The extent of the cloning and the completeness of the process will be determined by a num-

$$I \longrightarrow C \longleftrightarrow S$$

**Figure 11.1. The Instructor/Computer/Student
Communication Paradigm**

ber of factors, including whether the courseware is supplementary to the instructor in the classroom or functions in an independent and stand-alone fashion. The philosophy taken by the majority of authors of PLATO lessons is that courseware would fit into the latter category.

$$I \longrightarrow C$$

In this model, "I" represents the instructor or team of authors responsible for "delivering" the instruction or courseware. In those cases in which the instructor and courseware author are one and the same, communication about the courseware itself is not needed. If they are different, however, a great deal of communication and probably an extensive amount of exposure to the courseware by the instructor will be required. To properly deliver the courseware, the instructor needs to know its content, instructional methodology, and installation and operating parameters. Instructors are likely to improperly use or even stop using the courseware if their expectations of it are substantially different from how the courseware actually functions.

The left side of Figure 11.1 indicates a one-way communication arrow from I to C, the computer or CBI tutor. This represents the production or authoring phase of the courseware that will tutor the student. Notice that little communication flows back to the instructor in this basic model. As a communication enterprise, a sophisticated form of the systematic design of instruction (ISD), with special attention paid to the delivery features (strengths and limitations) of the computer is required. I call this art form Computer-Based Instructional Systems Design or CBISD. A partial list of those adaptations, over and above standard ISD elements, would contain the following:

1. Design that optimizes the unique features of the computer (among media that is) in eliciting information-processing thinking from the student.
2. A clear and graphical representation of the complete range of individual paths and options available to the student in completing the lessons.
3. The plan for creation and integration of visuals with text pre-

sentation, including drawings, photos, animations, audio, and video.

4. Specification of the distinct roles and functions provided by the computer and the instructor in the case of synchronous delivery.

5. Thorough and extensive validation of the courseware prior to release. This is particularly important in the asynchronous delivery format.

6. Communicate as to the role of each team member, as well as the form and nature of what each produces and the time frame for producing it.

An Example: Lower Division Engineering Curriculum

An example from PLATO will serve to illustrate. During the 1980s, CDC's Education Company developed thousands of hours of courseware. One of those projects was the creation of a 1-year course for first-year inorganic chemistry students. The course was to be developed by a team at the University of Alberta, and the 45 component lessons were to be reviewed at three different stages of development by six different subject experts, located in five different states and Canada with a budget limited to three face-to-face meetings.

The communication problem was easily solved as all six sites were linked into a complex network that could handle the bandwidth needed to transmit graphics-based data files quickly and easily. Each lesson was created in electronic format on the PLATO system. When each lesson was ready for review, it was transmitted electronically and received by the reviewers. The whole process took less than a few minutes.

The reviewers were able to immediately begin the review. But could they communicate their editorial suggestions back to the author as easily? To do this they used a built-in feature called "Comment." This is an online notes file linked specifically to the current lesson. When the reviewer wants to make a suggestion at any time during a lesson review, he simply invokes Comment and types his suggestion while the screen is visible. The comment is tagged with vital information, such as the lesson name, unit, and exact screen from which the comment was made, and sent to an electronic notes file where it is instantly available to developers, reviewers, authors, and project managers at each distant location.

Using this tool, the 1-2 week mail turnaround time for each lesson was cut to seconds (facsimile transmission was not widely available at this time, would not have been as fast, and was considerably more expensive). Multiplied by the number of lessons, number of reviews, and number of reviewers, the time savings were enormous.

$$C \longleftrightarrow S$$

The two-way arrow between computer and student in Figure 11.1 represents several events or activities.

- Presentation of information through a wide means of communication media, including text, graphics, sound, animation, photographs, and video, to the student.
- Inclusion of process-stimulating activities to the student. These are activities that cause the learner to actively process the information to be learned in such a way as to optimize the learning process. An example would be to provide practice exercises in identifying the concepts or skills presented during the lesson or previously.
- Evaluation of student responses to items and activities and generalized student performance according to some criteria established by the author or student.
- Student responses to activities and exercises submitted to the computer for evaluation. Typical student response modes that can be evaluated by machine are click/touch, short answer, move object, time, tries, conditional, and some combination of these six modes. Student responses, which may be stored in the computer for later evaluation by an Instructor, include long essays, computer programs, attitude surveys, and so on, and will be discussed under the data storage addition to the model in Figure 11.3.
- Student queries to a database using a structured query language protocol. In some CBI lessons, the student must use the program to obtain information, which is then used to make decisions. Simulation programs often make extensive use of this technique. The database that can be queried is usually small enough to be contained as part of the CBI courseware. In some cases (e.g., Montgomerie et al., 1991), the subject of the training is how to search distant online library databases, and the practice involves actual searches of external, distant library databases as an integral part of the lesson.
- Student control over the scope or sequence of sections of a lesson to be completed. When the decisions to be made are relatively few, it is called *student control*. When, however, the options are extensive and tied to large databases of visual and textual data and the student is permitted free access to any resource at any time, the process is called *navigation*. An example of navigation is found in Apple's CD-ROM program called "The Virtual Museum."

Communication between computer and student is currently limited by the artificiality of the interface, for example, no voice or complex language input recognized or output created, the experience or creativity of the author, and the lack of intelligence of the machine.

There are also limits in the nuances observed when one attempts to impart humor or sarcasm in a communication. Because these often depend on context, body language, and the inflections and tone of voice, they are extremely difficult to communicate using only text/graphics media. On the other hand, there is little chance of transmitting errors by having a student take seriously a comment meant to be lighthearted or sarcastic.

Adding Instructor Communication to the Process

The involvement of the instructor is illustrated in Figure 11.2. Comparison with Figure 11.1 reveals the same relation between I and C and that a new double headed arrow has been added between I and S. This represents a communication link in which the instructor may be physically present with the student during CBI or in communication with the student through telephone, computer messaging, or even videoconferencing. Another dimension has been added.

The communication between I and S may be synchronous, that is, simultaneous. Alternatively, there may be a significant time delay in the loop as in, for example, a student input or submission and instructor response which are stored and retrieved by machine. This is referred to as asynchronous communication. The I-S communication may be categorized into four conditions as shown in Figure 11.2a. The intersections of the four conditions are represented by one of four numbered conditions.

Local instructor-synchronous time. In this case the instructor is present and able to communicate directly with the student. The instructor-student communication in this condition can take on a variety of forms, such as coaching, trouble-shooting, elaborating, extending the topics being studied, providing additional examples, and challenging/motivating students.

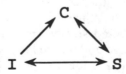

Figure 11.2. The IC/S paradigm with direct I-S communication

INSTRUCTOR

		Local	Distant
T I M E	Synchronous	1	2
	Asynchronous	3	4

Figure 11.2a. The intermediate CBI communication
paradigm with added I-S communication

In cases in which CBI is designed to operate in the absence of an instructor as is the case with most PLATO courseware, large student classrooms can be made available for learning. The classrooms may not need the physical presence of course instructors or even subject matter proctors. Thus, students taking different lessons and different courses could use the same classroom simultaneously. This has numerous scheduling and manpower loading implications and advantages for efficient or reconceptualized use of classroom space, such as schools without walls.

Distant instructor-synchronous time. Cell 2 provides for the same type of interaction as cell 1 if separate telecommunications facilities are available. If those facilities involve video, face-to-face communication is also possible. PLATO has several features that facilitate this mode of CBI communication.

The first of these is "Term-Talk," which permits interactive communication between an Instructor and Student signed on to a linked PLATO system anywhere in the world. Talk can be initiated by either party with a simple keypress, and the recipient's screen flashes a message. The recipient responds with a keypress and two scrolling lines for each communicator appear at the bottom of the screen.

The talk feature can be authorized by instructors and toggled on or off if one is busy and does not wish to be interrupted. This facility is also used extensively by authors when they experience difficulty and wish to avail themselves of the services of a consultant.

The "monitor" mode enables the instructor to provide a higher level of help by being able to directly monitor the screen of the student. The instructor can see the actual portions of the lesson where the student requests help. The protocol is that the monitor mode be used only with the advance permission of the student. While a screen is being monitored, a message flashes at the bottom of the screen indicating that monitoring is occurring and the name of the person who is monitoring.

If the Instructor feels it is important to "guide" or coach the student through a particular sequence in a lesson, the instructor can, with permission, take control of the student's screen and direct the flow of the lesson, just as if the student were operating the terminal. Once again, permission has to be obtained. Bear in mind that this happens when instructor and student are close or over a thousand kilometers apart.

Talk and monitor mode can be activated simultaneously so that the instructor and student can communicate about the specific events they are seeing simultaneously on the screen. In some cases, a separate telephone line enables the monitor mode to occur simultaneously with a telephone conversation.

Another mode allows people to interactively compete in real time in games and simulations. This application, of course, requires extensive and careful lesson design. The classic application is an interactive simulation of a military airfight between airplanes. Numerous educationally significant applications have been made of this facility, including one that allows numerous users to express their views on a topic and have the results build interactively as they vote. The purpose is to allow people to vote on an issue with varying levels of knowledge of how other people have voted, using a variation of the Delphi technique.

Although these PLATO features are described in terms of instructor-student interactions, they were also used quite heavily among lesson authors, programmers, systems analysts, and others responsible for maintenance and management of the system.

Local instructor-asynchronous time. Cell 3 of Figure 11.2a represents the case in which, although the instructor is physically present in the room, he is unable to communicate directly with a particular student. Perhaps the instructor is otherwise engaged or distracted, as is often the case in conventional instruction. In the case of remedial instruction, as much as 60% of the instructor's time is spent performing routine clerical chores.

Distant instructor-asynchronous time. Cell 4 of Figure 11.2a describes a situation in which the real-time communication described in Cell 2 is not useful. For example, when the instructor is in one time zone and the student is in another, and either is outside the normal 8-5 workday, online communication may be inhibited. A project in which this happened is described later in this chapter.

THE ADVANCED MODEL OF CBI
COMMUNICATION: ADDING DATA

The addition of data to the I-C-S model is illustrated in Figure 11.3. The various arrows represent unique forms of communication. In this context, communications and data may be stored in some format, to be recalled and acted on at some time after they were actually posted. In order for this to happen, there is obviously a need for sophisticated software to sort, route, classify, catalogue, and alert users to the existence of communication ("You have unread e-mail" or "Your in box is 75% full. Please take appropriate action."). Some have called these intervenors, intelligent assistants, personal support systems, or just plain pests.

In addition to this organizing and cross-referencing software, massive data storage capabilities were provided by PLATO. As microcomputers and local area networks become more powerful, the need for the software will re-appear, and programs will be created. Indeed, there are already several commercial products available on the market. As yet, however, they are quite separate and divorced from the interactive CBI environment. The storage space and software to manipulate them will simply be called "data" at this point. The S-D arrow indicates data generated by the student. This data may serve numerous purposes such as:

- student performance scores (item, objective, lesson, course, etc.)
- student decisions, such as choices of optional paths through the lesson
- lesson decisions in which, for example, a student's scores qualify him to skip a section of the lesson
- questions, notes, or messages sent as electronic mail to instructors, fellow students, or the author of the lesson.

The C-D arrow represents the fact that the data are stored in the computer memory, accessed, and manipulated in a dynamic way. One of the manipulations is to render the data easily accessible for examination, response, or further action.

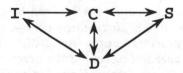

Figure 11.3. The advanced CBI communication paradigm with data
added to the I-S-C communication

Notes files. Several examples of the D interactions from PLATO are illustrated. The term Notes is an electronic mail facility that allows instructors and students to communicate either on a one-to-one personal and confidential basis or on a group bulletin board basis. The student simply invokes the notes option, specifies the recipient(s), types the message, and sends it on its way. The recipient would receive notification of the arrival of unread mail on the subsequent signon and could choose to read, discard, archive, or reply to the message. There are numerous support features involved, including an index to the names and group assignments of all registered users anywhere in the world. Paramount is the ease of use of the system. By typing a shifted character and entering the name and group of the recipient, the notation system could be accessed to send, receive, or manipulate messages using several different options.

Comment files. Student input is particularly important during formative evaluation and can be gathered through the use of the term *comment* as described earlier in this chapter.

A true story illustrates. An author was creating the first in a series of 32 modules of training for a large metropolitan area police force (Szabo, 1987). When asked about the progress of the project, the new author offered several comments, including one that caught the attention of the interviewer. It seemed that some of the officers expressed verbal concerns about the first lesson, which were dismissed as the grumbling of officers not used to this new form of training. The interviewer explained the feature to the author, who decided to make it available to the officers to voice their concerns. Within a week of the activation of comment, over 1,000 comments were logged! On inspection, it became clear that the majority of the comments identified numerous flaws of content and spelling in the lesson, which were subsequently and quickly corrected. Comments became a sought after and regular part of all subsequent lessons created for this project.

Progress and performance information. Because PLATO students interact with CBI from a central mainframe, performance records are stored centrally and instantaneously made available for all students in all lessons. Software is developed that organizes student performance data from a massive database and provides a wide range of reporting functions to the instructor. Information can be obtained on groups and/or individuals relative to curriculum, course, module, objective, or item performance. A structured query can identify students who were at the time of the query ahead of or behind the average performance of the class. These students can be singled out for additional assistance or enhancement.

Student routers. Another valuable use of the data is to provide not only performance feedback, but progress feedback to each individual student. When a student signed on to the PLATO Basic Skill Course, for example, he entered a massive curriculum which covered five course areas from grades 3 to 9. Of course, it is difficult for a student to keep track of his progress through several hundred lessons. A system was designed (Figure 11.4) that was invoked at each signon. The student was told which lessons he started, completed, and mastered. As well, he was informed which lessons were available (those whose prerequisites had been satisfied) and those which would be available after other prerequisites had been satisfied. At that point the student could ask for more progress information or proceed directly to the next lesson to study.

INTRODUCTION TO CONCEPTS OF MATHEMATICS	
WHICH MODULE DO YOU WANT TO WORK ON NOW?	
MODULES YOU CAN WORK ON NOW:	TESTS TAKEN
a. Solutions by Graphing	0
f. Solutions by simultaneous equations	0
MASTERED MODULES YOU CAN REVIEW	
c. Number Systems	3
e. Polynomials	1
MODULES YOU CAN WORK ON LATER:	PREREQUISITES
b. Conic Sections	a
d. Geometry	a
g. Trigonometry	f

1. See how well you're doing	3. Review Instructions
2. Work in a different course	4. Read and write notes

Figure 11.4. Sample student router

Performance data summaries. Individual performance data were also used to communicate information about a learner's progress, based on data collected from within the lessons. The value of this information in an environment in which the learner is separated physically from instructors or human tutors should not be underestimated. Furthermore, extensive research (e.g, Forsyth 1991; Tenneyson, 1981) has shown "computer advisement" to increase learning and possible metacognitive activities.

One of the major shortcomings of correspondence or distance learning is the lack of timely feedback on progress and performance available to the learner. With PLATO, on completion of a tutorial lesson, the student reviews personal levels of achievement relative to preselected mastery criteria on the objectives of the lesson just completed, the current module, and current course. In addition, the student can easily find out what lessons had been started but not completed as well as what lessons lay ahead. And with the prescriptive function of CMI in operation, he receives a wide array of study assignments, each of which focuses on the specific learning weakness of the individual.

On completion of each lesson, the performance and progress records are updated and results made available to the student with confidentiality. One example of the many performance feedback summary formats is shown in Figure 11.5. The student can quickly obtain an accurate picture of his level of learning on the specific module depicted.

The same data are available to the instructor through the I-D linkage. In this case, the instructor can examine the performance and progress records of individuals, classes, or groups of students for which he has responsibility. A powerful database query program extracts the data and equally powerful report functions format the data in an easy to

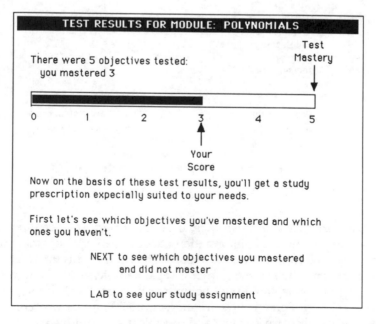

Figure 11.5. Sample performance data summary

access and understand format. The commands to access the data in numerous ways or formats are menu driven and can be learned in a brief instructor-training workshop. Figure 11.6 illustrates the choices available to view student performance information.

The same data are available to the instructor through the I-D linkage. In this case, the instructor can examine the performance and progress records of individuals, classes, or groups of students for which he has responsibility. A powerful database query program extracts the data and equally powerful report functions format the data in an easy to access and understand format. The commands to access the data in numerous ways or formats are menu driven and can be learned in a brief instructor-training workshop. Figure 11.6 illustrates the choices available to view student performance information.

The performance information for individual students can be examined as easily as the above information. In Figure 11.11, the progress of one hypothetical student is displayed. The instructor can quickly assess the progress of this student and decide what actions, if any, are needed. With paced instruction and the monitoring of time to respond or complete instruction, the instructor can obtain information about a given student's rate of learning. For situations or selection procedures in which speed of learning or performance is an important factor, this data communicates additional valuable information about the learner that can be used to modify the instructional environment or to select people for tasks. Inspection of Figure 11.7 provides a visual indicator of different rates of learning present in a typical classroom.

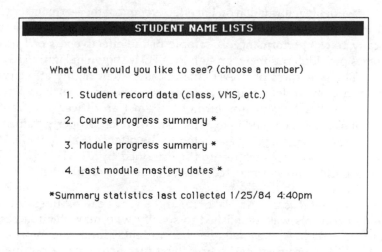

Figure 11.6. Instructor menu for student data

```
┌─────────────────────────────────────────────────────────────┐
│ Curriculum/Group:  obac/asdalg        1/25/84  4:30 pm        │
│                                                               │
│   COURSE #1      CLASS    A B C D E F G H I J K L              │
│   bill radke       1      ■ ■ ■ □ - - -       -               │
│   bruce myers      1      ■ ■ ■ ■ ■ ■ ■       -               │
│   bryan jeffries   3      ■ ■ ■ - - - - -                     │
│   kevin helfrick   3      ■ ■ ■ □ - - - - - -                 │
│   candy gentry     2      ■ ■ ■ □ - - - - -                   │
│   caroline petra   1      ■ ■ ■ ■ ■ - - - - -                 │
│   dan bettis       1      ■ ■ ■ □ - - - - - -                 │
│   darrel canterbury 3     ■ ■ ■ □ - - - - - -                 │
│   diane freeburg   1      ■ ■ ■ ■ ■ ■ ■ □                     │
│   doug boletto     3      □ - - - - - -   -                   │
│   john hartman     1      ■ ■ □ - - - - - -                   │
│   gerry stouthart  2      ■ - - - - - -   -                   │
│   gerry lee        3      ■ - - - - - -   -                   │
│   gwen lothar      1      ■ ■ ■ □ - - - - -                   │
│   joan lugios      3      ■ ■ ■ ■ ■ - - - - - -               │
│   judy schaeffer   3      ■ ■ ■ □ - - - - -                   │
│   vincent ortiz    3      ■ - - - - - -   -                   │
│                                                               │
│   ✓ = course mastered,   - = module assigned                  │
│   □ = module started,    ■ = module mastered                  │
└─────────────────────────────────────────────────────────────┘
```

Figure 11.7. Individual learner progress reports

Valuable information on the effectiveness of the learning activities used in CBI can be obtained through appropriate software which automatically tracks performance. A sample of the effectiveness of learning resources provided routinely through PLATO is shown in Figure 11.12.

These features of PLATO make the system highly attractive to agencies that must demonstrate training accountability, such as a police department. If a lawsuit was brought against an officer, the training department could be called in to demonstrate it had properly trained the officer in the specific objectives related to the offense (Szabo, 1987). With the extensive performance records maintained by PLATO, these data can be collected and summarized, often in a matter of minutes.

Controlled access. An elaborate and sophisticated but easy-to-use system of controls was established to specify who may obtain access to performance data. At the lowest level, a student is limited to information about only his progress and scores. The instructor may examine this information, as well as the data regarding all students under his direction. The security of the system is such that confidential testing can be done on the system with no concerns for breach of security. This issue arose when CBI was provided through PLATO to train inmates in a maximum security prison in Canada. Although public telephone lines were used, a thorough investigation by the Royal Canadian Mounted Police determined that the security of the system could not be breached.

The confidentiality feature was used at the University of Delaware's PLATO system for anonymous counseling. Anonymous notefiles were set up for students to discuss, in confidence, personal or social problems they were facing. Trained counselors would deposit their responses into linked notesfile in which a student could read them. The notefiles were only accessible by the individual student, and confidentiality was maintained at all times. The system was judged to be highly effective for students.

One clarifying fact makes these advanced forms of communication more amazing in light of today's stand-alone or local area networking. The PLATO communication can take place between individuals located anywhere in the world, so long as they have access to "linked" mainframe computers around the world. The computer communication uses public telephone networks and numerous local nodes which require only local telephone call charges. Currently, the same features are possible through a combination of one-way satellite communication (comput-

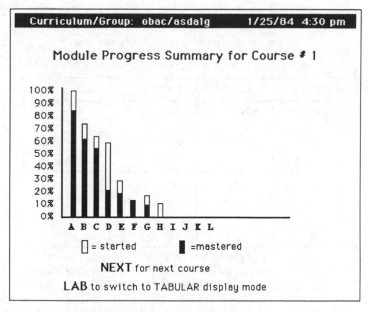

Figure 11.8. Class progress report

Figure 11.9. Class test performance on module A

| | Overall | Test | | |
		First	Second	Third
Tests Mastered*	20	10	8	2
Percent Score	67	59	80	100
Average Test Duration (min.)	4	3	4	5

Curriculum/Group: obac/asdalg   1/25/84 4:30 pm

COURSE #1   MODULE A

Students started: 23   Average number of tests: 2
Average number of tests taken before mastery: 1.65

* Only the first mastery by each student is counted.

Diane Freeburg / asdalg   1/26/84 5:54 pm

Course #1   Module A: "Integer Sum"

2 tests taken   Module mastered on 10/28/83

TEST	FIRST	SECOND	LAST
DATE	10/21/83	10/28/83	
TIME	12:40 PM	8:52 AM	
DURATION	1 min.	5 min.	
SCORE	0	100	
POSSIBLE	100	100	
PERCENT	0%	100%	

EDIT to change this record
NEXT for objective status   SHIFT-NEXT for next module
LAB for assignments   SHIFT-LAB for group averages

Figure 11.10. Module test history for one student

```
┌─────────────────────────────────────────────────────────┐
│ Diane Freeburg / asdalg              1/26/84  5:54 pm    │
│                                                          │
│ Course 1: Sets/Numbers                                   │
│ Started:  10/21/83  Last Test: Module H, 1/16/84         │
│                     Last Mastery: Module G, 11/07/83     │
│  ┌──────────────────────────────────────────────────┐   │
│  │ MODULE   STATUS    MASTERED    SCORE    TESTS      │   │
│  │   A     mastered   10/28/83   100 of 100    2      │   │
│  │   B     mastered   10/28/83   100 of 100    1      │   │
│  │   C     mastered   10/29/83   100 of 100    1      │   │
│  │   D     mastered   11/01/83   100 of 100    2      │   │
│  │   E     mastered   11/02/83   100 of 100    4      │   │
│  │   F     mastered   11/03/83   100 of 100    2      │   │
│  │   G     mastered   11/07/83   100 of 100    1      │   │
│  │   H     available              0 of 100            │   │
│  │   I     available                                  │   │
│  │   J     available                                  │   │
│  │   K     available                                  │   │
│  │   L     available                                  │   │
│  └──────────────────────────────────────────────────┘   │
│  LAB for next student       EDIT to change this record   │
└─────────────────────────────────────────────────────────┘
```

Figure 11.11. Course progress for one student

Learning Resource Effectiveness Stats		Times	%
*	TITLE	USED	SUCCESS
13	Read: Mathematics Guide, pp 1.3-1.5	6	33%
1	Read: M Series 10 pp 13-21	6	33%
2	Read: Mathematics Guide, pp 2.4-2.9	11	27%
3	Read: M Series 10 pp 34-49	8	25%
6	Read: Mathematics Guide, 658-660	9	22%
9	Visual:Film 32, Mathematics and People	5	20%
7	Lecure, Mathematics Applications	10	20%
4	CAI Lesson: Unit 6 B	5	20%
11	Read: Mathematics Puzzles, 54-59	6	17%
5	Read: Invitation to Math, pp 474-487	7	14%
8	Audio:Tape 21, Computers and Math	7	14%
10	Lab: Exeriment 1A: π	0	
12	Audio:Tape 25 C	0	

SHIFT-DATA to list resources by position
BACK   to option list
SHIFT-HELP to clear learning resource usage information

Figure 11.12. Effectiveness data on learning resources

er to learner) and dedicated telephone line return (learner to computer). The response time of 2/5 of a second is by and large maintained.

The recent trend to link microcomputers through local, campus, national, and international networks has brought us full circle; we are once again faced with establishing features and controls in order to maintain security, control viruses, and enforce copyright, ownership, and licensing agreements. More importantly, we are faced with rethinking the whole process of human-computer communication.

TRY TO REMEMBER THE FUTURE

To appreciate the enormity of the change we are facing and the rapidity with which it is taking place, we must take a look at where instructional computing is heading. Although the precise twists and turns are yet to unfold, there are some predictable trends from the hardware and communications industry. The tone is set by the forecast that the cost of computing will continue to decline at an annual rate of 25% for the foreseeable future, continuing an unbroken trend which began in the 1950's.

Powerful Microcomputers as Learning Workstations

The first of these changes deals with the power of desktop micros. Desktop computers are acquiring the power once capable only in mainframes. One implication is that these computers will be able to easily handle the full range of media required for effective communication, CBI or not.

Highly Integrated Worldwide Networks

The second major change deals with the distribution of data through networks. Today, computers share resources and files by being connected together using a combination of hardware and software known as networks. A network of 25-30 microcomputers doing moderate amounts of data processing will cause today's networks to run very slowly. When large files, such as those containing graphics or video, are sent over the network, the network grinds to a halt and becomes unusable.

Networks of the future will be fast and powerful enough to link every school, home, business, and office in large metropolitan areas and international regions. Communicating with students will be as easy as turning on a computer. Network "farms" will appear so that idle resources in anyone's microcomputer in the network can be accessed when others are busy (with appropriate privileges, of course).

The area known as multimedia will also receive a major boost. Currently, motion color video and animation occupy significant amounts of file space and require extremely high bandwidth to transmit. Networks are expected to be available to handle these requirements near the end of this decade. This means that telecomputers (microcomputers with video capabilities) will enable us to communicate with students using vast amounts of high-quality, full-motion, compressed video and audio. Students will carry pocket multimedia machines capable of the most sophisticated forms of information delivery and high-speed communications. And the machines will be equipped with cellular technology. A student will be able to, from a park bench, for example, dial distant databases around the world and learn.

The addition of multimedia will press design capabilities to the limit. For some time to come, electronic pageturners will be replaced by electronic graphics devices, which have little effect on learning but will be perceived by educators, media specialists, and administrators alike as indispensable to the learning process.

Object-Oriented Software Creation

A third change will be in the way we create software and courseware (program). Today's cumbersome computer languages, such as C and PASCAL, are being replaced by OOPS (Object-Oriented Programming Systems), higher level programming languages that deal with larger chunks of instructions that are grouped for more efficient programming and are represented visually. Object-oriented features have already appeared in authoring tools such as Authorware Professional™ and IconAuthor™.

These changes are practically guaranteed. Their speed of dissemination into widespread use is somewhat unpredictable, but they will occur (Martin, 1992). Even as this chapter is being written, the Los Angeles Times writes of a major consortium of six industrial giants who will develop personal digital assistants and associated software. These will be oriented toward the consumer market and be capable of communicating anywhere in the world using wire or wireless communications. The software base is already well under way, with a 10-year time frame targeted.

These technological developments will change in a major way how we produce and revise software and courseware, coupled with new ways of thinking about educational problems. New ways of thinking will be more difficult to grasp yet will change the way we handle educational information.

Implications for Education and Training

Consider a few simplistic and hypothetical examples of education. A student initiates a telecomputer call to his instructor. By the time the call is put through, the student's academic records have appeared on the computer screen of the instructor, next to the student's image. The student is in Caracas, the instructor in Ohio.

An instructor finishes a videoconference with the curriculum development team of an open learning institution. He then sits down at his workstation to send off a lesson design to colleagues, after which he searches several libraries in distant cities for the latest information on the topic for which he is developing a set of interactive multimedia lessons.

Consider the training of new salespersons. A 3-week trip to a major center with all the attendant costs can be reduced to one or two weeks using CBI and distance education. The cost savings are impressive indeed.

The major questions become: What should the "school" of the future look like? How will we get there? We must be careful that our limited view of the future does not cause us to dismiss technological change as unrealistic. How limiting was the comment of the early visitor to Henry Ford's first assembly line when he asked, "But where will we get enough chauffeurs to drive all these cars?" Equally limiting was the mentality that persisted until the late 1940s, which said that airplanes would make their mark as a personal means of travel, rather than carry hundreds of passengers at a time over thousands of miles (Soffo, 1992).

At least two lessons are clear from these observations. First, training must have top priority, for untrained people will hinder progress. Second, as we look back on some our finest achievements and learn from them, we must not forget the future as we move toward it.

Lessons From History about Innovative Change and Time Frames

A closing note about remembering the past. People and organizations pass through three stages of adaptation to new technologies or innovations. In Stage 1, they play with and learn about the innovation. Many of the things they do with the technology are of little value other than for purposes of learning and finding out how the thing works. Next comes Stage 2 in which they employ the technology to assist them in their daily vocational and personal chores to do the things they currently do, only more efficiently or effectively. After some time, they begin to use the innovation to help them achieve goals or solve problems that were never considered in the past because solutions were out of reach. At this stage, creativity comes into full play, and the possibilities are limitless.

Finally, dismiss those who criticize technological applications on the grounds that they have not delivered what was promised or when it was promised. Such comments are made by people who do not understand the time-lag factor in innovation. There is a time period between the development and widespread application of an innovation. The industrial revolution time lag was 150 years! For high technology (the mouse and laser, for example), the time lag was about 20 years. For educational innovation, the time lag is longer, probably about 40-50 years. Soffo (1992) estimated the time lag at 30 years.

If we consider CBI and telecommunications as hybrids between educational and technological innovations, it is reasonable to predict widespread adoption (Stage 2) will occur sometime after 20 years from invention, but before 50 years have elapsed. As CBI was "invented" around 1960, we can expect to see widespread implementation between 1980 and 2010. We are probably in the right place at the right time to witness, be a part of, and influence this development. And some will undoubtedly be around after 2010 to carry the development through Stage 2 and on into Stage 3. To those, I say, remember the future.

REFERENCES

Bloom, B. S. (1984). The 2 sigma problem: The search for methods of group instruction as effective as one-to-one tutoring. *Educational Researcher, 13,* 4-16.

Alessi, S. M., & Trollip, S. R. (1991). *Computer-based instruction: Methods and development.* (2nd ed.). Englewood Cliffs, NJ: Prentice-Hall.

Anderson, T., Anderson, R., Dalgaard, B., Paden, D., Biddle, B., Durber, H., & Alessi, S. M. (1975). An experimental evaluation of a computer based study management system. *Educational Psychologist, 11,* 184-190.

Bangert-Drowns, R. L., Kulik, J. A., & Kulik, C. C. (1985). Effectiveness of computer-based education in secondary schools. *Journal of Computer-Based Instruction, 12,* 59-68.

Forsyth, K. E. (1991). *Computer assisted instruction: Advisement and interactions with selected learner characteristics in learning 10th grade mathematics.* Unpublished masters thesis, University of Alberta, Edmonton, Canada.

Kulik, J.A., Kulik, C.C., & Cohen, P.A. (1980). Effectiveness of computer-based college teaching: A meta-analysis of findings. *Review of Educational Research, 50,* 525-544.

Kulik, J.A., Kulik, C.C., & Schwalb, B.J. (1986). The effectiveness of computer-based adult education: A meta-analysis. *Journal of Educational*

Computing Research, 2, 235-249.

Lee, W.C. (1990). *The effectiveness of computer-assisted instruction and computer programming in elementary and secondary mathematics: A meta-analysis*. Unpublished doctoral dissertation, University of Massachusetts.

Martin, J. (1992, November 8). An evening with James Martin. A public lecture presented at the Pacific Palisades Hotel, Singapore.

Montgomerie, T.C., Szabo, M., Johnson, D., Russell, F., Housch, E., Rempel, P., & Maxwell, F. (1991). Online access to information. *Dispatch*. Edmonton: Newsletter of Computing Systems, University of Alberta.

Niemiec, R., Samson, G., Weinstein, T., & Walberg, H.J. (1987). The effects of instructional technology in elementary schools: A quantitative synthesis. *Journal of Research on Computing in Education, 20*, 85-103.

Soffo, P. (1992). Paul Soffo and the 30 year rule. *Design World, 24*, 16-23.

Szabo, M. (1987). A cost-effective implementation of computer based training within a large government training organization. *Interactive Learning International, 4*, 81-84.

Szabo, M., & Montgomerie, T.C. (1992). Two decades of research on computer managed instruction. *Journal of Research on Computing in Education, 25*, 113-133

Tenneyson, R.D. (1981). Use of adaptive information for advisement in learning concepts and rules using computer-assisted instruction. *American Educational Research Journal, 18*, 425-438.

Chapter Twelve

Internetwork Resources*

Fay Sudweeks
University of Sydney
Mauri Collins
Pennsylvania State University
John December
Rensselaer Polytechnic University

NETWORKING

"I have a network account, a computer and a modem," you say, "but they aren't much use to me. I don't know what to do when I get connected, I don't understand networks. I don't even know how this modem works."

Let's take a step-by-step introduction to internetworking and learn how to transfer files, connect to remote machines, exchange mail, talk to distant people, and find out just about anything you need to know. If you try our instructions and have difficulties with them, please consult your site's network consultants or system administrator for access information that may be specific to your site.

---

*The authors thank Zane Berge, Georgetown University, Sheizaf Rafaeli, Hebrew University of Jerusalem, and Brian Logan, Cambridge University, for their support and constructive comments.

Modems

A *modem* is a piece of equipment that plugs into a computer and a phone jack to connect the "stand-alone" computer to a network of computers. When you are connected, messages you type on the computer are sent over a phone line to communicate with other computers and computer users. A modem that transmits information back and forth at 2400 bits of information a second (bps) is fast enough for most needs. There are also slower modems and much faster modems.

Networks

Having established a connection with a network of computers, either with a modem or with a direct link to a fileserver or mainframe, we now need to understand a little more about networks. In one sense, *network* refers to the actual physical connections between and among computers: the wires, fiber-optic cables, microwave links, phone lines, and so forth, that physically tie computers together and allow their users to communicate with one another.

These directly connected networks come in all sizes from local area networks (LANs) of two or three machines linked together in a single room to international wide-area networks (WANs) that span the globe and include satellites and microwave transmission to move the information. The physical setup of networks can be likened to a patchwork of independent telephone companies, serving their own area and yet linked together so that they can exchange the virtual equivalent of long-distance phone calls.

The Internet

The first wide-area computer network in the United States was established more than 20 years ago. Known as ARPANET, this network linked research universities and military installations so that researchers could communicate with one another and share expensive resources (like computers and databases).

Over the years, ARPANET was joined by an ever-increasing number of national, regional, and local networks and became known as the Internet, the backbone of which is the NSFNET. National networks, such as AARNET (Australian Academic and Research Network), have a layered structure: local networks connect to one of six regional hubs, regional hubs connect to a national hub, and the national network becomes part of the Internet with a link to California. More than 10,000 of these individual networks connect more than 20 million users worldwide, and it is this vast network of networks that is known as the Internet.

Protocols

A composite network of the complexity and diversity of the Internet is possible because the computers responsible for circulating the messages among and between them use a common "language" or standard for sending and receiving information. The standard, or set of instructions, is TCP/IP (Transmission Control Protocol/Internet Protocol) and is followed by all Internet-linked computers for transmitting information. BITnet (Because It's Time Network) and UUCP (Unix to Unix Copy Program) networked computers are, on the other hand, physically interconnected by leased telephone lines. They use different sets of protocols (RSCS/NJE in the case of BITnet) and are connected to the Internet by "gateways." "Gatewaying" computers is vital to the successful transmission of data between networks because they translate alternative protocol sets into TCP/IP and allow messages to pass through the backbone transparently between networks.

Transmission Lines

The backbone of the Internet network in the United States is made up of what AT&T calls their "T3" communications lines. These lines comprise the NSFNET, managed by the National Science Foundation (NSF), and refer to the high-speed data transmission lines permanently connecting the major routing computers in the network. These T3 lines can be considered the super highways of data transmission. The T3 lines, carrying 44.736 megabits (million bits of information) a second, have been upgraded recently from T1s, which carried only 1.544 megabits a second. This upgrade has significantly increased the available "bandwidth," which translates to the number and complexity of messages that can be carried simultaneously. Initially, all messages transmitted were just text; now data sent over these lines encode everything from plain text to interactive, two-way audio/video conferencing.

IP Numbers

Each computer that is connected to the Internet has a unique address called an IP (Internet Protocol) number. Each site with a national network connection is given a specific range of numbers that it can use for its internal machine addresses. The numerical address is in the format of 128.118.58.11, with the last one or two sets of numbers pointing to a specific machine. We rarely use the IP numbers, preferring instead to use machine and domain names. It is much easier for us to remember Mauri's machine as "cac.psu.edu" than 128.118.58.11. The Internet knows about both formats because there are computers (called *nameservers*) within each domain that match IP numbers to computer names and locations and make the translations transparent to the user.

Moving Traffic

Internet and BITnet use different protocols to pass messages and files between computers. Internet uses a packet-switching system. This means that information is broken down into packets that are sent via the least heavily loaded route. Each packet can be likened to one page of a multipage letter that is placed in an envelope. On the envelope is the information (e.g., destination address, sequence number of page) needed to reassemble the "pages" at the destination point. BITnet uses a "store and forward" system to move messages and files. Information "hops" from one computer to another in a linear fashion, rather like a bus that stops at every bus stop on its route. If a machine is temporarily offline (broken in some way, or being fixed or upgraded), then the messages just sit patiently until the way is open again. Some mailer software will even thoughtfully report to the sender that mail is being delayed and that efforts to deliver will continue, sometimes up to 30 days.

UUCP is a store-and-forward network of machines running the Unix operating system, whose messages are carried over regular voice telephone lines. Mail and files are moved in hops from one UUCP-connected machine to another and stored on disk until a telephone connection is made to the next computer on the network. Each UUCP computer only knows the address of those closest to it, and a map of the whole network must be consulted in order to correctly address mail to a distant site via UUCP. Mail transmission time can sometimes be counted in days, and there are no interactive facilities like FTP or Telnet on the UUCP network.

Some sites run software that dials the nearest switching center during the early morning hours, downloads all the files and mail that has accumulated for that site during the previous day, and then uploads any outgoing data. That one phone call may be the only connection with the outside networked world. Fido is one example of this kind of software. Fidonet is the collective name for the thousands of individually owned, personal computers throughout the world that run Fido software. Each computer has its own specific address so that messages can be routed to the correct place. The existence of Fidonet is not dependent on university or government funding. There are no permanent connections between these computers; all traffic is transferred over regular phone lines. There are gateways between Fidonet and the Internet. Fidonet provides electronic mail, file sharing, and hosts a large number of discussion groups called "Echomail." For details on how to get more information on Fidonet, see the Services section of the Information Sources appendix at the end of this chapter.

GETTING INFORMATION

There are two TCP/IP programs that are essential for moving around the network—FTP and Telnet.

FTP and Anonymous FTP

FTP (File Transfer Protocol) is both a program and a protocol for transferring files from a remote computer to your own local computer. Many Internet sites set aside diskspace on their computers to store a wide variety of information and computer software that are public domain, freeware, or shareware. You can copy these files without having an account on the archival site by using "anonymous FTP." This means you can log onto another computer "anonymously," just for the purpose of transferring files. Computer usage at most sites is heaviest in the daytime hours, so FTP sites encourage users to transfer files during late evening or early morning hours.

A useful file to transfer initially is:

FTP host: nic.sura.net
File: pub/nic/network.service.guides/how.to.ftp.guide

This is a cryptic description you will often see for the location of a file, and it is the format adopted in the Information Sources (see Appendix) at the end of this chapter. Let's take this step by step. First of all, in this case, the FTP archive site is "nic.sura.net." You connect to this machine using the FTP program from the system prompt by typing

[: ftp nic.sura.net]

When the connection is established, you will be asked for a user name and password. Type "anonymous" (without the quotation marks) as the login name, and your e-mail address as the password. You will get an ftp> prompt when the system is ready to use.

Next, the file name is "pub/nic/network.services.guides/how. to.ftp.guide." The slashes in this long name are a convention for separating directory levels. Directories on FTP sites are hierarchical, and you move up and down the hierarchical tree to find the file you need. To get the "how.to.ftp" file, you move down the tree either one level at a time or three levels at once by using "cd" (change directory):

    cd pub/nic/network.service.guides

When you are in the right directory, type "dir" to get a list of the contents of the directory, and check the name of the file you want to copy. File names are case sensitive, so you type the name of the file exactly as it appears in the directory listing. To get the file, type "get <filename>":

    get how.to.ftp.guide

If the filename is too long or is the wrong format for your system, you can change the file name as you transfer it by typing "get <old.file.name> <new.name>":

    get how.to.ftp.guide ftp.doc

The "get" command is used to copy one file at a time, but you can ask for multiple files:

    mget file1 file2 file3

When you have transferred the files successfully, leave the FTP program by typing:

    bye (or "quit") (or "exit")

Files on FTP sites are stored in different formats. Text or "ASCII" files can be transferred with the FTP mode set to ASCII. This is the default mode, so no special instructions are needed. Large files, like postscript or tar archives, are often compressed to save space. Because you will need to get those files exactly the way they are stored, the files should be transferred in binary mode. To change to binary mode, type "bin" or "binary" at the ftp> prompt before typing "get <filename>". This special instruction changes the FTP mode to binary. Compressed files need special processing after transferring them to read, edit, and print. Information on compressing and uncompressing files is available from:

FTP host: ftp.cso.uiuc.edu
File: doc/pcnet/compression

If your site does not have an Internet connection (and thus no access to FTP or Telnet protocols), BitFTP is a mail interface that allows users to access FTP files from sites on the Internet. Most of the Internet FTP commands can be used with BitFTP. However, the commands are typed in the body of a mail message, not interactively as during an FTP session like the one just described. This service tends to be slow, and your requested files may take hours or days to reach you, so be patient. To get a brief guide to BitFTP, send a message in the following form:

To: BITFTP@PUCC (or BITFTP@PUCC.Princeton.edu)

HELP

This service is also available at no charge from Digital Equipment Corporation's western regional mainframes. You can receive information by sending a message in the following form:

To: FTPmail@decwrl.dec.com

HELP

TELNET

Telnet, like FTP, is both a protocol (TCP/IP remote login protocol) and a program for an interactive connection with another machine. It is commonly used for two purposes: to remotely login to a machine to which you have an account in order to use it as if you are actually at that site, and to remotely login to public access catalogues and databases. Some of these sites (library catalogs and computers holding public access databases) require a login name, but it is usually published with information about the service.

To Telnet to a site, type "Telnet <address>":

Telnet nic.ddn.mil

If you experience difficulties while using Telnet, ^] (hold down control, press]) is the escape sequence that will often return you to either the Telnet> prompt or your local prompt. Watch carefully when you login to a remote system because it will often state the particular escape sequence needed, and check with your local systems administrator for any special instructions for your site. Once back to the Telnet> prompt, you can terminate the connection by typing "close," "quit," or "exit." A brief description of Telnet is available from:

FTP host: nic.sura.net
File: pub/nic/network.service.guides/how.to.Telnet.guide

Further examples of the use of Telnet follow in other sections of this chapter.

COMMUNICATING WITH THE NETWORK COMMUNITY

The network is a microcosm of our broader society: an interface to a community of people who would otherwise be inaccessible. Most importantly, it bridges geographical, temporal, and cultural differences. Within the network community, you can join the "neighborhood" within which you feel most comfortable and discuss topics of mutual interest.

Electronic Mail

The first thing you have to know when you want to send e-mail to someone is their electronic address, and the easiest way to find out is always to ask the person to whom you want to send mail. Electronic mail addresses look very different from postal (called "snail mail" by e-mail users) addresses. In fact, at first an Internet address appears to be just a collection of random characters. But there is a method here. To send mail to Fay's postal address, you need to know:

name	fay sudweeks
a department	architectural and design science
a university	sydney university
city/state	sydney nsw
a country	australia

To send electronic mail to Fay's Internet address (in Australia), you need to know:

a user	fay
a machine	@arch
a location	.su
a domain	.edu
a country	.au

So, Fay's Internet address is: fay@arch.su.edu.au

Notice that there are no spaces in the address. Machines would read blank spaces in an e-mail address to mean the end of the address, so connecting characters are used between each part of the address to separate the parts, roughly equivalent to each line in a postal address. These separators can be the underscore, a hyphen, or dots (periods) as in:

fay_sudweeks@arch.su.edu.au or nori@east.east-slc.edu

Different domains one may see in Internet addresses are .com for business or industry, .mil for military addresses, .gov for government addresses, .org for nonprofit organizations, and .edu for educational organizations. Some, but not all, addresses have a country code; for example, "au" for Australia, "uk" for the United Kingdom. The country code for the United States is "us," but it is rarely used.

Reading from left to right, an Internet address goes from the most specific to the most general, or from small machine to large domain. The exception to this format is the addressing system used in the United Kingdom. If Fay lived in the United Kingdom, her address would be reversed and might be fay@uk.ac.su.arch.

On BITnet, each computer has its own distinct name, which may or may not be the same as its Internet name. Mauri's BITnet address is MMC7@PSUVM, and her Internet address is mmc7@psuvm.psu.edu. When sending mail from a computer that does not have a direct connection to BITnet, it is usually necessary to add additional routing information to the address:

MMC7@PSUVM.BITNET

If your local e-mail system is set up to recognize an address in this format, the message will be sent to a BITnet/Internet gateway. The gateway will use the appropriate protocol to send the message to the BITnet machine. If this does not work, you will need to address your mail to a specific gateway. The basic strategy for mailing to non-Internet networks is to use the full non-Internet address as the userid, change any @ symbol to a % symbol, and add the address of the appropriate gateway. So, for example, if you want to send mail to Mauri's BITnet address, you add one of the BITnet/Internet gateways:

MMC7%PSUVM.BITNET@UGA.CC.UGA.EDA

Using a UUCP gateway is a little like a BITnet/Internet gateway. For example, to route a message to mauri@cac.psu.edu through a UUCP gateway, you would use:

mauri%cac.psu.edu@uu.cp.uucp

If you want to send mail to someone with a Compuserve account of 71234,567, you change the comma to a period and add the Compuserve gateway:

1234.567@CompuServe.com

Fidonet, however, needs a little more thought to get it right. To mail John December at 1:234/567, you would translate that address to:

John.December@f567.n234.z1.fidonet.org

A guide for sending mail between networks is available from:

FTP host: ariel.unm.edu
File: library/network.guide

Finding E-Mail Addresses

For the new net user, one of the most frustrating experiences is trying to find a person's e-mail address. Where is the network equivalent of a telephone book and directory assistance? The answer: There isn't one. A database of e-mail addresses is less useful than a telephone book because e-mail addresses are far more dynamic; domains change, hosts change, systems change, and user names change. The easiest method is to phone, fax, or write and simply ask for a person's e-mail address. If that is not possible, there are a number of other methods you can try. One method that attempts a solution to the dynamic nature of e-mail addresses is the University of Colorado's Netfind Server. The server is not a database but, given a name and a few keywords, it selectively searches Internet hosts to find the most recent e-mail address for that person. In some instances, it displays much more information about users. To use Netfind, Telnet to one of the following servers, type "netfind" at the login prompt, and read the help program to get more information:

Australia:	archie.au
Chile:	malloco.ing.puc.cl
Singapore:	lincoln.technet.sg
Slovak Fed. Repub.:	sun.uakom.cs
United Kingdom:	monolith.cc.ic.ac.uk
United States:	bruno.cs.colorado.edu

Another way to find e-mail addresses is to use "white pages" services. The most convenient way to access them is by the Knowbot Information Server (KIS), a one-stop master directory that accesses smaller white pages datasets, for example, the NIC WHOIS, the PSI White Pages Pilot Project, NYSERNET X.500 database, and MCI mail. Telnet to "nri.reston.va.us 185" (the port number 185 must be included) and use the "man" command to get more information, or e-mail "kis@sol.bucknell.edu" with the single word "man" in the body of the message.

Finally, the *finger* program provides a "hit-and-miss" method to finding out information about users. If you think you know, or can guess, the userid and address of the target person, you can run the finger command for verification. Type "finger fay@archsci.arch.su.edu.au," and you will not only verify the e-mail address, but will find out idle time, login time, and information included in a plan file. Sometimes when you finger an address you will get a "Connection refused" response, which means the site has probably disenabled finger for security reasons.

Group Conferencing

One of the more popular uses of networks, after the exchange of electronic mail, is to join electronic group conferences. These conferences come in many varieties. Some are like bulletin boards in local grocery stores where messages are posted and left for people to read and comment on. Some focus on topics ranging from postcard collecting to scuba diving. Some are for the dissemination of computer code or electronic journals and involve no discussion at all. And others read like the transcript of a cocktail party. It is a very popular medium that has been likened to newspapers or talk radio.

Many people just read or listen (or to use the network's term "lurk"), and a relative few contribute. However, readership in a group conference can bring people together from all over the world who might never have a chance to talk; it fosters the exchange of ideas and information and engenders a sense of cooperation and friendship. Many of these discussion groups are handled by a program called LISTSERV that runs on IBM mainframe computers. The groups are often called discussion lists because essentially what the LISTSERV software holds is a subscription list of electronic mail addresses. You might also see them referred to as BITnet groups because they were originally circulated among the IBM computers that comprised the BITnet network, but are now gatewayed to the Internet.

When you send a message to LISTSERV, depending on the instructions it has been given, it will send your message on to the moderator/listowner or, if the list is unmoderated, copies the incoming message to each of the addresses on its subscription list. If the list is moderated, the moderator will check the message against whatever formal or informal criteria exist that govern what goes out to the list's readership and either send it on, edit it, or return it to the sender. Most moderators see their primary role as controlling the signal-to-noise ratio. This involves making sure that the discussion is kept within the limits set in the group's charter and that discussion is conducted in a civil manner.

To join a LISTSERV group conference, send mail to the listserv at the address given for the discussion group (e.g., listserv@...) with a single line in the body of the message, substituting your own first and last names for YourFirstname and YourLastName:

> To: LISTSERV@guvm
> --------------------------------
> SUBSCRIBE IPCT-L YourFirstName YourLastName

A complete list of more than 4,000 Listserv groups is available from:

> FTP: ftp.nisc.sri.com
> File: netinfo/interest-groups

Be sure you have enough disk space before you get it, however, because the file is huge (more than a megabyte).

Usenet Newsgroups

Another type of group conference is the Usenet newsgroups. Usenet can be defined as computers that exchange messages with Usenet headers, and many of these machines are the same ones that carry BITnet and/or Internet traffic. There are some significant differences between the Usenet newsgroups and the discussion groups residing on BITnet and the Internet, most of which show up from the computer user's perspective. A user subscribes as an individual to Listserv and similar groups, and the messages are received in his or her personal mailbox. In order to read the netnews newsgroups, a site has to receive the "feed," which is stored at a central location on the site's mainframe and accessed by some kind of reader software. Sometimes Usenet newsgroup messages are available on campus through the same system that handles on-campus computer conferencing. Messages are held for whatever period of time the site administrators decide is appropriate, and this is often dictated by the amount of storage space available. There is no central authority for Usenet newsgroups, although protocols have grown that govern the creation of new groups.

A site may receive some, all, or none of the Usenet newsgroups.

There are currently over 2,000 different groups divided into a number of major streams such as .alt (alternative), .comp (computer), .soc (social), .rec (recreation), and .bit.listserv (groups that are mirrors of Listserv groups). A complete list of newsgroups is available from:

FTP host: rtfm.mit.edu
Files:
List_of_Active_Newsgroups,_Part_I
List_of_Active_Newsgroups,_Part_II
Alternative_Newsgroup_Hierarchies,_Part_I
Alternative_Newsgroup_Hierarchies,_Part_II

IRC

Another popular way to get to know other people on the network is to use an interactive messaging system. Internet Relay Chat (IRC) is conceptually like CB radio in that it is a multiuser chat system in which people get together on "channels" and participate in an interactive dialogue on topics of interest. It is a public forum, and like all public forums is open to abusive and offensive communication. The most frequent users of IRC are people in their late teens or early 20s, so it is not surprising that much of the communication has a sexual or fantasy quality. This has given IRC a dubious reputation, but it can, and is, a powerful medium for allowing isolated people to communicate interactively.

To use IRC, you run a "client" program by typing "irc," which connects to a "server" on the IRC network on Internet. If you get an error message when you try to run IRC, it probably means you do not have a client installed on your system. There are public clients and servers, but they are disappearing rapidly, so if you do not have your own client program, you are encouraged to get the source code and compile it or get it compiled for you. Check with your local network administrators regarding the acceptable uses of IRC on your system.

Check "Archie" (see later in chapter) for the nearest FTP location where the IRC source is archived. When you are connected to the IRC network, type "/list" to get a list of current channels in use. Choose a channel that interests you, and join by typing "/join #<channel>". Once you have joined a channel, anything you type that does not begin with a slash (/) is displayed to everyone on that channel with your "nick" as an identifying prompt. It's a good idea for new users to type "/help" when first connected to get more information, but here are some basic IRC commands to get started:

```
/help                  online help
/nick <name>           establish a nickname
/list                  list available channels and their topics
/join #<channel>       connect to the specific channel
/who                   list all persons on the current channel
/quit                  exit from IRC
```

A brief description of IRC is available from:

> FTP host: nctucca.edu.tw
> File: Usenet/faq/news.answers/irc-faq

and tutorials on IRC are available from:

> FTP host: cs.bu.edu
> Files: irc/support/tutorial.*

Talk/Tell/Send

There are various interactive communication systems available for different platforms, and again, check with your system's administrator to see which, if any, are available at your site. The UNIX programs *talk* and *ntalk*, when enabled, allow two people who are using different UNIX machines at the same time to "talk" in "real time." When a connection is established, each user's screen is split horizontally, and the two communicants type simultaneously with their output appearing in separate windows. *Talk* is a popular program for interactive dialogue because there are fewer distractions than with other similar programs. The words appear character by character, and there are no identifying labels against each line of text, as in IRC.

To run the program, type "talk <userid@internet.address>", for example:

> talk mauri@cac.psu.edu

If Mauri is not logged on, you will receive a message: "your party is not logged on." If Mauri is online, talk sends a message that a connection is requested by you. Mauri can either ignore the request or respond by typing "talk your_name@your_address." A talk session is terminated with ^C (control-C). Remember to be thoughtful about sending an unexpected talk request, as the message may be distracting and interfere with work in progress.

One-line messages can be broadcast to other users using the

"tell" or "send" command. *Tell* is available on IBM VM/CMS systems and works within and between the IBM mainframes. *Send* is a similar facility available within and between Digital Electronic Corporation's VAX computers. Check with your site administrators for specific instructions on how to use these facilities, if it is implemented on your site's platform.

Sending frivolous or threatening "tell" or "send" messages to people you do not know is a major breach of "netiquette" and can sometimes, depending on the position of an offended person in his or her organization's hierarchy, cost you your computer privileges.

FINDING INFORMATION

You can find just about any information you want—and more—on the Internet. The problem rapidly becomes one of knowing how to deal with an overload of information. Be selective as you explore the following services.

Archie

The Archie service combines a number of resource tools for locating information on the Internet. Archie can search the contents of a large proportion of the world's anonymous FTP archive sites. If you have an Archie client installed on your local machine (check with your friendly system administrator), just type "archie." Otherwise, Telnet to one of the following archie servers:

Australia:	archie.au
Finland:	archie.funet.fi
Israel:	archie.cs.huji.ac.il
Japan:	archie.wide.ad.jp
United Kingdom:	archie.doc.ic.ac.uk
United States:	archie.sura.net

At the login prompt, type "archie." It is always a good idea for first-time users to get information from Archie's online help program by typing "help." To get information on a particular command from the displayed list, type "help <command name>":

archie> help prog

The basic search command of the Archie program is "prog," and it is used to search for a file title that contains the string of characters specified: archie> prog <string>. When the search is completed, Archie will list the files containing the string and the FTP locations. A copy of the results of the search can be e-mailed to you by typing:

archie> mail <your email address>

Archie also supports FTP transfers by mail for non-Internet people. You can send your search request to one of the Archie servers in the same form as the help request below, substituting prog <string> for HELP. To get a brief guide to the mail Archie server and details of the e-mail-based FTP server, send a message to "archie@<archie.server>" in the following form:

```
To: archie@archie.au
-----------------
HELP
```

Gopher and Veronica

Gopher is another network information tool for retrieving information from the Internet. The name *Gopher* comes from the mascot of the University of Minnesota, where Gopher was developed. It also reflects the main function of Gopher: to "go for" network resources. Gopher uses a client-server communications model in which the server accepts queries and responds by delivering a document to the client. The value of Gopher is that, as a distributed document delivery service, it finds various types of information on many different computers. Gopher include services such as FTP archive searches, online books through Project Gutenberg, and university news and phone directories. If you have a Gopher client on your system (again, check with your system administrator), it can usually be accessed by typing "Gopher" at your system's prompt. If not, Telnet to a Gopher client, for example:

Telnet consultant.micro.umn.edu

This will connect you with the University of Minnesota's main client. When you get the login prompt, type "Gopher." A system of menus will then be displayed. You choose the menu entries until you come to a specific piece of information that you view. You will have the option to view the information online and/or have it mailed to you.

Each Gopher client (there are now hundreds of clients on the network) may offer different menus. Moreover, there is no standard subject classifications for the information on Gopher menus. Therefore, if you do not know what Gopher client to connect to and do not know the wording of the menu item, you cannot find your information easily. This is where Veronica (Very Easy Rodent-Oriented Net-wide Index to Computerized Archives) comes in. Veronica, developed by the University of Nevada, Reno, allows you to keyword search many Gopher menus for words appearing in the titles of files at all levels of the menus. This gives you the chance to quickly try out keywords that you think will be appropriate for your item of interest and find files without having to know where they are actually archived. You can access Veronica by choosing the following menu option from the University of Minnesota's Gopher:

Other Gopher and Information Servers /

This selection will then enable you to use Veronica. You can scan the Gopher menus of many clients for the occurrence of a keyword. Gopher will return with all the menu lines containing that keyword. You can then follow the paths down these menu options to find information.

Wide-Area Information Server (WAIS)

Like Gopher, WAIS is a network application tool to find information. The main benefit of WAIS is that it makes Internet-wide information accessible through a single, common user interface. For a simple search using WAIS, you first choose some databases that are likely to contain information for which you are looking. Once you have chosen the databases, you instruct the WAIS application to search those databases for items that contain your keyword(s). After the database(s) is searched, you are presented with a list of documents that match your keywords(s). You then have the option to retrieve the text associated with these headlines.

The databases on WAIS range widely: full text of journals (like *Communications of the ACM*), ERIC (Educational Resources Information Center) digests, texts of speeches by President Clinton, Department of Energy Climate Data, poetry archives, movie reviews, and many more.

Online Public Access Catalogs (OPACs)

Many national and international libraries have computerized their card catalogs and made them available to researchers via Telnet. There are several directories of OPACs that are available via anonymous FTP. These directories give specific access information for each library listed and also contain lists and access directions for other useful resources. You can obtain these lists via anonymous FTP from:

>FTP: ariel.unm.edu
>File: library/internet.library
>
>FTP: ftp.unt.edu
>File: library/libraries.txt

While you are there, take a look in their library directories for many other useful files.

HYTELNET

This program is designed to help you to reach all the Internet accessible libraries, Freenets, CWISs, Library BBSs, and other information sites accessible via Telnet. There are several versions of this program available, including versions that will run on IBM and compatible personal computers, Macintoshs, and DEC computers using the VMS operating system. The IBM PC version gives information on more than 400 different sites. Hytelnet is available from its creator Peter Scott.

>FTP: access.usask.ca
>File: pub/hytelnet/pc/README

This file will give you specific information for downloading the various versions of Hytelnet and the appropriate decompression programs. There are several programs of this nature, and many have already been installed on site mainframe computers, so please check with your local site administrators to see what is already available.

GETTING MORE INFORMATION

There is a vast amount of information describing the Internet and the activities that occur on it. Much of this information is online and free. However, the information and its location changes, sometimes on an almost daily basis.

John December (decembj@rpi.edu) has compiled a comprehensive and highly regarded list of Information sources, which he updates on a regular basis. The plain text (ASCII) version is available via anonymous FTP from host ftp.rpi.edu, file/pub/communications/internet-cmc.txt. There are several other formats available for those who can use them. Many of the entries on his list give more information about items discussed in this chapter. To get the list you only need to know how to FTP, but to make use of the list, you need to know how to use anonymous FTP, electronic mail, and Usenet newsgroups. If you are still not sure how to use FTP, send a request by email to:

> To: FTPmail@decwrl.dec.com
>
> --------------------------------------
>
> connect ftp.sura.net
> chdir /pub/nic/network.service.guides
> get how.to.ftp.guide
> quit

A starting point from which to learn more about the Internet is the introductory information for new users in the following list. The next recommended step is to work your way through John December's recommended Internet Starter Set:

Internet Starter Set
John December

PURPOSE: to list resources that a new user to the
                    Internet can obtain to start exploring.
ASSUMPTIONS: the user knows how to use anonymous ftp.
CONTENTS: Orientation, Guides, Lists, Exploring

* Section -1- Internet Orientation

What is the Internet?:	ftp nic.merit.edu	documents/fyi/fyi_20.txt
Surfing the Internet:	ftp nysernet.org	pub/resources/guides/ surfing.2.0.3.txt
New User's Questions:	ftp nic.merit.edu	documents/fyi/fyi_04.txt
Net Etiquette:	ftp ftp.sura.net	pub/nic/internet.literature/ netiquette.txt

* Section -2- Guides to the Internet

Big Dummy's Guide:	ftp ftp.eff.org	pub/EFF/papers/ big-dummys-guide.txt
Email 101:	ftp mrcnext.cso. uiuc.edu	etext/etext93/ email025.txt
Zen :	ftp csn.org	pub/net/zen/zen-1.0.PS.Z
De Presno Guide:	ftp ftp.eunet.no	pub/text/online.txt

* Section -3- Internet Lists

Internet Services FAQ:	ftp rtfm.mit.edu	pub/usenet/news.answers /internet-services/faq
Information Sources:	ftp ftp.rpi.edu	pub/communications/ internet-cmc.txt
Internet Services:	ftp csd4.csd.uwm. edu	pub/inet.services.txt
Internet Tools:	ftp ftp.rpi.edu	pub/communications/ internet-tools

* Section -4- Internet Exploring

Internet Hunt:	ftp ftp.cni.org	pub/net-guides/ i-hunt/00README
Merit NIC:	ftp nic.merit.edu	READ.ME
InterNIC:	ftp ds.internic.net	dirofdirs/0intro.dirofdirs
NSF Guide:	ftp ds.internic.net	resource-guide/overview

John December/decemj@rpi.edu/Rensselaer Polytechnic Institute/Troy, New York. PhD Candidate/Department of Language, Literature, and Communication.

THE NEXT STEP

Finding your way around the network is both frustrating and rewarding. This introduction is not intended to be inclusive or comprehensive, but is intended to provide the new networker with sufficient information and skills to know where and how to find more. For system specific information, try your computer support people; for hints on many aspects of networking, try subscribing to nettrain@ubvm.cc.buffalo.edu or helpnet@templevm; for more detailed information acquire John December's list mentioned above.

We welcome you to the network community.

Glossary

Compiled by Zane L. Berge, Mauri P. Collins and Michael Day

Academy One. National Public Telecomputing Network's (NPTN) Academic Projects area. It includes special areas for teachers, parents, and students, and features globally interactive projects, such as simulated space missions and an annual Teleolympics. Academy One promotes the educational use of the entire worldwide Free-Net system. For more information, contact NPTN's Director of Education, Linda Delzheit, on the Internet at aa002@nptn.org.

Address. There are two forms of machine addresses that will commonly identify any computer connected to the Internet. They are in the form or either words or IP numbers (dotted quads). For instance, GUVAX, a VAX computer at Georgetown University, is known as either 141.161.1.2 or guvax.acc.georgetown.edu.

Anonymous FTP. A form of FTP (see FTP) that allows unregistered users (those without passwords to the account) access to files. When using, one logs in as "anonymous" and uses one's e-mail address (e.g., BERGE@GUVAX) as the password.

ARPANet. A packet switched network developed in the early 1970s. The "grandfather" of today's Internet. ARPANet was decommissioned in June 1990.

Archie. An internet service that allows one to search the offerings of many FTP sites. Archie tracks the contents of over 800 anonymous FTP archive sites containing over 1 million files stored across the Internet. Two archie sites are: archie.ans.net (147.225.1.31) and archie.unl.edu (129.93.1.14). Logon as "archie".

ASCII. American Standard Code for Information Interchange, pronounced "Askee." A standard data transmission code that the com-

213

puter uses to encode alphanumeric and other characters into a binary file.

Asynchronous. Transmission by individual bytes, or packets of bytes, not related to specific timing on the transmitting end. When used to describe computer-mediated communication, it indicates that communication can take place without both parties being logged on at the same time, as messages can be left for subsequent reading.

Backbone. The primary, or trunk connection, on a distributed hierarchical network system, such as the Internet. All systems connected to the backbone are assured of being connected to each other. This does not prevent systems from setting up private arrangements with each other to bypass the backbone for reasons of cost, performance, or security.

Bandwidth. Used generally to refer to the capacity or throughput of a communications link. High bandwidth implies high data throughput, which can provide a very high speed to a few users at a time, or lower data rates to many users.

BITnet. Acronym for "Because It's Time Network." Begun in 1981, BITnet is a worldwide academic and research network that connects many universities, colleges, and collaborating research centers, and is restricted to the noncommercial exchange of information. It is operated by EDUCOM. BITnet differs from the Internet in the types of services (e.g., FTP and Telnet) its users can access. BITnet uses the RSCS protocol set and provides electronic mail, file transfer, and "Tell/Send" messaging.

Boolean searching. A method of searching in some electronic databases that allows the searcher to combine terms and/or phrases by using the Boolean operators "and," "or," and "not."

Bug. A bug is a programming error that causes a program not to work or to work differently than intended.

Bulletin-Board Systems (BBS). A network-based filesharing system in which users may enter information, usually in the form of messages, for others to read or download. Many bulletin boards are set up according to general topics and are accessible throughout a network.

Campus-Wide Information System (CWIS). A tool that allows users to navigate through and retrieve data from a variety of campus sources (e.g., library, news bureau, events center, admissions and registrar, computing center).

Client. In network terminology, client can have two meanings. Sometimes it is synonymous with "user". At other times it is used to denote a relationship between two computers in which one computer is a host and is serving a client machine. In this situation, the client computer becomes a guest on the host computer in order to use the host computer's resources. The program on the client machine that provides the user interface for those resources is typically called the client software.

Client-server interface. A program, running on a host computer, that provides an interface to remote programs (called clients), most commonly across a network, in order to provide these clients with access to some service such as databases, printing, and so on. In general, the clients act on behalf of a human end user (perhaps indirectly).

Computer-Based Instruction (CBI) or Computer-Mediated Instruction. Refers to using computers to instruct human users. CBI includes Computer-Assisted Instruction (CAI) (tutorial, review and practice, simulation, etc.); computer-managed instruction (diagnostic and prescriptive testing functions); and electronic messaging, which is generally associated with networked computer classrooms.

Courseware. Software, including documentation and workbooks, that is marketed for educational purposes.

Cross-Posting. Posting a BBS message to multiple subject groups or conferences.

DEC VAX Notes. *see* **Vax Notes.**

Domain. Usually the last term in an address (q.v.). Domains are usually functional or national. Functional domains include EDU for education, GOV for government, COM for commercial, and ORG for nonprofit organizations. National domains identify a country, such as CA for Canada, MY for Malaysia, SG for Singapore, and TH for Thailand.

Download. The electronic transfer of information from a remote computer to a local one. Upload refers to the transfer from the local machine to the remote one.

Electronic Bulletin Board. *see* **Bulletin Board Systems (BBS).**

Electronic Journal (ejournal). An electronically distributed publication which, like a print journal, includes a table of contents, numerically defined issues, and an ISSN number. Recipients can reformat text as they wish and print only what they need to print.

Electronic Mail (e-mail). Transmitting textual and nontextual messages in machine readable form from one computer terminal or computer system to another. A message sent from one computer user to another is stored in the recipient's mailbox, a file on the host machine where that person receives mail.

Emoticon-(smiley). Electronic text likenesses of human faces used in mail and news to indicate a variety of emotions and reactions. You read the "face" from left to right, as if it were rotated 90 degrees counter-clockwise. The most common smiley is :-) connoting a smile or happiness. You will also often see :-(meaning sadness or disappointment, and ;-) meaning irony or sarcasm.

ENFI (Electronic Networks For Interaction). A real-time writing environment for the networked computer classroom in which synchronous communications software allows teachers and students to explore, collaborate, and expand on ideas in class in writing. They see each other in the process of for developing ideas; they write for each other and not just to "the teacher".

FAQ. *see* **Frequently Asked Question.**

Fiber optics. The technology of connecting or networking communication devices, such as computers, by means of optical fiber cable instead of copper wire.

File Transfer protocol (FTP). A TCP/IP protocol and program that one can use to transfer files over the network.

Flame. To express a strong opinion and/or to criticize someone (or something), usually in a frank, inflammatory statement couched in language often vulgar or profane, in an electronic message.

FrEdMail Network. Free Educational Electronic Mail. One of the pioneering networks of microcomputer-based BBS systems serving K-12 educators, FrEdMail was begun in 1986 by Al Rogers in San Diego, CA and has spread to include more than 150 electronic bulletin boards systems across the United States and as far away as Australia and Ireland. FrEdMail offers collaborative activities designed to help students become better writers and learners and promotes the sharing of resources and experiences among teachers. FrEdMail can now be accessed through the Internet. For more information, contact Al Rogers, FrEdMail Foundation, P.O. Box 243, Bonita, CA 91908-0243.

Frequently Asked Questions (FAQs). A document containing answers to frequently asked questions about some service, application, or function. These documents are generally updated as users gain experience with the service, application, or function.

FTP. *see* **File Transfer Protocol.**

Full Text Delivery. The ability of an information server, like Gopher, to deliver the full text of a document to a patron.

Gateway. A computer or device that acts as a connector between two logically separate networks. It has interfaces to more than one network and can translate data so that it can pass from one network to another, possibly dissimilar, network.

Gopher. An information management tool that allows users to search for specific kinds of information over a wide-area network by using a series of menus. Gopher was developed by the University of Minnesota and is freely available in client and server form. Many Gophers serve as useful front-ends to Internet databases, FTP archives, OPACs, and CWISs.

Groupware (Group Conferencing Systems). A program (often marketed for business) that permits simultaneous work on a common file by more than one networked user. All the users can see the changes made by any other person as they occur.

Host Computer. In the context of networks, a computer that provides service to a user who is typically running 'client' software that turns their computer into a "terminal" of the host.

HYTELNET. A menu-driven version of Telnet that serves as a guide to online library catalogs and other information sources, updated 2-3 times per year. It can be downloaded by Anonymous FTP and placed on a local machine. Information on Hytelnet is available from WAIS: hytelnet.src.

Informatics. A general term describing network-accessible information servers. These include data archives such as anonymous ftp sites, interactive databases such as library OPACs, and client/server systems such as Gopher and WAIS.

Internet Relay Chat (IRC). A worldwide synchronous multiuser chat protocol that allows one to converse with others in real time. IRC is structured as a network of servers, each of which accepts connections from client programs, one per user. Jarkko Oikarinen, a Finnish programmer, created Internet Relay Chat. IRC is a free program, that is, anyone with access to the Internet can get a client program and use it to talk with others.

internet. A collection of computer networks interconnected by a set of routers that allow them to function as a single, large virtual network.

Internet. (Note the capital "I") The largest network in the world consisting of national backbone nets (such as MILNET, NSFNET, and CREN) and a myriad of regional and local campus networks all over the world. The Internet uses the Internet protocol suite, including the TCP/IP protocol set that includes electronic mail, Telnet, and FTP. To be on the Internet you must have IP connectivity, that is, be able to Telnet to—or ping—other systems. Networks with only e-mail connectivity are not actually classified as being on the Internet.

Interoperability. That which allows different computer models from different manufacturers to communicate meaningfully with each other.

IP (Internet Protocol). *see* TCP/IP.

IP Address. The numeric address (a dotted quad) of a computer connected to the Internet; *also called* **Internet address**. It has the form 123.456.789.101. Guvax.georgetown.edu, to other computers and the network routers, is 141.161.1.2

IRC. *see* **Internet Relay Chat.**

KIDSNET. Has been renamed KIDSPHERE. See KIDSPHERE.

KIDSPHERE. The major mailing list for the discussion of K-12 computer networking. It was established in 1989 by Bob Carlitz under the name KIDSNET. In Spring 1993 it was renamed KIDSPHERE with this statement of purpose: "to stimulate the development of an international computer network for the use of children and their teachers. The first pieces of this network have already begun to take shape, and the mailing list now helps to guide its continuing evolution. Subscribers to the list include teachers, administrators, scientists, developers of software and hardware and officials of relevant funding agencies." To join the list, send your request to Bob Carlitz <joinkids@vms.cis.pitt.edu> and ask to be added to the KIDSPHERE mailing list.

LAN. *see* **Local Area Network.**

LISTSERV. LISTSERV is the software that manages electronic discussion groups or computer conference distribution lists. These discussion groups are often called "lists" because, using what is called a "mail exploder" and a subscription list of electronic mail addresses, LISTSERV sends messages directly to the electronic mailboxes of many subscribers. Participants subscribe by sending a message to the LISTSERV hosting the list of interest. Eric Thomas originally wrote the listserv software for IBM mainframes, but there is now a similar program that runs on Unix systems.

Local Area Network (LAN). A network connecting machines at one site.

Lurking. Reading or "listening" to a mailing list discussion or Usenet newsgroup without actively participating (i.e., without contributing to the discussion). Lurking is encouraged for beginners who wish to learn the history and habits of the group.

Mail Exploder. Part of an electronic mail delivery system that allows a single message to be delivered to a list of addresses. Mail exploders are used to implement mailing lists. Users send messages to a single address (e.g., mygroup-L@somehost.edu) and the mail exploder takes care of delivery to each of the individual subscribers to the list.

Modem (MOdulator/DEModulator). A device that converts the digital signals in your computer to analog signals, and vice-versa, to enable computer communication through analog telephone lines.

Moderator. The person who is "in charge" of the Listserv or a Usenet newsgroup. On a moderated list, the moderator collects the messages posted to the list, edits them, and forwards them to the list. On an unmoderated list, the moderator just steps in when things get out of control. The moderator may also subscribe and unsubscribe people on the list, if is not a public list.

National Education and Research Network (NREN). The National Research and Education Network is a proposed national computer network to be built on the foundation of the NSF backbone network, NSFnet, the current internet backbone. NREN would provide high speed interconnection between various national and regional networks.

Netiquette. A contraction of "network" and "etiquette" referring to proper behavior on a computer network.

Netweaving. When a human volunteer (netweaver) must move individual messages from network to network because there is no direct electronic connection or gateway.

Network. A group of computers connected together for the purpose of transmitting information to one another.

NIC (Network Information Center). An internet host computer designated to provide useful information services to network users.

Node. A computer that is attached to a network; also called host.

NREN. *see* **National Research and Education Network.** NSFnet-National Science Foundation Network. TCP/IP-based network that is the backbone for data transmission in the United States.

OPAC (Online Public Access Catalog). Most large academic and many public libraries have converted their card catalogs to electronic or "machine-readable" format. These online catalogs may be searched from remote locations via modem or remote login, and so they truly have become public reference sources.

Postmaster. The person responsible for answering questions about users and electronic mail addresses at a site. Can sometimes be reached by sending mail to "postmaster@host.subdomain.domain" if you are having trouble reaching someone at that host machine or subdomain.

Protocol. A formalized set of rules governing the format, timing, and error control of transmissions on a network. The protocol that networks use to communicate with each other. TCP/IP is an example of a network protocol.

Remote Access. The ability to access one computer from another, from across the room or across the world. Remote access requires communications hardware, software, and actual physical links, although this can be as simple as common carrier (telephone) lines or as complex as a Telnet login to another computer across the Internet.

RFC (Request for Comments). The document series, begun in 1969, in which the Internet's standards, proposed standards, and generally agree-upon ideas are documented and published.

Server. A dedicated computer that shares its resources, such as files and applications programs, with other computers on a network.

Shareware. Microcomputer software, distributed through public domain channels such as ftp, for which the author expects to receive compensation.

Signature (often .sig). The three or four lines at the bottom of a piece of e-mail or a Usenet article that identifies the sender. Often contains addresses, telephone numbers, e-mail addresses, and, sometimes, ingenious graphics built from keyboard characters. Long signatures (over five lines) are generally frowned on.

SMTP. Simple Mail Transfer Protocol. The Internet standard protocol for transferring electronic mail messages from one computer to another.

Snail Mail. A pejorative term referring to the postal service.

Synchronous. Data communications in which transmissions are sent at a fixed rate, with the sending and receiving devices synchronized. Synchronous communication occur in real-time, for example, with two or more users communicating online at the same time to one another.

Sysop, sysops. System operator, person in charge of maintaining a host, server, or network.

Talk. A protocol that allows two people on remote unix computer systems to communicate in real time. When you issue the "talk user@machine.place.domain" command, and the individual is logged and accepts your request, the screen display divides horizontally and you can type at each other in real time.

TELL. The interactive real-time messaging protocol for IBM mainframes running VM/CMS and with BITnet connections. (SEND is the equivalent protocol for BITnet-connected VAX/VMS systems). At the system prompt one types:
tell (or "send") user@machine a single line message
and the message will appear on user@machine's screen if they are logged in. It is unwise to send TELL or SEND messages to persons one does not know because, depending on the rank and mood of the recipient, they could result in revocation of one's access privileges.

TCP. Transmission Control Protocol. The set of transmission standards on the Internet that provides the reliable communication service on which many applications depend for accurate data transfer. It allows the transfer of data between computers that have TCP/IP, and it supports other services (protocols) such as Telnet, FTP, and

SMTP. TCP/IP is also often used for other networks, particularly local area networks that tie together numerous kinds of computers or engineering workstations.

TCP/IP. *see* **TCP**

Telecommuting. The practice of employees working partially or primarily from home, using microcomputers and modems to access information systems and perform their daily duties without regard to their actual physical location.

Telnet. A basic function provided by the TCP/IP protocol on the Internet is Telnet, or remote login, or remote terminal connection service. This allows a user to interact with another computer as if she or he were directly connected to the remote computer.

Terminal Emulation Software. Communications software that permits your personal computer or workstation to communicate with another computer or network as if your machine were a specific type of terminal directly connected to that computer or network.

Terminal Server. A computer that connects terminals to a network by providing host Telnet service.

Thread. A series of postings to an electronic bulletin board or other discussion group (e.g., Listserv) that have a common subject heading. A thread normally consists of responses to an original posting to a discussion topic, or an offshoot of another thread.

TN3270. A version of Telnet providing IBM-3270 full-screen support.

UNIX. An operating system developed by Bell Laboratories that supports several users logged into a computer or workstation at the same time, and which supports multiuser and multitasking operations. That is, this operating system allows many people to share the processing capabilities of the computer on which it is running and allows those people to use several programs at once.

Usenet (NETNEWS). A computer bulletin board system, originally distributed over computers running the unix operation system that many computer systems on and off the Internet now subscribe to. Where LISTSERV software delivers discussion group messages as mail to individual mailboxes, messages from some or all of the over 2000 Usenet newsgroups are typically stored on a site's mainframe computer. Readers can then log in to read the accumulation of messages which may amount to 15 to 20 megabytes of text a day. With the number of groups growing daily, there is truly something of interest to everyone on Usenet.

UUCP (Unix to Unix Copy Program). A protocol used for communication between unix systems, on which mail and Usenet news services were built. Internet has largely taken over the transmission of such date exchange.

VAX (pl. VAXen). Mainframe and personal computers manufactured by the Digital Equipment Corporation and in wide use on the Internet. One of the prevalent terminal emulations used on the Internet is named for the VT100, an early DEC video terminal.

VAX Notes. VAX Notes is essentially a computer bulletin board set up with a series of topics numbered 1, 2, 3 and so on. Replies to each topic are attached to each topic note. Replies to topic 3 would be numbered 3.1, 3.2, and so on. This permits users to read and respond to several different discussion topics simultaneously. It also saves and stores all topic notes and replies, permitting readers to connect at any time, even after a several day hiatus and catch up on the entire series of transactions.

Virtual Reality. Systems that transform the computing environment by immersing the user in a simulated world, which also can include movement and tactile control. Virtual reality systems permit users to interact with computer systems in a manner that more closely mimics how humans naturally operate in the real world.

VMS. A Digital Equipment Corporation operating system for VAX machines.

VT100. *see* **VAX.**

Wide-Area Network (WAN). A distributed network spanning hundreds or thousands of miles, connecting a number of Local Area Networks.

Wide-Area Information System (WAIS). An information retrieval tool developed by Thinking Machines, Inc. WAIS provides a simple-to-use interface that allows a patron to search multiple sources for information with a single natural language question.

World-Wide Web (WWW or W3). A hypertext-based, distributed information system created by researchers at CERN in Switzerland. It allows users to create, edit, or browse hypertext documents. The clients and servers are easily accessible and available.

SOURCES

Ask ERIC InfoGuide. (1993). *K-12 educators and the Internet.* Available via anonymous FTP at ericir.syr.edu.

Day, M.J. (1993). Private correspondence.

Jacobsen, O., & Lynch, D. (1991). *A glossary of networking terms.* RFC 1208.

Kehoe, B.P. (1992). *Zen and the art of the Internet.* Available via anonymous FTP on host FTP.CS.WIDENER.EDU, directory PUB/ZEN, filename ZEN-1.0.PS (Postscript file) and other formats.

Krol, E. (1991). *The whole Internet user's guide and catalog*. Sebastapol, CA: O'Reilly and Associates.

Longley, D. (1986). *Dictionary of information technology* (2nd ed). New York: Oxford University Press.

Malkin, G., & LaQuey Parker, T. (1993). *Internet users' glossary*. RFC 1392.

Mitchell, M. & Saunders, L. (1992). *Glossary*. Sent via private correspondence.

Mulliner, K. (1993). *Internet glossary*. Prepared for a workshop in Columbus, OH. Sent via private correspondence.

Other miscellaneous glossaries from unidentified sources that were sent to us as private correspondence.

Author Index

Subject Index